THE IRAQ LIE

HOW THE WHITE HOUSE
SOLD THE WAR

The Iraq Lie
Testimonials

"Congressman Hoeffel offers his readers a candid and unsparing insider's account of one of the most consequential Congressional votes in modern history—the fateful decision to authorize war with Iraq. This wrenching and detailed assessment of the misleading case for war presented to the American people provides an important new perspective on the rush to invade Iraq."

–House Minority Leader Nancy Pelosi, (D-CA)

"This very important book will make readers understand that dedicated and intelligent Members of Congress—like author Hoeffel—thought their vote on the Iraq War was right but with hindsight are willing to admit the vote was wrong and analyze why it was wrong. If we can't learn from history—we are doomed to repeat it."

–Former House Minority Leader Dick Gephardt, (D-MO)

"*The Iraq Lie: How the White House Sold the War* is centered on the fundamental illness of Washington: the absence of accountability by our leaders, no matter how you feel about the Iraq War. Hoeffel calls for both the political courage and transparency needed for Congress to focus on facts, not political expediencies, to do its job. And, sadly, he leaves us with an awareness that even in a decision to take our nation to war, Diogenes continues to carry his lantern in our Capitol."

–Former Congressman and retired Admiral Joe Sestak, (D-PA)

"Every American who was drawn to support America's attack upon Iraq needs to read Congressman Hoeffel's honest, straight-forward reappraisal of the vote on the Iraq War resolution. Congressman Hoeffel grappled with the decision to go to war. His reflection marks a courageous call to conscience by a man who loves America."

–Former Congressman Dennis Kucinich, (D-OH)

"Joe Hoeffel, as a Member of Congress, voted for the Iraq War. In this thoroughly researched book, Hoeffel takes us inside the White House and behind the scenes to document the extent of the Bush Administration's lies that dragged our nation into its biggest foreign policy blunder since WWII. Unlike the men and women who sent us to war, Hoeffel has the courage to admit he made a mistake, and states if he could take back one vote in his long career of public service, it would be his 'Yes' for war in Iraq. That's a powerful admission, and this book tells us why. Hoeffel deserves a large audience, to prevent us from making the mistakes of Iraq again."

–Peter Van Buren, author, *We Meant Well: How I Lost the Battle for the Hearts and Minds of the Iraqi People*

"This book should be a reminder to the American people that no administration or Congress should commit young men and women to war based on manipulated intelligence—the people must demand the truth!"

–Congressman Walter Jones, (R-NC)

"This book serves as an incredible chronicle of the debate surrounding the worst foreign policy disaster in our nation's history. It is a well-timed reminder of the consequences of war as we work to achieve a more peaceful and secure world."

–Congresswoman Barbara Lee, (D-CA)

"Joe Hoeffel was well respected by members of both parties in Congress and his book shows why: Here is a thoughtful, insightful and compelling account of the run-up to the war in Iraq told by someone who was there. It is as important as it is page-turning, and a good primer for those studying the Congress and issues of war and peace."

–Congressman Adam Schiff, (D-CA)

"I worked with Joe Hoeffel in Congress to demand answers from the Bush Administration for its policies leading up to the invasion of Iraq and its aftermath. Joe provides a well-informed insider account of that effort. The book discloses the truth about our involvement in Iraq and simultaneously holds both the Bush Administration and Congress accountable for the debacle in Iraq and demonstrates how to prevent such a colossal failure from reoccurring."

–Former Congressman William Delahunt, (D-MA)

THE IRAQ LIE

HOW THE WHITE HOUSE
SOLD THE WAR

by
Joseph M. Hoeffel

ProgRESSive
Independent Media.
ProgressivePress.com

2014

THE IRAQ LIE

HOW THE WHITE HOUSE
SOLD THE WAR

Release date, July 28, 2014
ISBN 1-61577-792-X, EAN 978-1-61577-792-1
Length: 268 pages, 6 x 9 in., 86,000 words
List Price: $14.95
Mobi and Epub ebook editions: $5.99
Epub ISBN 1615778721, 9781615778720
Mobi ISBN 161577873X, 9781615778737

Subject: Nonfiction, Politics, History
LC classification DS79.76. Dewey class no. 956.7044/3
Subject Headings
    1. Iraq War, 2003–2011—Moral and ethical aspects—United States
    2. U.S. foreign relations—Iraq
    3. Weapons of Mass Destruction—Iraq
    4. Deception—Political aspects—United States

BISAC Subject Area Codes
HIS027170   History / Military / Iraq War (2003-2011)
POL030000   Political Science / American Government / National
POL061000   Political Science / Genocide & War Crimes

Distribution: Ingram, Baker & Taylor, Gazelle Book Services UK
Typesetter: Scribe, Inc.

Publicist: Ms. Rowe Carenen Copeland
The Book Concierge, LLC
675 North Main Street #313, Winston-Salem, NC 27101
www.thebookconcierge.com
Email: rowecopeland@thebookconcierge.com

How deceptive can Washington be? And how damaging is this deceit for our foreign policy? Former Congressman Joseph Hoeffel reveals how the Bush White House twisted arms and distorted intelligence to get support for their war. In *The Iraq Lie: How the White House Sold the War*, Hoeffel recalls how Congress struggled and failed to resist the war drums—and calls for intelligence reforms to prevent it from happening again. This first-person account of one Congressman's vote to defend his country, and his regret at believing the lies, comes as Iraq descends into civil war, and the debate flares up anew.

To my beloved wife
Francesca

And our beautiful granddaughter Elsa.
May she grow up in a peaceful world.

Acknowledgments

To the late Bob Silverstein, the first literary professional who believed in my story and this project,

To my agent, Anne Devlin, and my publisher, John-Paul Leonard, who brought this project to the printed page,

To House Democratic Leader Nancy Pelosi and her National Security Adviser Wyndee Parker, former Chairman of the House Intelligence Committee and former Director of the Central Intelligence Agency Porter Goss, and former Congressman and former three-star Admiral Joe Sestak for their wise counsel, helpful information and insightful advice,

To my friend Michael Sullivan and author Peter Van Buren for their very helpful suggestions,

To my golfing buddies, particularly Brookie, Pete, Whipple, Luvo and Euro, whose continuing interest in my work meant more than they know,

And to my wonderful family: my long-suffering wife Francesca and our two children Mary and Jake, and their spouses Steve and Erin, for years of love, devotion and encouragement. Francesca, Mary and Steve invested many hours of invaluable proofreading and editing, and all offered good advice. I could not have completed this book without their support. We share whatever success occurs, and any mistakes or failures are mine alone.

Table of Contents

THE IRAQ LIE

HOW THE WHITE HOUSE
SOLD THE WAR

Introduction

This is my story, from inside Congress, of how I came to vote for the Iraq War, and how I soon realized it was the worst vote of my career, as we were led into war under false pretenses by the Bush administration. This is how one Congressman saw the truth, the lies and the consequences of the Iraq War.

In the fall of 2002, I was completing my second term in Congress representing Pennsylvania's 13th district, and I was deeply interested in the legislative consideration of the Iraq War resolution. George W. Bush and his team told us that Saddam Hussein had weapons of mass destruction and was an imminent threat to America. I believed it and voted to disarm Saddam Hussein of weapons of mass destruction, but it turned out he did not have any. I had made the biggest mistake of my career.

I now firmly believe my colleagues and I never would have voted to approve the war had we known that the classified intelligence reports on Hussein's weapons were as uncertain and full of doubts about the Iraqi threat as they actually were. I also believe that next time we must disclose the intelligence before Congress authorizes any preemptive war.

The Iraq War was a debacle for America.

On March 19, 2003, President George W. Bush took the United States to war against a virtually disarmed Iraq. The performance of our brave soldiers was excellent, and the victory over the Iraqi army was swift, but the price paid by the military and their families—4,500 dead, 30,000 wounded and maimed—was brutally high.[1]

Our government's performance in Iraq included the misuse of intelligence, poor post-invasion planning, cowboy diplomacy, arrogant decision-making, and a botched nine-year occupation. Direct military spending in Iraq reached at least $758 billion,[2] with total costs to the United States of more than $2 trillion.[3] America emerged from the Iraq

War with reduced status and waning influence in much of the Middle East and throughout the Muslim world.

Estimates of Iraqi military personnel and civilians killed during the war run well over 100,000.[4] Iraqi citizens surely have more personal liberty after the downfall of the murderous tyrant Saddam Hussein, which is a very good thing, but they also have less personal security, increased sectarian strife and bleak economic opportunities. The post-war government of Iraq is dysfunctional and increasingly influenced by the hard-line clerics who rule Iran and oppose the United States. Our invasion, occupation and departure have allowed Al Qaeda to take root and flourish where they were not welcome under Saddam Hussein. Our misadventure in Iraq surely has created more extremists and terrorists than we brought to justice.

American citizens must wonder, after such a huge investment of American lives, treasure and prestige, how it all ended up like this and what can be done to make sure it never happens again.

It is hard to overstate how much George Bush and his top aides misled and hoodwinked the American people and their Congress about Iraq.

On September 26, 2002, President Bush made a speech in the White House Rose Garden stating with great certainty that Saddam Hussein had chemical and biological weapons of mass destruction and was developing more.[5] Not only did those statements prove to be untrue, but also those adamant claims were not fully supported by the classified intelligence then being received by the Bush Administration.

When George Bush asked Congress in a speech on October 7, 2002 in Cincinnati to authorize military action against Iraq, the President based the request on three definitive statements: Saddam Hussein had an active and growing program to develop weapons of mass destruction, Iraq was reconstituting its nuclear weapons program, and Hussein had an active connection to Al Qaeda and the attacks of 9/11 against America.[6] Those statements proved untrue as well, and also exaggerated the information in the underlying intelligence reports.

When President Bush asked for the military authorization to invade Iraq, he made three promises to the country about prior steps he would take before using that authority to go to war: he would exhaust all diplomatic options, allow the international weapons inspectors to finish their search for dangerous weapons, and assemble as large a coalition of international supporters as his father had done in the earlier Persian Gulf War. The President broke all those promises as well.

The Iraq War certainly was a debacle for the United States. President Bush's decisions and actions cost the country dearly.

However, George Bush was correct about one thing. He proclaimed the doctrine of preemptive use of military power to be essential to America's survival in a dangerous world.[7] I agree. The preemptive use of American force, a first-strike by our military, could prove necessary in the future to protect our country, our friends and our vital national security interests around the world. But George Bush's performance regarding Iraq has done more to undercut, rather than support, his doctrine of preemption.

Future military and security threats will not all be telegraphed ahead of time. In the ongoing war against terrorists, and in an age of rogue states and unstable leaders, we cannot count on an enemy's army massing on our borders or his armada forming off our shores to provide the alert.

Someday a U.S. president, based upon classified intelligence, may seek congressional authority to preemptively strike Iran to prevent a nuclear attack on Israel, or to stop North Korea from attacking South Korea or Japan, or to stop an irrational regime from using chemical weapons on its own people or its neighbors. Our intelligence community may advise the President that our homeland is in imminent danger of an attack from a rogue nation or terrorist group. The President may feel compelled to act, and to seek congressional authority to act, based upon secret intelligence reports in order to keep the country safe.

That President's request for congressional support to strike first, valid or not, will likely be met with disbelief and resistance, after the Bush administration's misuse of intelligence in Iraq. Congress and the public will be highly skeptical the next time classified intelligence is cited as the basis for starting a war. However, unlike Iraq, the next time could actually represent a dire and desperate threat to America.

It is time to embrace one critical lesson of Iraq. Congress must never again authorize the preemptive use of American military power without prior public disclosure of the intelligence reports that demonstrate the imminent threat and the need for action.

Only public disclosure—and public scrutiny—of those intelligence findings, with appropriate protection of intelligence sources and methods, will allow that President to win congressional support for preemptive use of American force. If the disclosed intelligence findings make the case that America or our allies face a serious and imminent threat, then the President will win essential public and congressional support for America to strike first to protect our vital national security interests.

If the findings cannot withstand public scrutiny in the light of day, then Congress and the public will resist the rush to war, and another foreign policy debacle may be avoided.

It is important to note the difference between a war authorized by Congress and the emergency military action that a President may order under his constitutional powers as Commander in Chief to protect the country or retaliate against an enemy. It would be unwise and impractical to require prior disclosure of intelligence findings in such emergency situations, when time is of the essence and the President has clear constitutional authority to direct our armed forces to act without prior congressional authority.

But when the situation calls for Congress to declare war under the Constitution or to otherwise authorize military action around the world, such as an invasion of another country, clearly the lesson of Iraq must be that Congress should never again authorize preemptive war without public disclosure beforehand of the intelligence findings on which the executive branch is relying.

Make no mistake. The Bush Administration did not tell the truth to Congress or the public about the classified intelligence regarding Iraq. And when the truth is kept from the public, little public pressure comes to bear on Congress to discover the truth for itself.

I strongly believe that Congress, which is entirely dependent on the executive branch for intelligence information, would not have authorized the Iraq War if the classified intelligence findings regarding Hussein's weapons of mass destruction were available to all rank and file members before the vote on the war resolution. I also believe that prior disclosure of the intelligence findings about Iraq to the press and public would have generated enormous pressure on Congress to slow down, to question the intelligence reservations and inconsistencies about weapons of mass destruction, and to reassess the President's march to war.

The classified National Intelligence Estimate on Iraqi weapons was issued on October 1, 2002,[8] and was circulated by law only to top Administration figures, and to eight congressional leaders and the members of the House and Senate intelligence committees who were sworn to secrecy under the law and committee rules and not allowed to discuss the findings with their congressional colleagues.

It is true that the intelligence analysts wrongly concluded that Hussein probably had weapons of mass destruction, but the analysts weren't so sure about it and they clearly expressed their doubts in the National Intelligence Estimate. There were many reservations and much uncertainty stated in the classified report, which was not publicly known until months after our invasion of Iraq started. Four intelligence agencies dissented from some of the key findings, and the Estimate was full of caveats.

None of those reservations were shared with the public or most of Congress. In fact, President Bush and his senior advisers actively misled the country by repeatedly claiming with absolute certainty that Hussein possessed weapons of mass destruction, was rapidly acquiring more and was willing to use them. These adamant statements were not fully supported by the classified intelligence reports that the Bush Administration was receiving and inaccurately citing, and some of the claims of the President and his team were not substantiated by any intelligence findings at all.

I was part of a small group of members of Congress briefed on Iraq by Director of Central Intelligence George Tenet and National Security Adviser Condoleezza Rice on October 2, 2002 in the Roosevelt Room of the White House, one of a series of Iraq briefings conducted by the Bush Administration for members of Congress.

Tenet and Rice insisted with absolute certainty that Hussein had weapons of mass destruction, was ready to use them and was developing nuclear capability. Little did we know that the classified National Intelligence Estimate produced the day before by the National Intelligence Council was filled with uncertainty and reservations on all these points. George Tenet had ultimate responsibility for preparing the Estimate, and Condoleezza Rice was a primary consumer of the Estimate. They both had to know that their verbal certainty in the White House on October 2, 2002 was not an accurate reflection of the uncertainty of the classified Estimate circulated on a very limited basis the day before.

Tenet made matters even worse by publicly releasing a White Paper on Iraq on October 4,[9] which purported to summarize for press and public the secret National Intelligence Estimate. Tenet's White Paper intentionally misled the country by removing all the reservations and dissents from the key findings of the still-classified Estimate on Iraqi weapons, and thus presented a false picture of the actual assessments of our intelligence agencies regarding Iraq and Saddam Hussein's weapons of mass destruction.

Under our national security laws and congressional procedures, the public and most members of the House of Representatives were only able to read the whitewashed White Paper before the congressional vote to wage war against Iraq. George Tenet acknowledged in his 2008 memoir that the White Paper was a "major error" because it sounded far too assertive about Iraq's weapons of mass destruction, but that admission was too little, too late to provide accurate information and guidance to the country whether to go to war.[10]

On October 10, 2002, I voted to authorize the use of force against Iraq. At that time, I believed this preemptive military action was necessary to disarm Saddam Hussein of weapons of mass destruction. I have been kicking myself ever since the truth came out about misused intelligence. I was wrong to vote for the Iraq War. I cast about 10,000 votes in my twenty-five year public career, and surely in my voting record I made some poor judgments and stupid mistakes. But my vote for the Iraq War is the only vote I want back.

Shortly after the American military defeated the Iraqi army in April 2003, the Defense Department and the Central Intelligence Agency assembled a team of 1,400 military experts and weapons inspectors and sent them to Iraq to find the weapons of mass destruction. This team, the Iraq Survey Group, came up empty. Their final report on September 30, 2004 stated that when America started the war, Iraq did not possess chemical and biological weapons, was not reconstituting its nuclear program, and was not making any active effort to achieve those goals. The Group concluded that Saddam Hussein abandoned his weapons of mass destruction programs in the mid 1990s under the pressure of United Nations sanctions and inspections.

So, when I voted to send American troops to disarm Saddam Hussein of weapons of mass destruction, he was already disarmed.

The Senate Select Committee on Intelligence issued a series of reports from 2004 to 2008 regarding the use and misuse of prewar Iraq intelligence. Their final bi-partisan report of June 5, 2008 stated that the Bush Administration made significant claims about Iraq that were not supported by the intelligence, leading the American people to believe that the threat from Iraq was much greater than it actually was.[11] The 2008 Senate report concluded that the Bush Administration led the nation into war under false pretenses.

So, when I trusted President Bush and his top advisers regarding the imminent threat posed by Saddam Hussein, I was both misled and wrong.

The Bush team, in post-war statements and in their memoirs, proclaims that they truly believed before the war that Saddam Hussein had weapons of mass destruction. Perhaps they did, and I have no information to the contrary. But I cannot accept their absolute refusal to admit that they distorted and manipulated the intelligence to bolster their case for war, despite all the evidence that they did just that. And I abhor the attempts of some of them in their memoirs to continue to mislead the country about what really happened regarding the intelligence, and what they really did to misuse that intelligence.

I don't want George W. Bush and his top people to get away with it. It is time they are held accountable for leading us under false pretenses into war with Iraq. It is time for a transparent review of how we decided to go to war, and time to adopt thoughtful reforms so we do not make such a mistake again.

My goal for this book is to set the record straight. This book will review many of the statements and public speeches by the Bush team, will analyze the effect those statements had on me, my congressional colleagues and the public, and will present in detail the critical, damning conclusions of the Senate Intelligence Committee and reports by American and international weapons inspectors regarding the false and exaggerated claims about Iraqi weapons of mass destruction.

We must never again go to war based on inaccurate or distorted intelligence.

Congress must act now to mandate the public disclosure of any intelligence findings that a President cites when seeking congressional authority for preemptive use of American military power. We must learn the lesson of Iraq: disclose the intelligence before starting a war.

This is my story, told as it was happening with events unfolding around me, about how I was both misled and wrong about Iraq. These are the events that led me to vote in Congress for the war resolution, then to realize how mistaken that vote was, and finally to conclude what we need to do to make sure a debacle like Iraq never happens again.

ONE

The Hard Sell

I walked up the famous driveway, feeling edgy and tense. The horse-shoe drive was off to my left, leading to the familiar portico with its soaring white columns and black hanging lantern. I was headed up the shorter drive on the right toward the low-slung office wing of this world-renowned residence. It was a hot and humid morning in the nation's capital, and my shirt was sticking to my back under my suit, but it wasn't the warm weather that was bothering me. I was thinking about war and peace and was in a skeptical frame of mind. My guard was up.

I knew it wasn't every day that a rank and file Democratic congressman was invited to a Republican White House. This day, Wednesday, October 2, 2002, a bi-partisan group of a dozen House members was scheduled for a private briefing at the White House. President George W. Bush had been beating the drums for war with Iraq for several months and was pushing Congress hard to give him the necessary authority. The President had ordered top administration officials to make the case for war directly to members of Congress, and I had accepted the White House invitation to the briefing. I was expecting the hard sell at the hands of the administration briefers.

My colleagues and I walked past the stiff Marines guarding the north entrance of the West Wing of the White House. Well-dressed young staffers greeted us, efficiently checked our credentials and organized us into a tight grouping in the lobby. Most of us were furtively gawking, never having stood in the West Wing lobby. The walls were covered with oil paintings of nautical scenes and Revolutionary events.

I spotted a painting of George Washington crossing the Delaware River, which is near my home in southeastern Pennsylvania. I was impressed by my surroundings, and a bit intimidated.

I knew this was not just a nice, friendly social visit to the White House. The Bush Administration had made it clear that they wanted to get rid of Saddam Hussein, and I expected to be lobbied hard to give the President the authority to go to war in Iraq.

The hushed tone and calm atmosphere in the West Wing was so different from the noisy hustle and bustle of any workday in the Capitol and the congressional office buildings. As the young staffers shepherded the members of Congress down a short hall to the Roosevelt Room, I realized that I didn't fully trust any of the Bush team that would be lobbying us today.

I knew a sales pitch for war was coming, and I knew the congressional vote was fast approaching to give George W. Bush the war authority he wanted. I knew my constituents, after months of administration pressure, seemed to support the President. I knew I really liked my job representing the suburbs of Philadelphia in Congress, and didn't want to recklessly jeopardize my chances for re-election, just five weeks away. What I didn't know was whom to trust, or how I was going to vote on authorizing war in Iraq. It was making me anxious.

The congressional delegation settled around the beautiful mahogany table in the Roosevelt Room, just a few steps from the Oval Office. In my second term in the House, I had been to the White House several times for ceremonial public events in the East Room. But this was my first time in the West Wing, where the President and his top staffers work.

Presidents and their senior advisors routinely use the Roosevelt Room for internal meetings and for briefings for foreign dignitaries and special guests. I looked around the room, painted a buff color with white trim, windowless with a false skylight in the ceiling. I knew that President Nixon had renamed the room after President Theodore Roosevelt, who built the West Wing, and President Franklin D. Roosevelt, who expanded it. I thought that TR looked particularly dashing in his Rough Rider uniform on a rearing horse in the oil painting hanging over the mantel on the curved east wall of the room, with his Nobel Peace Prize on display on the mantel, while FDR looked somber in a dark, formal portrait on a side wall. I wondered what the Roosevelt presidents would make of the threat posed by Saddam Hussein, and what they might do about it if they were sitting in the Oval Office instead of hanging on the walls.

CIA Director George Tenet and National Security Advisor Condoleezza Rice swept into the room, trailed by several self-important aides. After quick, solemn greetings around the table, Tenet and Rice got right to the point. Saddam Hussein had to go, they said. Tenet was blunt and matter of fact, and was the only man in the room in his shirtsleeves. Rice was focused and unsmiling, every hair in place. They opined with absolute certainty that Hussein had weapons of mass destruction, was rapidly acquiring more, and was willing to use them. They proclaimed that Hussein's Iraq was an imminent threat to regional peace and stability, and to our national security, and must be stopped as soon as possible.

Tenet and Rice then reviewed with us the public statements recently made by leading administration figures on the dangers posed by Saddam Hussein.

On August 26, 2002, in a speech to the Veterans of Foreign Wars, Vice President Dick Cheney had said:

> Simply stated, there is no doubt that Saddam now has weapons of mass destruction. There is no doubt he is amassing them to use against our friends, against our allies, and against us.[1]

I remembered that speech well, for it had received tremendous press attention and shocked the country out of its summer doldrums.

I had heard from several colleagues about Defense Secretary Donald Rumsfeld's testimony on September 10, 2002 to the House Armed Services Committee. Rumsfeld had testified:

> No terrorist state poses a greater or more immediate threat to the security of our people and the stability of the world than the regime of Saddam Hussein in Iraq . . . his regime has amassed large, clandestine stocks of biological weapons . . . his regime has amassed large, clandestine stockpiles of chemical weapons . . . his regime has an active program to acquire and develop nuclear weapons. And let there be no doubt about it, his regime has dozens of ballistic missiles.[2]

I knew that most of the Armed Services members were greatly influenced by the Defense Secretary's presentation.

Tenet then called our attention to the so-called Rose Garden speech of the President on September 26, just the week before. With some members of Congress by his side in the White House Rose Garden, President George W. Bush had said:

> The danger to our country is grave. The danger to our country is growing. The Iraqi regime possesses biological and chemical weapons. The Iraqi regime is building the facilities necessary to make more biological and chemical weapons. And according to the British government, the Iraqi regime could launch a biological or chemical attack in as little as 45 minutes after the order was given . . . and there are al Qaeda terrorists inside Iraq.[3]

I recalled two takeaways from this speech. First, how much it had scared my friends and constituents who discussed it with me afterward. Second, how silly some of my colleagues had looked on TV that night as they jostled and elbowed each other in the Rose Garden to position themselves in the best camera angles right behind the President.

Clearly, George Tenet and Condoleezza Rice were pulling out all the stops and were wrapping their presentation in as much presidential and national security aura as possible. As I looked around the room, my Republican colleagues and many of the Democrats seemed totally sold on the necessity of taking out Hussein, while a few of the Democrats looked skeptical. I wasn't sure whom to believe. This presentation was powerful.

Tenet spoke at length about the nuclear threat posed by Hussein. My friend Congressman Adam Schiff of California asked him, "Director, on a scale of one to ten, what is your level of confidence in the intelligence that Iraq has an ongoing nuclear weapons program?"

George Tenet instantly replied, "Ten."

This exchange set off Condoleezza Rice. The National Security Advisor began to mutter darkly about the horrors of a nuclear war and the dangers of waiting for ironclad proof before acting to prevent one. She intoned, "We don't want the smoking gun to be a mushroom cloud."

I knew this was not the first time Condoleezza Rice had used her "mushroom cloud" rhetoric. In preparation for this White House briefing, my staff had shown me the transcript of her interview with Wolf Blitzer on CNN on September 8, 2002, where Rice said:

> There is no doubt that Saddam Hussein's regime is a danger to the United States and to its allies, to our interests. It is also a danger that is gathering momentum, and it simply makes no

sense to wait any longer to do something about the threat that is posed here . . .

We do know that he is actively pursuing a nuclear weapon. We do know that there have been shipments going into Iraq of aluminum tubes . . . that are only really suited for nuclear weapons programs . . . we don't want the smoking gun to be a mushroom cloud.[4]

But I had never before heard George Tenet express himself with such absolute certainty on the nuclear question. I took a quick glance around the table and surmised that none of my colleagues had heard this before either. I remember thinking that a "ten" on a one to ten scale is about as certain as you can get.

Adam Schiff would say later that Tenet's absolute certainty was "meaningful and carried a lot of weight" since he considered the Director of the CIA less political and more credible on intelligence matters than the National Security Adviser.[5] I agreed.

The presentation wound down to its conclusion, and after quick, obligatory handshakes the delegation left the cool quiet of the White House and walked back down the driveway in the October heat and humidity. The members of Congress talked quietly in small groups, discussing what we had just heard and trying to assess its impact.

I was impressed by the presentation. I remember saying to no one in particular, "Those guys make a very convincing case."

A couple of my colleagues thought the Bush advisors were overstating their case and exaggerating their claims. There was a skeptical comment or two about George Tenet's assertion of "ten" about Iraqi nukes, with the doubters wondering how the CIA Director could be so positive since international weapons inspectors had been thrown out of Iraq four years earlier. There was some worry that President Bush wanted to invade Iraq just to avenge the assassination attempt on his father's life, and to get Saddam's oil in the process. But most of my fellow members of Congress seemed convinced that Saddam Hussein and his weapons of mass destruction posed an imminent threat to America and our allies.

There were also hard feelings among some of my colleagues about the comments of Vice President Dick Cheney the previous month on the PBS show *Newshour* that the Administration couldn't trust Congress with classified intelligence about Iraq because we would just start leaking it to the press.[6] Sure enough, George Tenet and Condoleezza Rice had not shown us any hard intelligence evidence or reports.

Little did we know that the day before our briefing, on October 1, 2002, the National Intelligence Council issued the National Intelligence Estimate entitled "Iraq's Continuing Programs for Weapons of Mass Destruction." This was the definitive and comprehensive statement of the country's Intelligence Community regarding the state of Hussein's weapons, and it was circulated on a classified basis only to the upper levels of the administration and to the eight leaders and intelligence committee members of Congress, all sworn to secrecy under the law.

Our congressional delegation would have been astonished, and furious, to learn how many caveats and reservations were expressed in the National Intelligence Estimate about the status of Iraq's weapons programs, and how the document contained dissents from four intelligence agencies to some parts of the findings. We had not heard any uncertainty or any dissenting opinion from Tenet and Rice about Saddam Hussein or his weapons of mass destruction.

That day, it seemed to me that the President's chief advisor on national security and the President's intelligence chief must have all the necessary information about weapons of mass destruction in Iraq. I figured they had to know what they were talking about.

It was inconceivable to me that the President of the United States and his top people would distort the intelligence to secure congressional votes to invade Iraq.

I thought that my eyes were wide open. After all, Saddam Hussein had already proven himself to be a murderous tyrant by using chemical weapons during the Iraq-Iran War to kill thousands of innocent Iranian and Kurdish-Iraqi civilians. It seemed both prudent and reasonable to me to believe the administration's firm statements that Hussein still had weapons of mass destruction, was actively developing more and was willing to use them again.

I kept wondering that if you can't trust the President and his top national security team on the fundamental issue of going to war, then who can you trust?

I also was thinking about the failure of England and Western Europe to stand up to Germany in the mid 1930s, when early, decisive action against Hitler before he gained such military strength might have avoided the necessity for World War II. If Saddam Hussein was truly the imminent threat to peace that the Administration claimed, then the sooner we acted, the better.

I still wasn't sure I could completely trust the President or his top people. But I was sure that a general mistrust of George Bush was not an adequate basis to determine my vote on a matter of war and peace.

The day after my White House briefing, on Thursday, October 3, I was visited in my office in the Longworth House Office Building by Ahmed Chalabi, founder and spokesman for the Iraqi National Congress, a group of Iraqi exiles who had long opposed the tyrannical rule of Saddam Hussein. Financially supported by the Pentagon, and vigorously promoted by the Bush White House, the Iraqi National Congress was providing much of the insider information used by the Bush administration to build its case for war. Chalabi was meeting with members of the House International Relations Committee on which I served to lobby for military action to remove Saddam Hussein from power. I did not learn anything new from my private meeting with Chalabi, except that the Iraqi exile had expensive tastes in clothing. Chalabi's suit was made of the finest material and was well tailored over his chubby body. His shoes were highly polished and his French cuffs sported what I thought were White House cuff links. Chalabi made the same arguments that I had heard the day before in the Roosevelt Room of the White House. I thought that the man sitting on my office couch could be a White House staffer for all the similarities in the arguments I was hearing. After Chalabi left, I told my young Chief of Staff, Josh Shapiro, that the Iraqi talked a good game, but he struck me as a four-flusher.

Josh said he agreed that Chalabi was glib, but asked me what I meant by "four-flusher."

I thought for a moment and responded that my grandfather used to use that phrase in the context of someone being a braggart. I thought it must come from poker, which my grandfather loved to play, where you need five cards of the same suit for a flush, so if you have just four cards of the same suit you don't really have anything at all.

The next day, Friday, October 4, 2002, George Tenet's Central Intelligence Agency publicly released a White Paper entitled "Iraq's Weapons of Mass Destruction Programs." Tenet presented this document to the public and Congress as a summary of the national intelligence reports on Iraq. Most of my colleagues and I, the media and the public had no idea that the White Paper we read on Friday removed all the caveats, reservations and dissenting opinions about Hussein's weapons contained in the classified National Intelligence Estimate that had been issued on Tuesday. We had no idea, and would have been outraged, that the Bush Administration had intentionally misled us.

I returned home to Abington, Pennsylvania that weekend to see my wife and to do some campaigning for re-election around the congressional district. Friday night my wife Francesca was cooking a late dinner after my arrival on the train from Washington. I described for her the persuasive power of the briefing at the White House. I admitted my inclination to accept the arguments of the top administration figures that were making the case for war based on the imminent threat posed by Iraq's weapons of mass destruction.

Francesca wasn't happy and she wasn't mincing any words. "You can't vote for this war. These guys are lying about all of this. And you know that you can't trust George Bush."

I told her I was worried about the threat posed by Hussein. I tried my argument that the Allies should have stood up sooner to Hitler. I discussed that week's briefing at the White House and that day's release of the CIA White Paper. I did not admit to my wife that I was also worried about my re-election, now just over a month away. But I did recount for her that the strong majority of opinion I was hearing from my constituents was I should support the President and stop the threat posed by Saddam Hussein.

Francesca wasn't buying any of it. She dismissed my arguments with a wave of her hand. She said she didn't care what my constituents thought because I was elected to exercise my own judgment, and I shouldn't trust George Bush.

I told her I didn't want to end up on the wrong side of history by failing to act when we were able to eliminate an imminent threat to the country. She told me I was about to end up on the wrong side of my family, since our daughter Mary had called from Missoula, Montana, where she was teaching as an AmeriCorps volunteer, and was threatening not to vote for me or come home again if I was stupid enough to vote for the war. I said I couldn't believe that my wife and daughter were putting such pressure on me and were being so unsupportive. I questioned her about how they could be so sure they were correct.

Francesca simply looked at me and said, "You can't trust George Bush."

I replied, "If George Bush is lying about the weapons in Iraq, it will ruin him."

I didn't realize at the time that Francesca and I were both right.

TWO

Intelligence Truth and Lies

The crux of the case against George W. Bush for taking the country to war in Iraq under false pretenses is that the certainty of the Bush administration's public statements, public documents and private briefings about the Iraqi threat did not match the uncertainty of the classified intelligence that the administration was receiving.

I believe Congress would not have authorized the Iraq War if most members had been able to read the classified National Intelligence Estimate on Iraqi weapons before we took our vote, rather than just the public White Paper purportedly summarizing the key findings of the Estimate. The uncertainties, reservations and agency dissents expressed in the classified Estimate, which were removed from the public White Paper, would have created too much doubt and raised too many questions in Congress to win a majority vote for the war authority requested by the Bush Administration.

I know that if I knew then what I know now, I would have voted no.

By way of background, a National Intelligence Estimate is the authoritative written assessment of United States intelligence analysts on a particular national security issue. Produced by the National Intelligence Council under the direction of the Director of National Intelligence (before 2004, by the Director of Central Intelligence), Estimates express the considered and coordinated judgments of the Intelligence Community, the group of 16 U.S. agencies that gather and analyze intelligence. Estimates are classified documents prepared for policymakers, typically at the request of senior civilian and military officials, including congressional leaders.

The Intelligence Community strives to produce accurate, timely and useful strategic intelligence assessments. Because of the needs for inter-agency coordination and analytic rigor, National Intelligence Estimates often take from several months to more than a year to complete.[1]

In the fall of 2002, facing the looming vote demanded by the Bush Administration to authorize war against Iraq, Senate leaders requested the Intelligence Community to prepare an Estimate on Iraqi weapons. The October 1, 2002 Estimate on Iraqi weapons was the rushed result, and was prepared in less than a month.[2]

As stated, any National Intelligence Estimate is generally consid-ered to be the most comprehensive and definitive intelligence report available to national policymakers in the White House and Congress. Accordingly, the unusually short preparation period for the National Intelligence Estimate on Iraqi weapons raises the question of whether the Bush Administration paid any attention at all to the key findings of the Estimate. All of the major figures of the Administration, includ-ing the President himself, were already on the public record as fully con-vinced that Saddam Hussein had weapons of mass destruction, and were publicly committed to eliminating the threat posed by Hussein and his weapons, long before the classified Estimate was privately circulated on October 1. It seems the Bush team was determined to invade Iraq long before the preparation of the Estimate even began in early September.

A detailed comparison of the two intelligence documents, one clas-sified and the other prepared as a public summary of the classified one, reveals the case against George W. Bush and his team for intentional distortion of intelligence findings. Excerpts of the two documents are contained in the appendix of this book.

The classified document is the National Intelligence Estimate enti-tled "Iraq's Continuing Programs for Weapons of Mass Destruction," 90 pages, published October 1, 2002 by the National Intelligence Coun-cil.[3] The Estimate remains classified to this day, but excerpts were partially declassified by the White House on July 18, 2003 in an off-the-record press briefing by a "senior administration official", in an appar-ent but unsuccessful attempt by the Bush team to demonstrate they had not distorted the intelligence. When the off-the-record briefing created a storm of controversy and press demands for accountability, the White House communications director Dan Bartlett identified himself for the record on July 22 as the "senior administration official" of the briefing. It is the partially declassified Estimate presented by the Bush White House that is analyzed in this book and contained in the appendix.

The second document is entitled "White Paper: Iraq's Weapons of Mass Destruction Programs", 25 pages, publicly released October 4, 2002 by the Director of Central Intelligence George Tenet.[4] Many Members of Congress and representatives of the media were asking for an unclassified version of the Iraq intelligence on which the Bush team was relying, and George Tenet presented the White Paper as that public summary.

A close comparison of the documents uncovers the reservations and dissents contained in the classified Estimate, and identifies the removal of those expressions of uncertainty in the public White Paper. The comparison shows how the White Paper was whitewashed.

For example, the White Paper consistently dropped the phrases "we judge" and "we assess" from the text of the Estimate, thus changing cautious expressions of opinion to firm statements of fact.

"We judge that Iraq has continued its weapons of mass destruction programs" in the Estimate is changed in the White Paper to "Iraq has continued its weapons of mass destruction programs".

"We judge that we are seeing only a portion of Iraq's WMD efforts" in the Estimate becomes "Baghdad hides large portions of Iraq's WMD efforts" in the White Paper.

"We assess that Baghdad has begun renewed production of mustard, sarin, cyclosarin, and VX" in the Estimate becomes in the White Paper "Baghdad has begun renewed production of chemical warfare agents".

"We judge that all key aspects—R&D, production, and weaponization—of Iraq's offensive BW program are active" in the Estimate becomes "All key aspects—R&D, production, and weaponization—of Iraq's offensive BW program are active" in the White Paper.

"We judge Iraq has some lethal and incapacitating BW agents" in the Estimate becomes "Iraq has some lethal and incapacitating BW agents" in the White Paper.

These changes have large significance in the language of intelligence analysis. They change the meaning of the classified intelligence document by morphing uncertain expressions of opinion into statements of fact. The uncertainty of the classified intelligence is changed into the "certainty" of the public document.

But this is not what the intelligence analysts intended. The National Intelligence Council offered a clear expression of the meaning of their language in their January 2007 National Intelligence Estimate on Iraq's prospects for stability. In a section titled "What We Mean When We Say: An Explanation of Estimative Language," the Council wrote:

When we use words such as "we judge" or "we assess"—terms we use synonymously—as well as "we estimate," "likely" or "indicate", we are trying to convey an analytical assessment or judgment. These assessments, which are based on incomplete or at times fragmentary information are not a fact, proof, or knowledge. Some analytical judgments are based directly on collected information; others rest on previous judgments, which serve as building blocks. In either type of judgment, we do not have "evidence" that shows something to be a fact or that definitively links two items or issues.[5]

When the Director of Central Intelligence, George Tenet, publicly released the White Paper on Iraqi weapons as a summary of the secret Estimate, he knew what he was doing. He was changing uncertain classified opinions into factual statements for public consumption.

Director Tenet certainly didn't stop there. He also excluded from the White Paper certain key sentences and important sections in their entirety that were contained in the Estimate.

The sentence in the classified Estimate, "We lack specific information on many key aspects of Iraq's WMD programs" was dropped in its entirety from the public White Paper, thus completely omitting a major reservation.

In the section on mustard gas and other chemical weapons, the White Paper drops this entire qualifying clause from the Estimate, "Although we have little specific information on Iraq's CW stockpile . . ." Omitting this huge caveat kept out of the public discourse the truth about our lack of knowledge of Hussein's chemical weapons.

Significantly, this important qualification in the Estimate about our lack of knowledge regarding Hussein's chemical weapons stockpiles was similar to a glaring reservation contained in an underlying defense intelligence report. The Defense Intelligence Agency circulated a classified report to the Intelligence Community on Iraq's weapons facilities in September 2002, and the report was used to prepare the National Intelligence Estimate of October 1. The defense report was declassified by the Department of Defense on June 7, 2003 after it had been leaked the previous day, causing a media uproar. The classified report stated:

There is no reliable information on whether Iraq is producing and stockpiling chemical weapons, or where Iraq has—or will—establish its chemical warfare agent production facilities.[6]

This critical reservation from an important underlying intelligence report is reflected in the classified National Intelligence Estimate in the key qualifier, "we have little specific information on Iraq's CW stockpile."

But, shockingly, no such caveat about unreliable chemical weapons information was repeated in the October 4 public White Paper. Nor were any such uncertainties about chemical weapons contained in any of the public statements at this time by the President or any of his top aides. To the contrary, the Bush team was insisting the Hussein had chemical weapons and was ready to use them.

Whole sections of the classified Estimate containing caveats and reservations were omitted in their entirety from the public White Paper. An example is the elimination from the White Paper of the entire section from the Estimate entitled Confidence Levels for Key Judgments in This Estimate. This section of the Estimate admitted that the intelligence analysts had "low confidence" in three of their "key judgments":

- When Saddam would use weapons of mass destruction
- Whether Saddam would engage in clandestine attacks against the U.S. Homeland
- Whether in desperation Saddam would share chemical or biological weapons with Al Qaeda.

Of course, all three of these terrifying prospects were repeatedly trumpeted by the President and his top advisers as imminent threats to America, as realities that warranted the extraordinary step of authorizing a preemptive first strike to eliminate these threats, despite the deep uncertainty, the "low confidence", of the intelligence analysts regarding the likelihood of these three risks. Omitting from the White Paper the section on Confidence Levels for Key Judgments in This Estimate drastically changed the meaning and the impact of the uncertain intelligence analysis as stated in the Estimate.

Finally, the public White Paper completely excluded the actual statements and any specific references to four agency opinions dissenting to parts of the classified Estimate.

First, both documents contain the statement '[Iraq] probably will have a nuclear weapon during this decade'. But the public White Paper omitted the long section contained in the Estimate from the State Department's Bureau of Intelligence and Research (INR) indicating that the intelligence gathering and analyzing arm of the State Department disagreed with that conclusion about Iraq's nuclear readiness. The omitted section stated:

INR believes that Saddam continues to want nuclear weapons and that available evidence indicates that Baghdad is pursuing at least a limited effort to maintain and acquire nuclear weapons-related capabilities. The activities we have detected do not, however, add up to a compelling case that Iraq is currently pursuing what INR would consider to be an integrated and comprehensive approach to acquire nuclear weapons. Iraq may be doing so, but INR considers the available evidence inadequate to support such a judgment . . .

In INR's view, Iraq's efforts to acquire aluminum tubes is central to the argument that Baghdad is reconstituting its nuclear weapons program, but INR is not persuaded that the tubes in question are intended for use as centrifuge rotors. INR accepts the judgment of the technical experts at the U.S. Department of Energy (DOE) who have concluded that the tubes Iraq seeks to acquire are poorly suited for use in gas centrifuges to be used for uranium enrichment and finds unpersuasive the arguments advanced by others to make the case that they are intended for that purpose. INR considers it far more likely that the tubes are intended for another purpose, most likely the production of artillery rockets.

This dissenting opinion from State, the leading foreign policy agency, incorporating the dissent from Energy, casts considerable doubt on the insistence of the President, the Director of Central Intelligence and the National Security Adviser that Saddam Hussein was reconstituting a nuclear program. But all reference to this dissent was eliminated from the public White Paper.

Second, the White Paper omitted the specific statement in the Estimate that the Department of Energy (DOE) disagreed that those high-strength aluminum tubes were intended for a nuclear program. This is a troubling omission, since DOE is the federal agency with the most knowledge and specific responsibility for nuclear development, safety and non-proliferation programs, and serves as the nuclear experts for the Intelligence Community. DOE's dissenting view, had it been known, would have strongly influenced public opinion, as we have seen how the DOE dissent influenced the State Department.

Third, the Estimate contains two statements:

- Iraq maintains a small missile force and several development programs, including for an Unmanned Aerial Vehicle (UAV) probably intended to deliver biological agents.

- Baghdad's UAVs could threaten Iraq's neighbors, U.S. forces in the Persian Gulf, and if brought close to, or into, the United States, the U.S. Homeland.

But the Estimate also contained a key dissenting opinion regarding the two statements quoted above regarding Iraq's UAV program:

The Director, Intelligence, Surveillance, and Reconnaissance, U.S. Air Force, does not agree that Iraq is developing UAVs *primarily* [emphasis in original] intended to be delivery platforms for chemical and biological warfare (CBW) agents. The small size of Iraq's new UAV strongly suggests a primary role of reconnaissance, although CBW delivery is an inherent capability.

The White Paper removed this dissenting opinion in its entirety. This omission is particularly glaring because the intelligence, surveillance, and reconnaissance branch of the U.S. Air Force is the agency with primary responsibility within the Intelligence Community for technical analysis on unmanned aerial vehicle programs. But the readers of the White Paper never knew that Air Force intelligence dissented from the findings of the Estimate and the repeated hype of the President and his political appointees that unmanned aerial vehicles from Iraq posed a clear and present danger to the United States.

Fourth, the White Paper also totally omitted a section of the Estimate that contained this dissenting statement from the State Department's Bureau of Intelligence and Research (INR) on the issue of African uranium as part of Iraq's weapons programs:

Finally, the claims of Iraqi pursuit of natural uranium in Africa are, in INR's assessment, highly dubious.

No intelligence branch of any federal agency would have a more qualified opinion on the overseas adventures of Saddam Hussein than the department charged with our nation's diplomacy and foreign policy. And yet the State Department's dismissive opinion of the claim that Hussein was seeking uranium for nuclear enrichment, "highly dubious", was omitted from the public White Paper.

The White Paper was a whitewash. It was an intentional attempt by the Bush Administration to keep the Congress and the American people from knowing of the numerous uncertainties and professional doubts within the Intelligence Community regarding Saddam Hussein, the status of his weapons and his actual threat to the United States.

On July 9, 2004, the Senate Select Committee on Intelligence issued a report on prewar intelligence assessments which identified many failures by the Intelligence Community in both the gathering of intelligence and its analysis regarding Iraq, failures that misled both government officials and the general public.[7] The Report's first conclusion was:

> Most of the major key judgments in the Intelligence Community's October 2002 National Intelligence Estimate (NIE), Iraq's Continuing Programs for Weapons of Mass Destruction, either overstated, or were not supported by, the underlying intelligence reporting. A series of failures, particularly in analytic trade craft, led to the mischaracterization of the intelligence.

But in addition to the flawed intelligence, the Senate Intelligence Committee also found problems and discrepancies between the intelligence reports themselves. The 2004 Senate Report compared the classified October 1, 2002 National Intelligence Estimate on Iraqi weapons with the unclassified White Paper, which followed three days later on October 4. The Senate Report stated:

> . . . The key judgments of the unclassified paper were missing many of the caveats and some references to alternative agency views that were used in the classified NIE. Removing caveats such as "we judge" or "we assess" changed many sentences in the unclassified paper to statements of fact rather than assessments.

The 2004 Senate Intelligence Committee Report reached three Conclusions regarding the White Paper:

- The Intelligence Community's elimination of the caveats from the unclassified White Paper misrepresented their judgments to the public . . .
- The names of agencies which had dissenting opinions in the classified National Intelligence Estimate were not included in the unclassified White Paper . . . excluding the names of the [dissenting] agencies provided readers with an incomplete picture of the nature and extent of the debate within the Intelligence Community regarding these issues.

- The key judgment in the unclassified October 2002 White Paper on Iraq's potential to deliver biological agents conveyed a level of threat to the United States homeland inconsistent with the classified National Intelligence Estimate.

There is no doubt that the Intelligence Community produced flawed intelligence analysis about Iraqi weapons for use by the White House and other high level federal policymakers. This failure is both unfortunate and unacceptable, because flawed intelligence generates bad policy decisions, and there is really no excuse that the best intelligence operation in the world was so wrong about Iraq. Our analysts thought Saddam Hussein probably had weapons of mass destruction, but he didn't. They thought he probably was building and acquiring more, but he wasn't.

But the Intelligence Community also expressed its doubts. They weren't so sure about Hussein and his weapons of mass destruction. These reservations were expressed, as we have seen, in numerous caveats, doubts and dissents included in the flawed October 1, 2002 National Intelligence Estimate, which was the comprehensive statement by the Intelligence Community about Iraqi weapons of mass destruction. The analysts were wrong when they concluded in the Estimate that Hussein probably had weapons of mass destruction, but they freely expressed their doubts and identified their uncertainties in the same document.

President Bush's appointee as Director of the Central Intelligence Agency, George Tenet, took out all the uncertainties and reservations of the Estimate when the CIA published the public White Paper three days later. As the Senate Intelligence Committee unanimously concluded, the White Paper "changed many sentences in the unclassified paper to statements of fact rather than assessments", "misrepresented (the Intelligence Community's) judgments to the public", "provided readers with an incomplete picture", and "conveyed a level of threat to the United States homeland inconsistent with the classified National Intelligence Estimate."

But George Tenet's misrepresentations in the White Paper certainly were not the only sordid examples of intelligence hype and abuse by the President and top Administration figures in their public statements urging military action against Saddam Hussein. The bipartisan final report of the Senate Intelligence Committee on June 5, 2008 studied whether public statements by the Bush administration were accurately based on the available intelligence.[8] Senator John D. (Jay) Rockefeller IV, chair of the committee, made the following public statement:

Unfortunately, our Committee has concluded that the Administration made significant claims that were not supported by the intelligence. In making the case for war, the Administration repeatedly presented intelligence as fact when in reality it was unsubstantiated, contradicted, or even non-existent . . . Sadly, the Bush Administration led the nation into war under false pretenses.[9]

If I knew in October 2002 what I know now, if I knew then that the flawed findings of our nation's key intelligence report on Iraqi weapons of mass destruction had been secretly changed from uncertain opinion into statements of fact, if I knew then that the Bush Administration was leading us into war under false pretenses, I would have opposed going to war against an already virtually disarmed Iraq.

If they knew the truth in October 2002, I am convinced that a majority of the members of Congress also would have opposed the war in Iraq. And so the history of Iraq, our role in the Middle East and our stature and influence around the world would be very different today.

THREE

The Run-Up to War

Saddam Hussein was a murderous tyrant. He was an unstable leader, a danger to neighboring countries and a menace to his own citizens. He murdered political opponents, abused human rights, started wars, committed war crimes, and used chemical weapons of mass destruction against innocent civilians in the 1980s.

Hussein served as the fifth President of Iraq from July 16, 1979, when he seized power from the ailing, elderly President Ahmed Hassan al-Bakr, until Baghdad fell to U.S.-led coalition forces on April 9, 2003.

On July 22, 1979, soon after assuming the presidency, Hussein convened a meeting of the top leaders of the ruling Ba'ath Party. Hussein announced at the meeting that he had uncovered disloyalty among many of those present, and he had the names of 68 alleged co-conspirators read aloud. As names were called, the individuals were escorted from the room and placed under arrest. At the end of the meeting, Hussein congratulated those who remained for their loyalty and patriotism. The 68 who were arrested were subsequently tried as a group, found guilty of treason, and many were sentenced to death. By August 1, 1979, hundreds of high-ranking Ba'ath Party leaders had been executed, often with other top party leaders serving as the firing squad.[1]

Hussein started wars against Iran in 1980 and Kuwait in 1990. Probably over a million people died on all sides of those wars—nobody knows for sure.

Hussein's campaign of genocide against the Kurds in Northern Iraq, in which he used chemical weapons against his own citizens, led to the death of between 50,000–150,000 people[2]—nobody knows for sure.

Hussein's regime was responsible for the deaths of at least 250,000 Iraqis, and committed war crimes in Iran, Kuwait and Saudi Arabia.[3]

At the end of the Persian Gulf War in February, 1991, after U.S. and British armored and infantry troops with the support of the United Nations ousted the Iraqi Army from Kuwait, President George H. W. Bush decided not to march on Baghdad and left Saddam Hussein in power.

Finally, after the subsequent and successful military invasion of Iraq under President George W. Bush, Hussein was captured on December 13, 2003 by United States forces. On June 30, 2004, the United States transferred power to the interim Iraqi government, including legal responsibility for the former Iraqi president.

On November 5, 2006, after a long, contentious trial, Saddam Hussein was found guilty of crimes against humanity and was sentenced to death by hanging.

On December 30, 2006, while exchanging curses with newly trained members of the Iraqi National Police, Saddam Hussein was hanged until dead.[4]

For many years, the international community was aware of the evil nature of Saddam Hussein and of the threats he posed to regional stability in the Middle East. The Security Council of the United Nations, charged with maintaining peace and security among nations, passed at least 50 Resolutions from 1980 through 2007 addressing security and humanitarian crises caused by Iraq.[5]

These Resolutions called for an end to the Iran-Iraq War, deplored the use of chemical weapons in that war, condemned the Iraqi invasion of Kuwait and demanded a withdrawal, placed economic sanctions on Iraq for invading Kuwait, condemned the repression of Iraqi Kurds, and gave Iraq a final chance to disarm.

Two of the most important Security Council Resolutions regarding Iraq involved the invasion of Kuwait in 1990. The first, Resolution 678 on November 29, 1990, authorized the use of force to implement the Security Council's earlier demand that Iraq leave Kuwait and "to restore international peace and security in the area." President George H. W. Bush used this international authority, which he had secured through deft diplomacy at the United Nations, to justify American use of force in January 1991 to expel Iraq from Kuwait in the Persian Gulf War.

The second key Security Council action was Resolution 687 on April 3, 1991, which declared a formal ceasefire ending the Persian Gulf War, with the conditions that Iraq must destroy all chemical and biological weapons and long-range ballistic missiles, agree not to develop nuclear weapons, and permit on-site weapons inspections. Iraq agreed to all terms, and Saddam Hussein stayed in power. But in 1998, in violation of his commitments to the international community, Hussein ousted all United Nations weapons inspectors from Iraq.

The most important United Nations Security Council resolution about Iraq was the one that never passed, the one that would have authorized the international use of force in 2003 to disarm Iraq of weapons of mass destruction.

The Security Council set the stage for possible United Nations intervention in Iraq on November 8, 2002 with passage of Resolution 1441 giving Iraq "a final opportunity to comply with its disarmament obligations" as set forth eleven years before in Resolution 687.

After years of refusing to comply with United Nations resolutions demanding compliance with weapons inspections and his obligations to disarm, Saddam Hussein finally complied. Weapons inspections by the United Nations resumed in Iraq on November 27, 2002, as a result of the passage of Resolution 1441.

The chief U.N. weapons inspector, Hans Blix, presented an interim report to the Security Council on March 7, 2003 stating the United Nations was conducting professional, no-notice inspections all over Iraq and had found no evidence of illegal weapons activity by Iraq. Chief Inspector Blix estimated the time needed to complete the inspection work and draw his final conclusions about Iraq's weapons of mass destruction "will not take years, nor weeks, but months."[6]

Most members of the Security Council wanted to allow the weapons inspectors the time they needed to complete their work. Accordingly, President George W. Bush was not able to secure majority support on the Security Council to authorize international military action against Iraq, and the President wasn't willing to wait for the U.N. weapons inspectors to complete their assignment. Instead, the President relied upon the congressional authority for the use of American armed forces that he secured in October 2002, and launched the invasion of Iraq on March 19, 2003.

The history of the Security Council resolutions on Iraq, and Hussein's open defiance of the United Nations, played a large part in the deliberations on the war authorization resolution in the House of Representatives on October 8–10, 2002, as we will see.

In the early days of the George W. Bush administration, the President and his top advisers did not seem all that alarmed by any threat posed by Saddam Hussein. Certainly, the Bush team considered Hussein a bad actor in the Middle East, but not an imminent threat to our security or to international peace.

During a press briefing on board his plane flying to Cairo on February 23, 2001, Secretary of State Colin Powell said:

> Though [the Iraqis] may be pursuing weapons of mass destruction of all kinds. It is not clear how successful they have been. We ought to declare [sanctions] a success. We have kept [Saddam Hussein] contained, kept him in his box.[7]

The following day, in Cairo, Powell made further comments about international sanctions against Iraq and Hussein:

> Frankly, they have worked. [Saddam Hussein] has not developed any significant capability with respect to weapons of mass destruction. He is unable to project conventional power against his neighbors. So in effect, our policies have strengthened the security of the neighbors of Iraq . . . [Hussein] threatens not the United States.[8]

Vice President Dick Cheney chimed in later that year. In an interview on September 16, 2001 on NBC, just after the 9/11 attacks on America, the Vice President was asked about Saddam Hussein by interviewer Tim Russert:

> Vice Pres. Cheney: "At this stage, the focus is over here on Al Qaeda and the most recent events in New York. Saddam Hussein is bottled up at this point."

> Mr. Russert: "Do we have any evidence linking Saddam Hussein or Iraqis to this operation?"

> Vice Pres. Cheney: "No."[9]

Well into 2002, the Bush Administration seemed unconcerned about any imminent threats posed by Hussein or his weapons of mass destruction. In CIA Director George Tenet's January 2002 review of the global risks of weapons-technology proliferation, Tenet mentioned an actual nuclear risk posed by North Korea but did not mention one from Iraq. In *The New Republic* article reporting on Tenet's January 2002 review, the magazine also quoted Greg Thielmann, former director for strategic proliferation and military affairs at the State Department's Bureau of Intelligence and Research (INR):

> During the time that I was office director, 2000 to 2002, we never assessed that there was good evidence that Iraq was reconstituting or getting really serious about its nuclear weapons program.[10]

On February 6, 2002, the *New York Times* also reported on the January 2002 CIA proliferation review:

> The Central Intelligence Agency has no evidence that Iraq has engaged in terrorist operations against the United States in nearly a decade, and the agency is also convinced that President Saddam Hussein has not provided chemical or biological weapons to Al Qaeda or related terrorist groups, according to several American intelligence officials.[11]

Clearly, the Bush Administration, and the Central Intelligence Agency, was not overly concerned about any imminent threat from Saddam Hussein in the spring of 2002. They still seemed focused on events in Afghanistan, which the United States and an international coalition had invaded on October 7, 2001, as a result of the 9/11 attacks, to pursue Al Qaeda and to dislodge the Taliban that was harboring the terrorists in that country.

On March 12, 2002, I hitched a ride on Air Force One that was flying President Bush back to Washington, D.C. after a speech promoting community service at the Kimmel Center in Philadelphia. I recall that my colleagues Congressmen Robert Borski, Robert Andrews and Curt Weldon were also on board. It is a tradition for Presidents to offer local congressmen a seat on Air Force One when the chief executive returns to the capital after a public appearance in or close to their districts. It is a thrill, an honor and a political boost for any member of Congress to fly on Air Force One, and it gives the President the opportunity if he so desires to lobby the members and twist some arms. President Bush was kind enough to invite the four of us to his conference room in the middle of the plane. He wanted to discuss the challenges presented by Afghanistan. The President made some remarks, quite forcefully, describing our need to root out the evildoers in Afghanistan. I had voted for the congressional war authorization in September 2001 to bring the terrorists to justice who had perpetrated the 9/11 attacks, which led to the invasion of Afghanistan. But by the following spring, with Al Qaeda on the run and the Taliban thrown out of power, I was beginning to wonder if the United States could use more international help to handle the security and public safety challenges we were then facing in Afghanistan. So, when the President asked for comments, I suggested that we put together an international force of peacekeepers to secure the country.

President Bush gave me a hard glare, pounded the conference table and barked, "We are war fighters, not peacekeepers!" A bit taken aback by the President's vehemence, I defended my suggestion, but to no avail. The President, although cordial, was unmoved. The conversation languished after that. When we deplaned at Andrews Air Force Base, and as the President helicoptered off to the White House, my congressional colleagues congratulated me with much amusement and ribbing for ticking off the Leader of the Free World.

But as 2002 wore on, the rhetoric heated up from President Bush and his top advisers about the threats posed by Iraqi weapons of mass destruction. As we have seen, by September 2002 the Bush team was positive in their public statements that Saddam Hussein had such weapons, was acquiring more, was ready to use them against us, and was likely to give them to terrorists. As we now know, these alarming and adamant claims were untrue, were not backed up by the underlying intelligence, and actually misrepresented what the Bush team was being told by our uncertain intelligence analysts.

During the summer of 2002, as the Bush Administration beat the drums for war, I began to hear more and more from my constituents who were voicing their concerns about the threat posed by Saddam Hussein. Some letter writers and callers advocated a cautious approach in dealing with Iraq based on international cooperation and diplomacy if at all possible, but most of my constituents urged me to support the President and do whatever was necessary to get rid of the Iraqi dictator and his threat to America.

I always paid close attention to the letters and phone calls I received from my constituents, and I asked my staff to do the same. I divided my staff allotment evenly with eight employees working in my two district offices, mostly dealing with constituent problems with the federal government such as missing Social Security checks, and another eight working in my Capitol Hill office, mostly focused on legislation, policy matters and related correspondence. My staffers were young, smart and idealistic, and they worked very hard and very effectively for the people of Pennsylvania's 13th District.

But I was really hard on them about preparing prompt, accurate and sympathetic replies to the letters and emails I received in Washington, D.C. about public policy and pending legislation. I stressed to my young staff that every letter writer had taken the time to compose a letter and share personal opinions or requests for action, and surely they wanted their correspondence treated seriously. Most of all, every letter writer wanted a reply. My standing rule was that every letter and email, no matter how disrespectful or nasty, deserved a written, signed reply. We received about 300 letters every week, so this kept everyone in the office busy.

My bright, young staffers seemed to have a collective problem with accurately proofreading their drafts. Some of them had bad cases of "commaitis" where they would routinely use too many commas, or not enough. I remember one time gathering the staff and lecturing them on the proper use of the comma as punctuation. They must have figured I was just a frustrated college English major.

But together we worked through all this and provided thoughtful and responsive replies to the correspondence from my district. I simply never wanted someone back home to ruefully say, "I wrote to my congressman but I never heard back."

As the war drums beat louder in the late summer of 2002, I heard more frequently from my constituents regarding Iraq. My standard written reply contained the following paragraph:

> There is no doubt the world would be a better and safer place without Saddam Hussein as leader of Iraq. He is a treacherous and dangerous bully. While I support the . . . United States policy to seek regime change in Iraq, I also believe that President Bush and his advisers should exercise caution when deciding whether to invade Iraq with American armed forces. Before an invasion, President Bush must present to Congress and the American people evidence of current Iraqi provocations and threats that would justify military action to depose him.

My letter further called for the President to explain his plans for governing a post-Hussein Iraq, and pointed out the danger that unilateral American military action would inflame the Middle East. Finally, I called on the President to seek specific congressional approval before ordering any military action in Iraq.

On September 12, 2002, President Bush spoke at the United Nations.[12] In a much-anticipated presentation, the President forcefully urged the United Nations to compel Iraq to comply with the numerous Security Council resolutions regarding weapons of mass destruction. The President warned that the United States was prepared to act militarily against Iraq without the approval of the United Nations, although Congress at that point had not authorized such use of American armed force. Bush called on the Security Council to require Hussein to honor his commitments to disarm and allow inspectors back inside Iraq.

President Bush extolled the virtue of international action by recalling the unity his father had achieved before the Persian Gulf War, saying:

> Twelve years ago, Iraq invaded Kuwait without provocation . . . Had Saddam Hussein been appeased instead of stopped, he would have endangered the peace and stability of the world. Yet this aggression was stopped by the might of coalition forces and the will of the United Nations.

After reviewing the long history of Hussein's human rights abuses and repression as well as the Security Council resolutions condemning those abuses, President Bush focused on Hussein's weapons:

> In 1991, the Iraqi regime agreed to destroy and stop developing all weapons of mass destruction and long range missiles and to prove to the world it has done so by complying with rigorous inspections. Iraq has broken every aspect of this fundamental pledge.

George Bush then made a series of positive statements about the status of Iraq's weapons of mass destruction that proved to be untrue. These assertions were far more positive than the actual, uncertain intelligence being produced for the Bush Administration by the country's Intelligence Community. The President said:

> Right now, Iraq is expanding and improving facilities that were used for the production of biological weapons. United Nations' inspections also revealed that Iraq likely maintains stockpiles of VX, mustard and other chemical agents, and that the regime is

rebuilding and expanding facilities capable of producing chemical weapons.

True, the President used the qualifier "likely" in announcing the existence of Iraq's chemical weapons stockpiles, and he identified facilities "capable of producing" chemical weapons rather than actually producing them. But even these modest caveats disappeared from Bush's public remarks after his appearance at the United Nations.

The President's U.N. speech quickly returned to the blunt, adamant statements of fact he used throughout the build up to war that were not supported by, and were often contrary to, the underlying intelligence reporting. For example, Bush asserted:

> Iraq has made several attempts to buy high-strength aluminum tubes used to enrich uranium for a nuclear weapon. Should Iraq acquire fissile material, it would be able to build a nuclear weapon within a year . . .
>
> Iraq also possesses a force of SCUD type missiles with ranges beyond the 150 kilometers permitted by the U.N. Work at testing and production facilities shows that Iraq is building more long range missiles that can inflict mass death throughout the region.

These statements were actually not true. That is fortunate for the world, but unfortunate for George Bush's credibility and place in history. And the President's statements did not accurately reflect his intelligence reports.

Then President Bush, after more criticism of Hussein's lack of compliance with U.N. resolutions, unwittingly disclosed the weakness of his own arguments with the following passage in his speech:

> As we meet today, it's been almost four years since the last U.N. inspector set foot in Iraq—four years for the Iraqi regime to plan and to build and to test behind the cloak of secrecy. We know that Saddam Hussein pursued weapons of mass murder even when inspectors were in his country. Are we to assume that he stopped when they left?

This statement and rhetorical question exposed this truth about our intelligence regarding Hussein's weapons of mass destruction: our analysts *assumed* Iraq had such weapons and suspected he was developing more, but they weren't sure. After all, Hussein had thrown the inspectors out of Iraq in December 1998, and now nearly four years later the United Nations didn't know for sure what Hussein was doing or what was the status of his weapons programs. As a result, American analysts were expressing that same uncertainty in their classified reports to the President and his top advisers.

But George W. Bush spoke with complete certainty about Hussein's weapons, even in the speech where he admitted that he was "assuming" that the Iraqi weapons program was moving dangerously forward. It remains surprising that so many people, myself included, failed to notice this fundamental discrepancy in the President's public statements.

President Bush hammered home his argument to the United Nations delegates:

The history, the logic and the facts lead to one conclusion: Saddam Hussein's regime is a grave and gathering danger.

George Bush then asked the international body:

Are Security Council resolutions to be honored and enforced, or cast aside without consequence? Will the United Nations serve the purpose of its founding or will it be irrelevant?

The President promised both cooperation and action. First, cooperation:

My nation will work with the U.N. Security Council to meet our common challenge. If Iraq's regime defies us again, the world must move deliberately, decisively to hold Iraq to account. We will work with the U.N. Security Council for the necessary resolutions.

Then, action:

But the purposes of the United States should not be doubted. The Security Council resolutions will be enforced, the just demands of peace and security will be met or action will be unavoidable, and a regime that has lost its legitimacy will also lose its power.

President Bush made his intentions very clear to the United Nations and to his own country. He wanted the U.N. to stand united against the threat to peace posed by Iraq. He wanted the Security Council to enforce its own resolutions demanding that Iraq disarm and allow inspections again. He asked the Security Council to authorize international military action to hold Iraq "to account." He would cooperate in that joint action. But, if the United Nations failed to act, George W. Bush was willing to act on his own, through the preemptive use of American military power, to remove Saddam Hussein from power.

The President's speech to the United Nations resonated deeply with many of my colleagues and with me. This was our national leader, and he had made a forceful argument for war to the international community of nations. But I wanted to learn more about the specific threats posed by Saddam Hussein, and I wanted to make sure that Congress was fully consulted and asked to give approval before any American forces were dispatched to Iraq.

The drumbeat for war got louder and louder during September 2002. As we have seen, President Bush followed up his speech to the United Nations with his Rose Garden remarks surrounded by members of Congress on September 26, in which he identified Iraq as a grave and growing danger to the United States. The President said that day:

> The Iraqi regime possesses biological and chemical weapons. The Iraqi regime is building the facilities necessary to make more biological and chemical weapons . . . the regime has long-standing and continuing ties to terrorist organizations. And there are Al Qaeda terrorists inside Iraq. The regime is seeking a nuclear bomb, and with fissile material, could build one within a year.[13]

We know now that these presidential statements were not true. We also know the statements exaggerated the findings and ignored the reservations of the analysts who were just then communicating their uncertain intelligence opinions to the White House.

But at the time of their delivery, these forceful Bush assertions had a significant impact on me. These were positive, certain claims by the President of an imminent threat posed by Iraq, a clear and present danger it would be foolish to ignore.

Interestingly, absent from the Rose Garden remarks were the President's own caveats from his United Nations speech two weeks before. No longer was it "likely" that Iraq maintains stockpiles of chemical weapons, now the President stated that Iraq "possesses biological and chemical weapons." No longer was Iraq rebuilding facilities "capable of producing chemical weapons", now the President stated, just two weeks later, that Iraq is building the facilities "to make more biological and chemical weapons." At this point, all reservations and qualifiers about the threats posed by Saddam Hussein and his weapons of mass destruction were dropped from the President's public advocacy to remove the Iraqi dictator from power.

The same day, September 26, Defense Secretary Donald Rumsfeld piped up. He said in comments to reporters:

> We do have solid evidence of the presence in Iraq of Al Qaeda members, including some who have been in Baghdad. We have what we consider to be very reliable reporting of senior-level contacts going back a decade, and of possible chemical- and biological-agent training.[14]

The following day, in remarks to a Chamber of Commerce luncheon in Atlanta, Secretary Rumsfeld said that United States intelligence had "bulletproof" evidence of links between Al Qaeda and Saddam Hussein's government in Iraq. Rumsfeld said that intelligence reports about suspected ties between Al Qaeda and Iraq, including the presence in Baghdad "in recent periods" of senior leaders of Al Qaeda, were "factual" and "exactly accurate."[15]

But then Rumsfeld did a curious thing. He weaseled on his positive statements, offering reporters after his speech the following caveats about the supposedly "bulletproof" sentences that intelligence analysts prepared for him:

> But they're not photographs. They're not beyond a reasonable doubt. They, in some cases, are assessments from limited number of sources.[16]

How those caveats match up with Rumsfeld's earlier insistence that the statements were "bulletproof", "factual" and "exactly accurate" is beyond my modest powers of comprehension. But, looking back, I do wish I had paid more attention to these inconsistencies. In the differences between Donald Rumsfeld's Atlanta Chamber of Commerce speech and his subsequent responses to the media regarding the speech can be found the unintentional admission that the adamant statements of the President and his top advisers were not always backed up by the uncertain intelligence those same officials were receiving.

During September and early October the Defense Department held several closed-door briefings for the entire membership of the House regarding weapons of mass destruction in Iraq. These briefings were usually held in the House Armed Services Committee room, and were led by Secretary Rumsfeld and a number of high-ranking, uniformed officers and White House officials. The "classified" briefings included all the claims about the Iraqi threat we were already hearing on the evening news, and included some grainy photographs that the briefers claimed were weapons sites. Most of what I heard in each briefing I would then read a day or two later in news reports that cited the same administration and military sources that had briefed the House members. These briefings were not particularly useful since they did not provide me with any hard intelligence or new information, but they were fully consistent with the relentless public message of the Bush administration that Saddam Hussein was an imminent threat to the United States.

The first week of October, as I described in Chapter One, I was briefed at the White House by the dissembling George Tenet and Condoleezza Rice, was visited by the four-flushing Iraqi Ahmed Chalabi, read the just-released public White Paper on Iraqi weapons that actively misled the country about the Iraqi intelligence, and was bluntly advised by my wife and daughter that I was a naive chump for leaning toward supporting the war.

I returned to the Capitol on October 7 for routine votes and office paperwork. The congressional votes on the Iraq war resolution were scheduled for later that week, and I was still leaning toward a Yes vote as the correct thing to do. I felt I was about 60% in favor of the war resolution, and 40% against. I was greatly influenced by the continuing public statements from the Bush Administration that Saddam Hussein had weapons of mass destruction, was acquiring more and was willing to use them. I still was worried whether I could trust George Bush and his top people, and wondered whether Hussein had really amassed such a formidable arsenal. The Bush Administration still had not offered convincing evidence that Iraq was about to attack the United States or our allies. But I also believed that sooner or later Saddam Hussein must be disarmed. It did not seem likely that he would disarm on his own.

I thought the best result would be a United Nations-backed international military action that would disarm the dictator and probably remove him from power. Perhaps the proposed congressional war resolution would give the United Nations enough motivation to act boldly and collectively, as they had done eleven years before in the Persian Gulf

War, so that the U.S. would not have to act alone. It did seem to me that somebody would have to act at some point to disarm Saddam Hussein.

On the evening of Monday, October 7, I settled in my Capitol Hill office to watch the President on television from Cincinnati, Ohio make his final appeal to the American people concerning the need to remove the imminent threat posed to world peace and security by Saddam Hussein. This speech was billed as the President's closing argument, his last opportunity to influence public and congressional opinion before the House vote scheduled for that Thursday and the Senate vote on Friday. I knew that the impact of this presidential speech would likely determine the outcome of the congressional votes later that week. A strong presidential performance tonight that clearly and convincingly made the case for disarming Saddam Hussein would surely solidify public opinion in favor of military action against Iraq, and the weight of that public opinion, in turn, would strongly influence the upcoming congressional votes.

I thought there was a lot at stake for the President that night. I wondered how precise the President would be in his claims about Hussein's weapons of mass destruction. Everyone on Capitol Hill, even Bush's harshest critics, understood that Hussein was a murderous, dangerous dictator. But many members of Congress were still asking, mostly in private, whether Hussein actually had dangerous weapons right now. Had Hussein really become an imminent threat to regional and world peace? Was U.S. military action necessary, and if so, how soon?

I watched on C-SPAN 2 as the President strode out to the podium in front of an invited audience, which gave him a warm welcome. In a dark grey suit and light blue tie, George Bush stood out sharply before the light grey marble background in the Cincinnati Museum Center. At 8:02 P.M. EDT, the president began his speech, reading slowly and carefully from the teleprompter.[17]

> Tonight I want to take a few minutes to discuss a grave threat to peace, and America's determination to lead the world in confronting that threat. The threat comes from Iraq. It arises directly from the Iraqi regime's own actions—its history of aggression, and its drive toward an arsenal of terror . . . it possesses and produces chemical and biological weapons. It is seeking nuclear weapons. It has given shelter and support to terrorism . . . [W]hile there are many dangers in the world, that threat from Iraq stands alone—because it gathers the most serious dangers of

our age in one place. Iraq's weapons of mass destruction are controlled by a murderous tyrant who has already used chemical weapons to kill thousands of people.

Well, that was certainly a forceful beginning to the speech, I thought. The President just identified Iraq as the most dangerous country in the world, as a threat that "stands alone." I wondered if the President would make the specific assertions now to back it up. George Bush continued:

If we know that Saddam Hussein has dangerous weapons today—and we do—does it make any sense for the world to wait to confront him as he grows even stronger and develops even more dangerous weapons? . . . [W]e know that the regime has produced thousands of tons of chemical agents, including mustard gas, sarin nerve gas, VX nerve gas. . . . Iraq possesses ballistic missiles with a likely range of hundreds of miles. . . . Iraq has a growing fleet of manned and unmanned aerial vehicles that could be used to disperse chemical or biological weapons across broad areas. . . . [and] for missions targeting the United States.

There they were, the specific assertions against Iraq—chemical agents, three types of gases, ballistic missiles, and aerial vehicles targeting the United States. It was a sobering catalogue of dangerous threats. The President was continuing:

Iraq and al Qaeda have had high-level contacts that go back a decade . . . Iraq could decide on any given day to provide a biological or chemical weapon to a terrorist group or individual terrorists . . . Saddam Hussein is harboring terrorists and the instruments of terror, the instruments of mass death and destruction. And he cannot be trusted. The risk is simply too great that he will use them, or provide them to a terror network.

There was the connection between Iraq and terrorists. I knew that nothing got the attention of Americans quicker than the subject of terror. It was only a year since the horror of 9/11, and the American people still had raw feelings about those attacks, and an abiding conviction that justice must be done.

Now the President was addressing the nuclear threat:

Iraq is reconstituting its nuclear weapons program . . . [I]t could have a nuclear weapon in less than a year . . . [K]nowing these realities, America must not ignore the threat gathering against us. Facing clear evidence of peril, we cannot wait for the final proof—the smoking gun—that could come in the form of a mushroom cloud.

Now the President was using the same mushroom cloud imagery that I had heard last week in the White House from Condoleezza Rice. He was leaving no emotional chord unstruck. I knew these remarks would have a big impact on the country.

George Bush continued:

After eleven years during which we have tried containment, sanctions, inspections, even selected military action, the end result is that Saddam Hussein still has chemical and biological weapons and is increasing his capabilities to make more. And he is moving ever closer to developing a nuclear weapon . . .

Saddam Hussein must disarm himself—or, for the sake of peace, we will lead a coalition to disarm him . . . [A]s Americans, we want peace—we work and sacrifice for peace. But there can be no peace if our security depends on the will and whims of a ruthless and aggressive dictator. I'm not willing to stake one American life on trusting Saddam Hussein. . . .

Later this week, the United States Congress will vote on this matter. I have asked Congress to authorize the use of America's military, if it proves necessary, to enforce U.N. Security Council demands. Approving this resolution does not mean that military action is imminent or unavoidable . . . Congress will also be sending a message to the dictator in Iraq: that his only chance—his only choice is full compliance, and the time remaining for that choice is limited . . .

By our resolve, we will give strength to others. By our courage, we will give hope to others. And by our actions, we will secure the peace, and lead the world to a better day. May God bless America.

I clicked off the television and realized that President Bush had just delivered a very powerful speech containing specific assertions about Hussein's weapons of mass destruction and connections to terrorism.

George Bush had made clear statements of fact and left himself no wiggle room. He had just made Saddam Hussein our Public Enemy Number One.

The President also had said that the military authorization he was seeking from Congress did not mean that war was "imminent or unavoidable." Those words suggested that Bush was still planning a vigorous diplomatic effort at the United Nations to deal with Hussein, which I found reassuring.

I still had some lingering doubts. It was hard to believe that Hussein really had all these weapons, and where was the evidence that he was willing to use them against America and our allies?

On the other hand, could President Bush and his senior officials be making up these claims, or exaggerating them? Was that even possible? That made no sense at all. Surely, if George Bush were lying about the weapons of mass destruction, it would ruin his presidency and his place in history. He had to know that as well as I did. He couldn't be lying.

There was no doubt about one thing. Election Day was November 5, 2002, just four weeks away. I enjoyed being a Member of Congress, and I wanted to stay one. I knew public opinion was firmly behind the President, and would be even more so after that night's speech. A "yes" vote in my district to authorize war in Iraq made good political sense. A "no" vote would be politically risky and would require a lot of explaining back home. While political considerations alone did not determine my vote, they were certainly a factor.

Most importantly, I was convinced that the lessons of history taught us that the sooner the international community stood up to a tyrant and a bully, the better. How many statesmen from an earlier era had regretted their failure to act early and decisively to stop Adolf Hitler? How much of the suffering and horror caused by Hitler could have been avoided? I did not want to be on the wrong side of history. I decided that night for sure that I would vote in favor of the war resolution later that week, in order to disarm Saddam Hussein.

FOUR

Voting for War

Dennis Hastert, Speaker of the House of Representatives, opened the debate on October 8, 2002 on the Iraq war resolution, which he had introduced in the House:

> On September 11 those who hate America tried to silence the voices of the American people as represented by this body. But free men cannot be silenced; and so once again today, as we have almost every day since September 11, we gather in this Chamber to do the people's business.[1]

And so began the debate on House Joint Resolution 114, the Authorization for Military Force Against Iraq Resolution of 2002. The floor action in the House would range over three days with an astonishing 26 hours of debate on the resolution itself, two proposed amendments and a motion to recommit to committee. This length of debate was highly unusual, as the regular rules of the House limit debate on routine bills and resolutions to just one hour, equally divided between the parties. Nearly every member of the House asked for time to offer his or her thoughts on the question of whether Congress should authorize preemptive war against Iraq, and they were granted at least three minutes to address their colleagues and the national C-SPAN television audience.

Dennis Hastert had taught sociology, economics and speech at Yorkville High School in Illinois for seventeen years, and coached the wrestling and football teams. Then he turned to politics, and would serve for over twenty years as a Republican member of the U.S. House of Representatives. He had an unassuming midwestern public demeanor, and as a backbencher in Congress representing the 14th District of Illinois, he compiled a conservative voting record and displayed a moderate temperament. Hastert was the compromise choice in January 1999 to lead the divided Republican Conference in the House, and once elected Speaker he ran the House with a firm hand, and always with the goal of preserving his Republican majority.[2]

Speaker Hastert was respectful and courteous to rank-and-file Democrats like me. He even came to my district once at my invitation to help raise money for Save the Speaker's House, Inc., a non-profit group working to preserve and restore the home in Trappe, Pennsylvania of the first House Speaker, Frederick Muhlenberg. Dennis didn't say much, as usual, during the trip, but he made a very favorable impression on the local folks in Trappe.

Unfortunately, Speaker Hastert and Minority Leader Richard Gephardt of Missouri had a strained relationship throughout their overlapping service in the House. This apparently started when Speaker Hastert was visiting the Democratic Leader's office and spotted a "Gephardt for Speaker" sign, and then was exacerbated by a disagreement over the selection of the House Chaplain, when Hastert thought he was charged unfairly with alleged anti-Catholic bias.[3] Accordingly, it was unusual and noteworthy that the two leaders agreed to introduce the war resolution together.

In his opening speech, the Speaker left no doubt where he stood on the dangers he saw from Saddam Hussein and from Iraq's connections with Al Qaeda. Hastert's remarks emphasized the impact of the September 11 attacks on America, and he wasn't shy about using that tragedy as a springboard to gather support for the Iraq war resolution. In fact, the Speaker used the phrase "September 11" six times in the first eight paragraphs of his floor speech. He argued that there was a clear connection between Iraq and the perpetrators of 9/11:

> Some may question the connection between Iraq and those terrorists who hijacked those planes. There is no doubt that Iraq supports and harbors those terrorists who wish harm to the United States. Is there a direct connection between Iraq and Al Qaeda? The President thinks so; and based upon what I have seen, I think so also.[4]

Speaker Hastert was one of the eight leaders of Congress allowed under law to review the most highly classified intelligence documents such as the National Intelligence Estimate on Iraqi weapons that had been secretly circulated at only the highest levels just one week earlier. When the Speaker, any Speaker, rendered an opinion on national security matters "based upon what I have seen," that opinion carried considerable weight.

Hastert addressed some of the concerns about the President's doctrine of preemptive use of force that he had heard from members of the House.

> For those Members who are worried about the doctrine of pre-emption, let me say this is not a new conflict with Iraq. Our planes which have been patrolling the no-fly zone since the end of the Persian Gulf War pursuant to U.N. resolutions have been fired upon by the Iraqi military hundreds of times.[5]

The Speaker was arguing that it was acceptable to use American force now since we had already been attacked by Iraq "hundreds of times," so we weren't the ones striking first. He then addressed the desire of many to see international action to meet the challenge of Saddam Hussein:

> For those who argue that we must build a consensus with the United Nations, let me say that we are taking an effective action here in this Chamber to perhaps help the U.N. do what is right in their own Chamber . . . [W]e must give the United Nations the backbone it needs to enforce its own resolutions. But if the U.N. refuses to save itself, and more importantly the security of its member states and the cause of peace in this world, we must take all appropriate action to protect ourselves.[6]

The Speaker of the House was clearly echoing the arguments of President Bush we had heard the night before from Cincinnati; it is time for the United Nations to enforce its own resolutions to disarm Saddam Hussein, and the United States will work to help supply that "backbone", but if the U.N. fails to act then the United States will act, on our own if necessary.

This was also the sum and substance of House Joint Resolution 114, the subject of the debate, which had been introduced by Speaker Hastert and Minority Leader Gephardt with 136 co-sponsors on October 2, 2002.[7] The resolution was the result of a bipartisan negotiation between House and Senate leaders and the White House, and different versions were introduced in both houses of Congress.

A joint resolution is legally the same as a bill in the legislative process of the United States Congress. They both must be passed in identical forms by both the House and the Senate and are presented to the President for approval or disapproval. Laws that are enacted by way of a joint resolution are not distinguished legally from laws enacted by a bill. The real difference between a bill and a joint resolution is in how they are used.

Bills are used to add, repeal or amend laws codified in the United States Code, and for the twelve annual appropriations bills that comprise the nation's budget. Joint resolutions are used, for example, to authorize small appropriations, create temporary commissions, for continuing budget resolutions and, of interest here, to declare or authorize war.[8] A House Joint Resolution is simply a joint resolution originating in the House, rather than the Senate.

H. J. Res. 114 started with a simple declaration of its purpose: "to authorize the use of United States Armed Forces against Iraq."

The resolution then set forth twenty-three "whereas" clauses outlining the long and often sordid history of Iraq's aggressive behavior on the world stage, and the world's attempt to deal with that bad behavior. The hostile actions described included Iraq's 1990 invasion of Kuwait, its use of weapons of mass destruction, its agreement and then violation of the 1991 ceasefire accord, its failure to disarm and permit inspections, its continuing threat to world peace, its possession and development of chemical and biological weapons, its ongoing search for nuclear weapons capability, even its attempt in 1993 to assassinate former President Bush.

The Congressional responses taken through the years to deal with the challenges posed by Saddam Hussein were listed in H. J. Res. 114. These public actions include Public Law 102-1, enacted January 12, 1991, the first congressional authorization for use of military force to expel Iraq from Kuwait under U.N. auspices; Public Law 105-235, August 14, 1998, declaring Iraq in "material breach" of Persian Gulf War ceasefire agreements and urging the President "to take appropriate action" to bring Iraq into compliance with its international obligations; Public Law 105-338, October 31, 1998, the Iraq Liberation Act stating it is United States policy to remove the current Iraqi regime from power and to encourage a democratically-elected replacement government; and Public Law 107-40, September 18, 2001, the Authorization For Use of Military Force Act to allow the President to use American armed forces against international terrorism and those that harbor terrorists following the attacks of 9/11.[9]

H. J. Res. 114 recounted the most recent congressional action in the House of the passage of House Joint Resolution 75 on December 20, 2001, demanding the resumption of United Nations weapons monitoring and inspections, and declaring Iraq's refusal to permit such inspections a "mounting threat" to the United States and our allies. This resolution had passed the House with my support, but was not acted upon in the Senate.

H. J. Res. 114 also recalled the long history of numerous U.N. Security Council resolutions regarding Iraq, particularly Resolution 678 of 1990, which authorized the use of force to implement international demands that Iraq leave Kuwait, used by the United States to justify our use of force against Iraq in 1991, and Resolution 687 of 1991, which declared a formal ceasefire ending the Persian Gulf War and required Hussein to give up all weapons of mass destruction and allow international inspections.

Following the "whereas" clauses, H. J. Res. 114 had three key sections. The first urged the President to continue his diplomatic efforts to work through the United Nations Security Council to "strictly enforce" all relevant Security Council Resolutions regarding Iraq and to "obtain prompt and decisive action by the Security Council" to enforce their own resolutions.

The second key section authorized the President to use American armed forces to "defend the national security of the United States against the continuing threat posed by Iraq," and to enforce all relevant Security Council resolutions regarding Iraq. The resolution required the President to officially make two determinations to Congress before using the war authorization to begin hostilities, or within 48 hours of doing so: first, a finding that further diplomacy "will not adequately protect" the U.S., and second, military action was consistent with efforts to combat international terrorists and respond to the attacks of 9/11. Further, the resolution proclaimed that Congress intended that the authorization of force was consistent with the "specific statutory authorization" required under the War Powers Resolution.

The third key section of H. J. Res. 114 required the President to submit a report at least once every 60 days to Congress on actions taken under this authorization, including the status of planning efforts for post-invasion activities.

The language of H. J. Res 114 is important for two reasons. First, it contains the actual provisions passed by the House and Senate and ultimately signed into law by the President on October 16, 2002. Secondly, it contained compromise language worked out primarily by House

Speaker Hastert and Minority Leader Gephardt in negotiations with Senate leaders and the White House. The Hastert-Gephardt language was more moderate and measured than the original proposals from the White House to secure military authorization from Congress. This successful search for common ground between these two competing leaders of the House was a rare example of bipartisan cooperation during my six years of service in Congress.

The original legislative language sought by the Bush Administration to authorize military force against Iraq was contained in an earlier Senate proposal, Senate Joint Resolution 45, introduced by Senate Majority Leader Thomas Daschle and Senate Minority Leader Trent Lott on September 26, 2002.[10] S. J. Res. 45 listed 16 "whereas" clauses similar in tone and assertion to those in H. J. Res. 114.

But S.J. Res. 45 contained only one key section, focused on just one purpose, compared to the later House version. The Senate resolution simply authorized the President "to use all means that he determines to be appropriate, including force" to defend the United States against the threat posed by Iraq and to enforce Security Council resolutions.

Unlike the House proposal, there was no encouragement in the Senate version for the President to continue his diplomatic efforts, or to keep working through the Security Council or to urge the Security Council to enforce its own resolutions.

There was no requirement in the Senate proposal for the President, before using force, to make an official determination that conducting further diplomacy would be inadequate to protect the U.S. against the continuing threat posed by Iraq.

There was no statement in the Senate version that the authorization for use of force in the resolution complied with the specific statutory authorization required by the War Powers Resolution, the Vietnam-era legislation intended by Congress to prevent any future President from engaging in war without either a congressional declaration of war or a specific authorization by law.

There was no requirement in the Senate version for Presidential reports every 60 days on the actions taken under the war authority or on the status of post-invasion planning.

It has never been clear to me why the bipartisan Senate leadership was willing to simply give to the President the broad war-making authority he wanted without also urging more diplomacy before going to war, and without demanding more accountability from the executive branch. The rush to war in the spring of 2003 without broad international support and before the weapons inspectors had completed their work, and the lack of post-invasion planning, would emerge as enormous failures by the Bush Administration. Many members of Congress, including myself, were unhappy in the fall of 2002 about the stark grant of war authority being requested by the White House and proposed in the original Senate version of the resolution. We felt more emphasis must be placed on continuing diplomatic efforts to avert war, and on efforts to get the United Nations to act multinationally to enforce its own resolutions against Iraq. We also wanted more accountability from the executive branch. House leaders heard these objections after the Senate resolution was introduced on September 26, and the result was the introduction by Speaker Hastert and Minority Leader Gephardt of H.J. Res. 114 on October 2.

Following Speaker Hastert's opening remarks on October 8, twenty-six additional hours of debate followed over the course of three days. Virtually every member of the House had the opportunity to address his or her colleagues and the nation about whether we should go to war against Saddam Hussein and Iraq. The speeches were spirited and heart-felt, and members freely expressed their views.

The debate also occurred while the Bush Administration was shouting loudly in the public arena that Saddam Hussein had weapons of mass destruction, was acquiring more, and was ready and willing to use them. Regrettably, the congressional deliberations on the Iraq war resolution unfolded under the false pretenses created by the Bush Administration concerning the status of Iraq's weapons of mass destruction.

On Tuesday afternoon, October 8, I left my office in the Longworth House Office Building and walked across Independence Avenue to the Capitol to join the debate. A copy of my speech was jammed into my suit jacket, and I felt the familiar tension and excitement that always preceded a speech on the floor of the House. The hot weather had broken the day before and it was a beautiful fall afternoon with the temperature in the mid 60s. The sidewalks and plazas weren't so crowded now that the summer tourist season was over, but there were always lots of people out and about on a beautiful day like this on Capitol Hill. There seemed to be extra energy in the air, shared by Hill staffers and tourists alike, as the House of Representatives was beginning debate on this historic resolution to authorize military action against Iraq.

I loved the walk across the street, onto the Capitol grounds, and up the wide marble outside steps to the second level of the southern end of the Capitol where the House chamber was located. It was a majestic walk up stately steps, past tall marble columns that framed the entrance portico. Once inside, it was a few paces through the elevator lobby and across a narrow hallway and then directly into the chamber of the House of Representatives. This walk to work, this grand approach to the People's House, never got old for me.

I took a seat in the far corner of the House floor to the Speaker's right hand side to wait my turn to speak on the war resolution. Every time I entered the House chamber I marveled at its majestic yet simple beauty. The chamber actually seemed bigger to me than it looked on television.

The first time I had set foot in the place was during the orientation session in late November 1998 for the recently victorious Members-elect who would be sworn in the following January. I couldn't contain myself that first time on the House floor—I borrowed a cell phone from my new friend and colleague Jan Schakowsky of Illinois to place an important call during a lull in the briefing. I spoke my first words on the floor of the House into the phone, "Hi Mom. Guess where I am?" and Jan had a good laugh. It took me awhile to live that one down.

The House chamber was a big rectangle with blue carpeting and brown leather benches with armrests arranged in a semi-circle around the Speaker's Rostrum, which was centered in the long southern wall. The ceiling was a great expanse of white plaster with a glass false skylight in the middle portraying a large eagle with wings spread. Galleries surrounded the floor below—the press gallery with plain wooden benches perched right above the Speaker's Rostrum, the public galleries with upholstered chairs encircling the chamber on all four sides. The walls above the galleries contained numerous sculpted reliefs of lawgivers and lawmakers throughout world history.

My attention was always drawn to the Speaker's Rostrum, a beautifully carved, wooden platform rising in three levels above the floor of the House. Behind the rostrum was the giant American flag that dominated the background during televised speeches from the House chamber, and above the flag, chiseled into the marble facing, the national motto, "In God We Trust".

On both sides of the flag, hanging from the marble walls, were large bronze fasces representing a classical Roman symbol of civic authority. The fasces portrayed an axe within a bundle of narrow rods bound together by a band, signifying strength, unity and the authority of Congress. I never would have known this were it not for that orientation briefing.

But the mace I would have understood even without the briefing. The mace was a symbol of the Speaker's authority and power, and that is what it looked like. About four feet high, the mace was a decorative version of the fasces hanging on the wall, comprised of 13 thin ebony rods, representing the original states, bound together by four crossing silver bands, with a silver globe on top, engraved with the seven continents, names of the oceans, and the lines of longitude and latitude, crowned by a solid silver eagle with a 15 inch wingspan. The Sergeant at Arms placed the mace on a pedestal to the Speaker's right when the House was in session, and removed it at the close of legislative business each day. The Western Hemisphere on the globe was always placed facing toward the chamber.[11]

The mace was a symbol of power, like the ancient war clubs that served as its model. The official Rules of the House provide that the Sergeant at Arms, at the direction of the Speaker, shall present the Mace before any unruly members with the unwritten expectation that those members would unfailingly and immediately come to order. None of the House staff could recall such dramatic use of the Speaker's Mace in modern times, but that didn't stop me from hoping to witness such a confrontation sometime, as long as I wasn't the unruly member in need of discipline.

I was sitting in what was unofficially dubbed "Pennsylvania Corner" on the House floor. There were no assigned seats on the long leather benches in the House, but by custom the Republican members sat to the left hand side of the Speaker and the Democrats to the right, with the center aisle separating the two partisan teams. For reasons lost to time, the Pennsylvania Democrats traditionally sat together in the back row or two in the corner seats farthest to the Speaker's right, with the senior Pennsylvania Democrat occupying the actual corner seat and the other Democrats from the state sitting in rough order of seniority along the back row. No other state's delegation in either party sat in such a designated space on the House floor. Frankly, the elevated back row afforded an excellent view of the full House, and was far enough from the well of the House, where most members chose to speak, and from the rostrum where the Speaker and the Parliamentarian kept a close eye on the proceedings, that the Pennsylvania Democrats could chat and joke without being chastised by the Speaker. Nobody seemed to know how the tradition started, but nobody questioned it. I enjoyed the camaraderie with my home state colleagues, as well as the bit of status conferred on Pennsylvania Democrats by the seating tradition, and I could tell from a few snide comments and smirks from some of my colleagues from other states that there were those in the House who were annoyed by the Pennsylvania Democrats' tradition, and even resented it. As far as I was concerned, that was the best part.

I arose from my seat and walked down to the two minority Democratic tables facing the well and the rostrum, where the Democratic leadership and senior staff sat and from which the Democratic floor operations were run. The Republicans had two corresponding tables on their side of the aisle. During floor debate, the ranking Democratic member from the committee responsible for the pending legislation would sit with his senior committee staff and manage the debate, allocate speaking time and make the final arguments for the Democratic side. When I was told that several Democrats were scheduled to speak before me, I left the House floor to check the newspapers in the adjacent member's room.

As always, debate on the House floor was highly structured and strictly limited by time. Unlike the Senate with its tradition of unlimited debate, every bill or resolution considered by the full House must first be approved by the House Rules Committee and be given a "rule" which would control the floor debate. This rule determined the amount of time allotted for floor debate, always equally divided and controlled by each party, as well as the specific amendments that were allowed. Usually, each bill was allotted one hour of debate time and each permitted amendment was allotted ten minutes of debate. By long-standing House custom, the minority was generally allowed the opportunity to offer a "substitute" amendment, which would change the entire bill, and a motion to recommit the bill to committee for further review. Usually, these legislative maneuvers failed and, after the minority had its say, the majority would have its way.

I was well aware that this war resolution was no routine piece of legislation. The Rules Committee, after consultations with the leadership, had originally allotted a total of 18 hours of debate over three days to House Joint Resolution 114.[12] Subsequently, an additional 6 hours of debate time was added since virtually every member of the House wanted to make a floor speech in support or opposition of the resolution. Everyone knew this was a defining moment for the nation, and for the careers of the Members. Everyone wanted to be heard on the subject of war in Iraq. Most of them, including me, were given just three minutes to make their speech on the floor of the House.

I walked through the swinging doors to the right of the rostrum that separated the chamber from the long narrow hallway immediately behind the rostrum that was known as the Speaker's Lobby. Only Members, senior staff and reporters were allowed in this space, and I always enjoyed the respite from the public eye that the lobby afforded. On the wall that separated the lobby from the chamber hung oil portraits of previous Speakers of the House, and the honored location in the center of the long wall was reserved for the painting of the first Speaker, Frederick Muhlenberg of Trappe, Pennsylvania, which was located in my district. I took great pleasure in pointing that out to any of my colleagues or reporters who were willing to listen. Most of them feigned interest or just smiled politely.

Part of the opposite side of the narrow Speaker's Lobby was actually a wide opening to what was officially called the Member's Retiring Room. My colleagues and I used the room with its high arched ceilings, painted murals and marble decorations to gab, read newspapers and smoke cigars. It was nice for a while not to have to worry about the prying eyes of constituents.

But the best place, my favorite spot in the Capitol, in all of Washington for that matter, was "the Beach", and that is where I was headed. Accessible by a single door on the far side of the Member's Retiring Room, the Beach was a long, narrow, open air marble balcony perched on the southern end of the Capitol building, surrounded by a massive marble balustrade and flanked by several of the soaring marble columns that dominate the Capitol's architecture. The roof high above the balcony gave some protection from bad weather, and the thick columns and heavy balustrade offered a surprising amount of privacy to anyone out on the Beach. You could see the southern grounds of the Capitol, the traffic on Independence Avenue and the pedestrians in front of the House Office Buildings, but they couldn't see you. By tradition, the Beach was reserved for Members only while Congress was in session, and I liked to go out there during House debates to get some fresh air and soak up some sunshine, particularly during the winter months. I must admit that I enjoyed the sense of entitlement and privilege that came with being one of only 435 people in the world who were allowed to be out there, on the Beach.

It was about time to make my speech. I left the Beach, walked back across the Retiring Room and the Speaker's Lobby, and reentered the House chamber. I approached one of the microphones located on the Democratic side of the floor and waited for recognition by the ranking Democrat on the International Relations Committee, the legendary Holocaust survivor Tom Lantos of California, who was managing the floor debate for the minority side. Tom survived two forced labor camps in his native Hungary during World War II and, after escaping from the second, joined the anti-Nazi resistance while still a teenager. Possessing Old World courtliness and unflappable calm, Tom Lantos was undoubtedly the most revered member of the House.

I was more nervous than usual. Only a handful of Members were actually on the floor during this part of the debate, most were back in their offices meeting with staff or doing paperwork. Some, I thought, who weren't scheduled to speak today might have taken the afternoon off and were playing golf or having a leisurely lunch somewhere. There were no committee meetings or hearings scheduled this afternoon that would otherwise occupy Members. The House was focused today, and for the next two days, on whether to authorize war against Iraq.

I was glad to be there, and proud to be part of this deliberative, democratic process, but I wished my hands would stop shaking the papers of my speech. I didn't want to just read my speech, since that could make me sound wooden and unconnected. Rather, I wanted to look out and make eye contact with my colleagues when I addressed the House, because that would improve my delivery and make my words more persuasive. Better to stumble a little or garble some syntax, or even to forget a phrase or two, but firmly connect with your audience than to precisely read your speech and put everyone to sleep in the process.

I was surprised by my jumpiness, since I was very used to public speaking and readily gave off-the-cuff remarks all the time. But I didn't quite have enough confidence this day to deliver these remarks with nothing at hand, even for three minutes, in case I lost my way or drew a blank. So I held on tightly to the text of my speech. It was amazing what speaking on live television on a matter of war and peace could do to your nerves.

Then, it was time. Representative Lantos said "Mr. Speaker, I am pleased to yield 3 minutes of time to the gentleman from Pennsylvania, a distinguished member of our committee."[13]

I began:[14]

Mr. Speaker, we face a toxic mix in Iraq: dangerous weapons controlled by a dangerous tyrant. From the beginning of this national debate, I have felt strongly that we must act through the United Nations, in concert with our allies, and with multi-national support, and focus on the weapons of mass destruction and disarming Hussein.

Clearly, we must rid Iraq of the weapons of mass destruction and the means of producing new weapons of mass destruction. If Saddam resists and regime change thus occurs, we must be prepared for what happens next, the very next day.

So far, so good. My words were actually clear and understandable, and I wasn't mumbling. Time to give the Bush team a little shot for their initial request as contained in the original Senate resolution:

[The Senate resolution] gave credence to the fear that we would, as a first step, act in a preemptive unilateral military strike, which I would not support and do not support in the absence of an imminent threat to the United States. That resolution was too broad, did not require the President to work through the U.N., and did not address our plans for the future of Iraq.

Since then, the House and the administration, in a bipartisan manner, have negotiated a compromise resolution that addresses many of these issues. I support the resolution now. It strikes a good balance between urging a multilateral approach and preserving America's right to defend our citizens.

Little did I know that the Bush team would virtually ignore all the provisions in the House resolution urging more diplomacy and imposing more accountability.

But was anyone paying attention to my speech? I didn't think so. Few members were on the floor and many who were there were engaged in quiet conversations of their own. Some members were watching me as I spoke, but I got the feeling they were thinking more about their own remarks they were waiting to give, or perhaps about what they were going to order for dinner. It was time to liven things up, time to get a little personal. So I switched gears:

The President has promised congressional leaders he will exhaust all options at the U.N. before taking military action. At a White House briefing last week, the National Security Advisor and the CIA Director made the same assurances.

The resolution, even with this balancing and moderating language, still represents a grant of broad military authority to the President, broad authority for the President to wage war. The question is: do we trust the President's judgment to use this authority wisely? This President came to office without much background in foreign policy and without much apparent interest in foreign policy. The President's initial steps in foreign relations were an isolating brand of unilateralism that told the world that America would thrive if we acted alone in our own interests.

There. That seemed to wake them up a little, particularly on the Republican side of the aisle. Not many Members of Congress were openly questioning the President's judgment those days on national security matters, not since the country had rallied together after 9/11. But I felt I had better not be too critical of the President, and shouldn't get too far out on the plank, because some Republicans back home might try to saw it off on Election Day, just one month away, with me out on the end. So I continued:

> Then came 9/11 and the President changed his policies, and I am glad he did. In the war on terror, the President resolutely has led this country, skillfully assembled the international coalition against terror, and has made necessary and appropriate use of America's military power . . .
>
> I urge the President in the strongest terms to adhere to the letter and the spirit of this resolution in exhausting all diplomatic options in order to disarm Saddam Hussein. But the use of American military power alone will not meet all of our challenges. We must be prepared for the challenges of nation building, prepared for the challenges of peacekeeping.

I was running out of time. I could see the Speaker on the rostrum checking with the timekeeper and preparing to tap lightly with his gavel to signal that my time was running out. Soon the Speaker would begin announcing, "The gentleman's time has expired" and would begin to really hit the gavel. You didn't want to finish a speech with the Speaker chastising you for being long-winded. I wanted to get in a short plug for my bill to create a modern-day Marshall Plan for Eurasia and the Middle East, so I plowed quickly ahead and picked up my pace, garbling a bit of my syntax.

> We must be prepared for the redevelopment of Iraq and other trouble spots around the world where people not just have to deal with the grinding poverty and the lack of day-to-day opportunity but they have to deal with day-in, day-out sense of hopelessness. We must consider the demand for a new, modern-day Marshall Plan to address the development needs, the food and educational needs, the hope that people must have to lead to democracy and self-government.

The Speaker was pounding on the gavel. I stepped back from the floor microphone and Tom Lantos was already yielding time to another speaker.

I looked around to assess the impact of my remarks, but nobody seemed to be paying much attention. The members and staff around the Republican leadership table had returned to talking among themselves. It was probably a mistake to cram into my speech the references to my modern-day Marshall Plan legislation. It was a damn good idea, but it had caused me to rush too much at the end of my speech. A frantic wrap-up is not the best way to persuade anybody. Well, I gave it my best and, on balance, the speech was a good effort. But it probably didn't change any minds.

Most of that day and the next two were taken up by statements from virtually every member either in favor or opposition to the underlying resolution. Unfortunately, the resulting floor "debate" consisted mostly of members talking past each other with prepared remarks that did not directly respond to what was said by the prior speakers. Accordingly, the twenty-six hours of debate on H. J. Res. 114 became rather repetitive and predictable. To paraphrase a saying often attributed to the late, great Congressman Morris Udall, after awhile everything on the subject of going to war with Iraq had been said, but not everybody had the chance to say it. So the House soldiered on until all members who had something to say had said it.

After general debate on H. J. Res. 114 had concluded, there was more time scheduled under the House Rule governing floor proceedings on the war resolution. Immediately following the close of general debate, two amendments would be considered and voted on, and were granted one hour of debate each. Then, one hour of final debate was scheduled on the resolution, generally reserved for major sponsors and caucus leaders. Finally, a motion to recommit to committee would be considered, and was allotted ten minutes of debate before a vote on the motion. Then the House would proceed to a final vote on the resolution, as amended. Usually, debate on amendments and motions in the House was livelier and more responsive to opposing comments than the remarks prepared for general debate on resolutions and bills, and that held true in this case.

Amendment Number 1 was offered on October 10 by Representative Barbara Lee of California, a feisty, funny and charming Democrat who entered the House with me in January 1999. Barbara was a brave politician. She was the only member of either house of Congress to vote against the authorization for the use of American armed forces following the September 11, 2001 attacks. She became a hero of the anti-war movement, and was a vocal opponent of the Iraq War. You always knew where she stood, and her firm opinions were usually delivered with a smile.

Barbara Lee's amendment, offered to entirely replace the underlying resolution, was disarmingly straightforward. Containing no authorization for the use of force, the amendment provided that the United States should work through the U.N. to seek to ensure that Iraq was not developing weapons of mass destruction, through "resumption of weapons inspections, negotiation, enquiry, mediation, regional arrangements, and other peaceful means."[15]

The Lee amendment noted that Hussein had accepted the ceasefire provisions of U.N. Security Council Resolution 687 in April 1991 ending the Persian Gulf War, but Hussein was not complying with the provisions requiring free access for weapons inspections.

The amendment provided that the "true extent" of Iraq's weapons development and the "threat posed by such development . . . are unknown and cannot be known without inspections." These were wise words. But most of the House was not paying attention.

Lee said as she presented her amendment:

My amendment provides an option and the time to pursue it. Its goal is to give the United Nations inspections process a chance to work. It provides an option short of war with the objective of protecting the American people and the world from any threat posed by Iraqi weapons of mass destruction . . . through United Nations inspections and enhanced containment.[16]

Lee argued that we did not need to rush to war, the President already had "all the authority in the world" to defend the country, and unilateralism was not the answer. She advocated for improved border monitoring, including the installation of surveillance technology to keep an eye on Hussein. She said the words "first strike" by the United States should fill us with fear.

In the middle of her remarks, Barbara Lee described the contents of a curious and confusing letter that C.I.A. Director George Tenet had sent to Senator Bob Graham (D-FL) on October 7, which was first published in the *Congressional Record* and the *New York Times* on October 9,[17] just the day before Barbara offered her amendment. Her summary of the Tenet letter was:

Our own intelligence agencies report that there is currently little chance of chemical and biological attack from Saddam Hussein on U.S. forces or territories. But they emphasize that an attack could become much more likely if Iraq believes that it is about to be attacked.[18]

The Tenet letter to Senator Graham resulted from a classified briefing given to the Senate Intelligence Committee by Deputy C.I.A. Director John McLaughlin on October 2, the date of my White House briefing. McLaughlin conceded to the Senate committee that the likelihood of Saddam Hussein launching an attack with weapons of mass destruction was "low." Chairman Graham was concerned that this secret testimony was not consistent with the public statements of top administration officials, and the Senator subsequently requested that the McLaughlin remarks be declassified. Certainly, such a comment by the Deputy Director of the C.I.A. was contrary to the Bush Administration party line that Hussein's weapons posed an imminent threat.

On October 7, Tenet wrote the following to Chairman Graham:

In response to your letter of 4 October 2002, we have made unclassified material available to further the Senate's forthcoming open debate on a Joint Resolution concerning Iraq . . .

Regarding the 2 October closed hearing, we can declassify the following dialogue:

Senator Levin: . . . If (Saddam) didn't feel threatened, did not feel threatened, is it likely that he would initiate an attack using a weapon of mass destruction?

Senior Intelligence Witness: . . . My judgment would be that the probability of him initiating an attack–let me put a time frame on it—in the foreseeable future, given the conditions we understand now, the likelihood I think would be low.

Senator Levin: Now if he did initiate an attack you've . . . indicated that he would probably attempt clandestine attacks against us . . . But what about his use of weapons of mass destruction? If we initiate an attack and he thought he was *in extremis* or otherwise, what's the likelihood in response to our attack that he would use chemical or biological weapons?

Senior Intelligence Witness: Pretty high, in my view.

In the above dialogue, the witness's qualifications—"in the foreseeable future, given the conditions we understand now"— were intended to underscore that the likelihood of Saddam using WMD for blackmail, deterrence or otherwise grows as his arsenal builds.[19]

At the time, I found the Tenet letter odd. Because of Senator Graham's insistence, Tenet was forced to publicly confirm that his deputy John McLaughlin, a career C.I.A. man, told the Senate Intelligence Committee on October 2 that there was a low likelihood of Hussein initiating an attack with weapons of mass destruction. McLaughlin's candor clearly contradicted statements from all the top Bush advisers and the President himself that Saddam Hussein posed an imminent threat to the United States and our allies.

But Tenet muddied the waters by writing in the letter that McLaughlin's numerous qualifications about the foreseeable future and current conditions were meant to "underscore" that the threat from Hussein was actually growing as the dictator built his weapons arsenal.

To further confuse matters, the New York Times on the day of Barbara Lee's speech reported George Tenet's public statement that there was "no inconsistency in the views in the letter and those of the president."[20]

All things considered, I thought at the time that the controversy over Tenet's letter to Senator Graham did little to change the administration's public position regarding Saddam Hussein and his weapons of mass destruction. The subsequent Tenet statement about "no inconsistency" the day before the House vote worked to tamp down any public speculation that the CIA disagreed with the White House over Iraqi weapons.[21]

But relative to the congressional debate, Deputy Director McLaughlin had said what he said, and Representative Lee used those declassified comments effectively in her speech.

Lee closed her remarks on October 10 by describing the intention and impact of her amendment:

> It states that we reject the doctrine of preemption, and it reaffirms our commitment to our own security and national interests through multilateral diplomacy, not unilateral attack.[22]

Representative Henry Hyde of Illinois, Chairman of the House International Relations Committee, was managing the floor debate for the majority Republicans, and stood to oppose the Lee amendment. Hyde served in Congress over 30 years, and rose to national fame as the chief prosecutor of the President during the Clinton impeachment trial in the Senate in 1999. He ran the International Relations Committee with a polite and respectful manner toward all members and witnesses, but possessed a sharp tongue and fierce partisanship that were never far from the surface, and both were on display during the debate on the Iraq war resolution.

Henry Hyde said of the Lee amendment:

> I think her amendment suffers from terminal anemia. It is like slipping someone an aspirin who has just been hit by a freight train . . .
>
> While Saddam repeatedly violates the myriad of U.N. Security Council Resolutions passed since 1991, the world watches, the world waits and the world does nothing . . .
>
> [T]he security of the United States cannot be held hostage to a failure by the United Nations to act because of a threat of a Security Council veto by Russia, China or France.
>
> The Lee substitute essentially advocates the futile policies of the previous decade and fails to recognize the United States as a sovereign nation with an absolute right of self-defense . . .[23]

Of course, Barbara Lee's amendment most certainly did not fail to recognize the United States as a sovereign nation. That was an absurd allegation by Chairman Hyde, and would not be the last overheated or partisan remark directed at the President's opponents during the closing hours of debate on the amendments to the war resolution.

But the Democrats were capable of giving as good as they got, and Representative Peter DeFazio of Oregon was the next to speak after Chairman Henry Hyde relinquished the floor. DeFazio, one of the most progressive and pugnacious members of the Democratic caucus, wasted no time defending the Lee amendment and taking a shot at the President and his allies:

> This [amendment] represents neither conciliation or negotiation. It is . . . for continued containment, deterrence, that would be bolstered by intrusive, effective, forced, unfettered inspections. They worked before. They can work again . . . This cowboy, go-it-alone, to-heck-with-our-allies, to-heck-with-the-rest-of-the-world principle with an attack before we try this alternative is wrong.[24]

Peter DeFazio got his point across effectively, even though the word "heck" probably wasn't his preferred term.

Next up was Representative John Linder, Republican of Georgia, and a conservative backbencher who served eight years in the House.

Linder suggested that if Saddam Hussein restricted future inspections, or if he killed several thousand innocent Iraqis, or if he gave a nuclear device to terrorists that was used against an American city, the Lee amendment merely said, "Let's talk." Then, in an apparent attempt to surpass Henry Hyde's analogy of slipping an aspirin to someone hit by a freight train, Linder said:

> The lack of enforcement contained in this amendment is a bit like a senior citizen trying to stop a mugging by suggesting they dance the polka.[25]

It wasn't always easy to figure out exactly what these Republican analogies actually meant. But their unified opposition to the Lee Amendment was crystal clear.

The debate on the Lee amendment surged forward, with several Democrats speaking in support and several Republicans speaking in opposition. All but one of the Democrats who planned to vote against the amendment refrained from speaking against it, out of respect for Barbara Lee and a desire not to add to the stridency of the Republican opposition. But that sole Democrat carried a lot of weight.

As the ranking Democrat on the International Relations Committee, and as a supporter of the underlying war resolution, Tom Lantos felt an obligation to defend the war resolution and to "regretfully and respectfully" oppose the Lee substitute amendment. He described Barbara Lee as "my friend and colleague from California" and praised her "active and valuable" work on the International Relations Committee, and agreed with her that "war can be only our very last resort." Lantos then said:

> The joint resolution before us supports the diplomatic process at the United Nations and it requires the President to exhaust all peaceful means before resorting to war . . . our distinguished Secretary of State, Colin Powell, is working nonstop at the United Nations to move towards a peaceful and diplomatic resolution to this crisis . . . I strongly believe that our diplomacy will achieve its purpose only if the Iraqi regime knows that a sword of Damocles hangs over its head.[26]

Tom Lantos misspoke. H. J. Res. 114, the Iraq war resolution, did not *require* the President to exhaust all peaceful means before using the war authority granted by the resolution. H. J. Res. 114 provided merely that the Congress "supports the efforts by the President" to work through the U. N. Security Council to enforce and secure Iraqi compliance with prior U. N. resolutions. The House joint resolution also required the President, before or within 48 hours of using military force, to provide to the Congress his "determination" that further diplomatic efforts would not adequately protect the United States. But in no way did H. J. Res. 114 require the President to exhaust his diplomatic efforts before going to war.

This was a curious and uncharacteristic mistake for Representative Lantos, who was known for his precise and thoughtful commentary on foreign affairs. But Tom certainly expressed the view held by a large majority of House members when he opined that Saddam Hussein was unlikely to change his ways and start to cooperate with the international community unless the Iraqi dictator thought that the United States meant business. Most of us thought that Hussein would only pay attention and mend his ways if he felt a military Sword of Damocles hanging over his head.

Representative Sherrod Brown of Ohio was recognized for just one minute of debate time to support the Lee amendment. Sherrod, a friendly colleague and hard-driving liberal, and ace centerfielder for the House Democrats baseball team, made good use of his 60 seconds to express the fears of many Bush critics regarding the consequences of American preemptive use of military power:

> For 40 years our policy was to contain and deter Joseph Stalin and the Soviets, to contain and deter Fidel Castro and the Cubans, to contain and deter and restrain Communist aggression by the Chinese, always without invasion . . . but if we go first strike into Iraq the message to the world and to Putin is he can go into Georgia and chase down the Chechnyan rebels and the message to China is they can go into Taiwan and they can come down harder on Tibet and the message to the Pakistanis and the Indians is that they can go into Kashmir, maybe even with their nuclear weapons.
>
> Mr. President, go slow. Mr. President, we need aggressive, unfettered inspections in Iraq, complete, thorough, aggressive, unfettered inspections. Then go back to the United Nations. War should be a last resort.[27]

The next speaker was a senior member of the House, Representative Jerry Lewis, Republican of California, who served as one of the

"Cardinals" of the House by chairing the Defense Appropriations sub-committee of the powerful Appropriations Committee. Representative Lewis started his remarks in opposition to the Lee amendment with a reasonable review of the recent work of the Defense Appropriations sub-committee in funding America's role as a "force for peace in our world." Lewis calmly noted that the underlying war resolution would not auto-matically take the country to war, but was a "tool" for the Commander-in-Chief to use to secure "our future hopes for peace."

But then, in his criticism of the Lee amendment, Lewis dipped into the well of small-minded partisanship and questioning of opponents' patriotism that so often poisoned the remarks of leading Republicans during the Bush years:

> Let us not as a result of these votes today have one of our par-ties be the party working with the President for peace and have the other party be the party of the United Nations.[28]

What was that supposed to mean? Was Jerry Lewis suggesting that only the Republicans working with the President could be the party seeking peace? Did he mean that the other party, the Democrats, par-ticularly those that wanted to continue to work through the United Nations, was somehow anti-peace and anti-American?

I am not sure what Jerry Lewis meant that day. But I do know that his remarks were typical of the shallow, mocking tone so often adopted by the Republicans during the first term of George W. Bush to suggest that the President's supporters were the only true Americans and his opponents, therefore, must be disloyal and unpatriotic.

Not to be outdone, Representative Steve Buyer, Republican of Indi-ana, took the floor and started his remarks with the following:

> I rise in strong opposition to the Lee amendment. This amend-ment is another abdication of the United States' leadership in the world. It is tantamount to saying that Congress should contract out decisions on national security to foreign govern-ments: Paris, Beijing, Damascus.[29]

Obviously, the Lee amendment said nothing of the sort. The Lee amendment called for the United States to continue to work through the United Nations to impose unfettered weapons inspections in Iraq, to determine for sure whether Hussein actually had any weapons. Nothing in the Lee amendment would have given control over our national security to any foreign government. Nothing in the Lee amendment would have reduced our leadership in the world or threatened our national defense. But nothing could stop many of the Republicans from making such outlandish claims.

There was also nothing that could make the House think clearly about the merits of the Lee amendment. Many Members clearly felt that the Lee amendment was simply not adequate, not tough enough, to meet the current challenge posed by the murderous tyrant, Saddam Hussein. Perhaps the House felt that the amendment's author, Barbara Lee, who had cast a brave but solo vote against military action after the September 11, 2001 attacks, was simply too consistent in her opposition to the use of military force. The view of Tom Lantos, that Hussein had to feel a real military threat, a Sword of Damocles hanging over his head, before he would comply with U. N. demands, carried the day.

The Lee amendment got hammered in the vote: 72 yes votes, 355 no votes.[30] An overwhelming bipartisan majority of the House said no. I voted no.

Looking back, I wish I had voted yes. Barbara Lee was right. Intrusive, unfettered weapons inspections in Iraq would have uncovered the truth without resorting to war: Saddam Hussein had no weapons of mass destruction, was no threat to the national security of the United States, and was still contained, "bottled up" in Dick Cheney's earlier phrase, by existing United Nations sanctions. The Lee amendment, if enacted into law, would have exposed the hollow threat of Iraq and stopped the rush to war.

As soon as the result of final vote on the Lee amendment was announced, the House moved immediately to the consideration of the second amendment to the war resolution authorized by the House Rules Committee. Amendment No. 2, also intended to replace the entire underlying resolution, was entitled the "Elimination of Weapons of Mass Destruction From Iraq Resolution," and was offered by Representative John Spratt of South Carolina.[31]

John Spratt was one of my favorite senior members of the Democratic caucus. He served in Congress for 28 years, chairing the Budget Committee and serving as the 2nd ranking Democrat on the Armed Services Committee. Avuncular and knowledgeable, he taught me a lot about the federal budget and Congress when I served as a new member of his Budget Committee. He was a respected moderate and a strong supporter of the military.

The Spratt amendment sought to encourage continued presidential diplomacy while authorizing the immediate use of American force but only under U. N. auspices, and required the President to seek a second congressional vote for war authority if the United Nations failed to act satisfactorily against Iraq. This requirement of a second vote by Congress to authorize any unilateral, preemptive war by the United States against Iraq was hailed by John Spratt and the amendment's supporters as an appropriate application of the "checks and balances" required by the U.S. Constitution concerning the exercise of executive and legislative power.

The Spratt amendment started with 17 "whereas" clauses reviewing the history of Saddam Hussein's offenses against humanity and non-compliance with previous United Nations resolutions demanding weapons inspections and Iraqi disarmament. The amendment announced the "sense of the Congress" that the President should continue his diplomatic efforts to win U.N. Security Council support to require Iraq to disarm and permit unrestricted inspections, and authorized an American military force formed under the auspices of the U.N. but commanded by the United States to force Iraqi compliance. Further, if the Security Council failed to act, or acted ineffectually, the Spratt amendment urged the President to return to Congress for a second vote to use American force unilaterally to compel Iraq to disarm and permit inspections, under expedited legislative procedures that would not permit a Senate filibuster. The amendment also required Presidential reports every 60 days regarding U.S. actions, expenditures and reconstruction efforts in Iraq.

The Spratt amendment made sense to me. I liked how the amendment urged the President to continue his diplomatic efforts with the United Nations, and I liked how it connected the authorization of the use of American force to prior action by the U.N. Security Council to move against Iraq with international force. Of course, this was the legal and political structure engineered through skillful diplomacy by the first President Bush, George H. W. Bush, who secured the passage in 1990 of Security Council Resolution 678 authorizing international action to expel Iraq from Kuwait, then followed that with congressional passage in January 1991 of legislation authorizing the President to use American armed forces against Iraq under the auspices of the United Nations resolution. It seemed to me that what was good for America and Bush the Father in 1991 should be equally good for our country and Bush the Son in 2002.

I also liked that the Spratt amendment did not immediately authorize unilateral American military action, but required the President to return to Congress for a second vote on the question if the United Nations failed to act against Iraq or did not act effectively. While the Bush Administration was painting a harrowing picture of the imminent threat posed by Saddam Hussein and his weapons of mass destruction, there were still questions in the public debate about how truly imminent the Iraqi threat was.

I was worried about the political motives of the Bush team for demanding this congressional vote so soon before the 2002 elections. Were the Bush political operatives counting on the upcoming elections to pressure uncertain members of Congress, particularly Democrats, to vote "yes" for war or face a patriotic backlash at the polls?

I preferred to delay voting on the requested military authorization until after the elections when, perhaps, the reality about weapons in Iraq might be more fully understood. Moreover, the Administration was making clear that they were not intending on taking military action in the immediate future, and I thought a congressional vote authorizing war should come just before the onset of hostilities, in order to give diplomacy as much chance as possible to avert war. The Spratt amendment seemed to me to offer the right balance of continuing diplomacy, achieving international unity if possible, honoring the "checks and balances" envisioned by the framers of our Constitution, and the necessity of defending the country.

Representative Spratt opened the debate on his amendment by reminding the House that his proposal called for the same approach used by the first President Bush; namely, to use American military force in an international action sanctioned by the Security Council. Further, Spratt called for a second vote by Congress if the United States would be "faced with going it alone." He explained:

> I know that some will say this is an imposition on the President's power, a second vote, but in truth it is nothing more than the age-old system of checks and balances built in our Constitution. It is one way that Congress can say what we believe, that any action against Iraq should have the sanction of the Security Council and the support of a broad-based coalition, and if it does not, we should have a further say on it . . .
>
> . . . the precedent it follows was the precedent set by President Bush in 1991. He turned to the United Nations first.[32]

The Republican leadership in the House must have realized that the Spratt amendment made a lot of sense, and might be attractive to some of the Republican rank-and-file because Spratt stressed the similarities between his proposal and the successful steps taken by the first President Bush in dealing with Saddam Hussein 1991. Accordingly, the Republican Chairman Henry Hyde wasted no time in attacking the amendment and bashing the United Nations, despite the success of international action in 1991 engineered by the current President's father.

Hyde spoke immediately after Spratt's opening comments, and after announcing his opposition to the Spratt amendment, Hyde proceeded to distort the proposal and to appeal to his party's isolationist, anti-international wing:

> First and foremost, this substitute neither recognizes nor protects American sovereignty. It clearly yields to the United Nations the right and obligation to protect America.[33]

The only truth contained in that absurd statement was that the "first and foremost" phrase actually did come at the beginning. But Henry Hyde wasn't finished distorting the amendment:

> Its primary focus is on approval of the U.N. before any military action can be taken against Iraq. It does not recognize the sovereignty of the United States . . . I do not propose that we subordinate our foreign policy to the Security Council whose permanent members include France, China and Russia.[34]

It was curious that an old Cold War warrior like Henry Hyde chose to disparage the Spratt amendment not only by incorrectly claiming that it subordinated our foreign policy to the Security Council, but also by lumping in our long-time although annoying ally France with our communist adversaries China and Russia. But it was a useful way for Hyde to appeal to the anti-Europe, know-nothing wing of the House Republican caucus. After all, France is the country that many Republican politicians love to hate, except when they are visiting there at public expense.

After several members expressed their view both pro and con regarding the Spratt amendment, Tom Lantos, the ranking Democrat on the International Relations Committee, again took the floor to oppose a Democratic amendment. After complimenting "my good friend . . . one of the most valued in this House, on a very thoughtful and creative amendment", Lantos spoke against Spratt's proposal:

[T]he amendment would weaken the hand of our Secretary of State in international negotiations that are occurring as we speak . . . both the Security Council and Saddam Hussein must perceive that diplomatic failure will lead to military action. This amendment fails to convey that critical message.[35]

Again, Tom Lantos was expressing a strong sentiment that seemed prevalent in the House: America had to show the United Nations as well as Saddam Hussein that we meant business.

Later during the debate Representative Dana Rohrabacher, Republican of California, rose to oppose the Spratt amendment. Rohrabacher first came to Congress in 1989 as a rock-ribbed conservative after seven years as a senior speechwriter for President Ronald Reagan, and he never lost his conservative principles or his ability to turn a phrase. I used to enjoy, although seldom agree with, his right-wing commentary on the International Relations Committee. After opening his remarks by quoting Patrick Henry, Rohrabacher said:

And when all is said and done, America's security and our freedom is in the hands of our people. We do not choose to put the future of this country and the security of this country into the hands of the United Nations . . . This amendment requires the United States to have the permission of the Communist Chinese and gangsters of other regimes to do what is necessary for our own security. That is ridiculous . . . Let us remember what George Washington told us: "Put only Americans on guard tonight."[36]

Rohrabacher used a great quote by Washington, and his description of the Spratt amendment as "ridiculous" would have been valid if his summary of the proposal had been true, but it wasn't true.

John Spratt wasn't proposing to put the Chinese Communists, or any other communists for that matter, in charge of America's security. Spratt just wanted to follow the procedure that the first President Bush had followed to win international support, if possible, for action against Iraq. If international support was withheld or was inadequate, Spratt wanted Congress to take a second vote to authorize preemptive, unilateral action against Iraq by the United States.

None of the Republicans who spoke and voted against the Spratt amendment were ever able to explain why the procedure used by the first President Bush to act under United Nations auspices, which they had supported, was so terrible when proposed by Democrats for use by the second President Bush. Their only reaction was to distort the meaning of the amendment and to bash the United Nations.

Representative Henry Hyde still wasn't done. Later in the debate on the Spratt amendment he addressed himself to the Democrats who were expressing support for Spratt:

> When you retire from Congress and the great summing up comes with your great-grandchildren or great-great-grandchildren, and people say, "What did you do in Congress," you say, "Well, I voted to yield sovereignty to the United Nations. I voted to have the decision to defend the United States" national interests [given] to the Security Council, which is composed of five members, three of which are France, China and Russia.[37]

There is poor France again, still a whipping boy for the Republican Chairman to mock the Democrats and rally the conservative Republicans to oppose the Spratt amendment.

Henry Hyde had one more argument to make in opposition to the Spratt amendment, this one a blatantly political attack on the motives of the Democrats who were supporting the amendment. Late in the debate, Hyde offered the following:

> History is an exciting adventure. On April 28, 1999, in this very Chamber, right where we are now, this House voted to allow the President, President Clinton, without any U.N. resolution, to take military action: bombing in Kosovo. And among those who voted to allow the President to do this, without a U.N. resolution, but to go ahead, gung ho, was virtually everybody that has spoken on that side of the Chamber.
>
> Absolutely, I applaud them. I do not know what changed them, why they now demand we process this through the U.N., but they did not feel that way back then, in April of 1999, and I have the roll call if anybody cares to see it. But everybody voted to bomb Kosovo. Now, is that because that was President Clinton? There must be some explanation.[38]

This was the low point of the debate, the snide suggestion by a Republican leader that those of us in the Democratic caucus who had voted to bomb Kosovo and who also supported the Spratt amendment were casting those votes, votes on national security issues, matters of war and peace, based merely on party loyalty to President Clinton and on party opposition to President Bush.

Well, Henry Hyde had said, "There must be some explanation." John Spratt gave it to him. At the close of the debate on his amendment, Spratt said:

> My good friend, the gentleman from Illinois (Mr. Hyde), has said that many of us on this side of the aisle voted for action in Kosovo. I did. And I am proud of it because we stopped another butchery in the backyard of Europe by doing so. We did not go to the U.N. then, and the gentleman knows why. Because the Russians are on the Security Council and they would have blocked us.
>
> Politics and diplomacy is a pragmatic thing. That is why we did not go there. But it was multilateral, because it was an undertaking by NATO, and we tried to use collective defense in that particular case. It simply proves the point.[39]

John Spratt was too much of a gentleman, and far too respectful of his colleagues in the House, to point out that the Republican caucus had largely failed to support President Clinton's request in 1999 for authorization to conduct military air operations and missile strikes against Yugoslavia to stop atrocities against innocent civilians, in the very same roll call vote to "bomb Kosovo" that Henry Hyde had brandished about moments before. On April 28, 1999, in the House vote on S. Con. Res. 21, the House Republicans voted against President Clinton's request for military authorization against Yugoslavia by a margin of 31–187, although Hyde to his credit voted yes.

John Spratt did not play the partisan game that Henry Hyde was playing by suggesting that the Republican opposition to President Clinton's policies in Kosovo was based on pure politics. It can be very tricky, and frequently inaccurate, to try to identify the private motivations for a politician's public actions, and Spratt wouldn't stoop to that level. But Spratt correctly pointed out that the successful U.S. air campaign in Kosovo in 1999 had "stopped another butchery in the backyard of Europe," and he was offering his amendment to the Iraq war resolution in an attempt to move forward again with international support to stop another tyrant.

Representative Spratt closed his argument on behalf of his amendment with a description of the actions taken by President George H. W. Bush at the time of the Persian Gulf War in 1991:

> But remember what he did then, just days after Iraq's invasion of Kuwait, President Bush . . . turned first to the United Nations and went to the Security Council and got the first in a series of resolutions that culminated in Resolution 678 which authorized the use of force. President Bush obtained all those Security Council resolutions, with our support, but without an express war powers resolution until literally days before the war began.
>
> Rather than asserting that he could go it alone, stiffing the Security Council, he sought the Security Council approval. He sought allies to stand with us and cover approximately $62 billion out of the $66 billion total cost of the war. The result, a successful military action, a successful diplomacy, and I think a model worth emulating. And that is exactly what this [amendment] does.[40]

Well, that is what the amendment would have done, or at least tried to do, if it was passed by the House and enacted into law. But the House voted against the Spratt amendment by a vote of 155 in favor and 270 against.[41] I voted for the amendment. The Republican members voted against the Spratt amendment by a margin of 7 in favor and 210 against. I wonder what Henry Hyde thought about that partisan split.

I was disappointed by the defeat of the Spratt amendment. I was sorry that the Republicans voted so overwhelmingly against giving the President the clear direction to confront the challenges in Iraq by working through the United Nations if at all possible, as the President's father had done so successfully twelve years before.

Following the defeat of the Spratt amendment, the House moved immediately to one hour of "final debate" on H. J. Res. 114, the Iraq war resolution. Such debate is generally reserved on major pieces of legislation for the party leaders and the proposal's chief sponsors to make their final arguments, and that was the case here.[42]

Representative Nancy Pelosi of California, then the Minority Whip, was the second ranking member of the Democratic Caucus. A party whip assists the leader of the caucus, and is primarily responsible for obtaining headcounts on important legislation tabulating how the members of the caucus plan to vote, and occasionally twisting arms to encourage balky members to support the party's position on a bill or to support or oppose a President's position. Pelosi did her job well. The daughter of a former Congressman from Maryland and a former Mayor of Baltimore, and sister of another former Mayor of Baltimore, Nancy had politics in her blood and performed her duties with great diligence, intelligence and charm. She was an articulate spokesperson for her progressive principles, and was the only leader of the House to oppose the Iraq war resolution. She said during the final hour of debate:

> I rise in opposition to the resolution on national security grounds. The clear and present danger that our country faces is terrorism. I say flat out that unilateral use of force without first exhausting every diplomatic remedy and other remedies and making a case to the American people will be harmful to our war on terrorism . . . these costs to the war on terrorism, the loss of life, the cost to our economy, the cost in dollars to our budget, these costs must be answered for. If we go in, certainly we can show our power to Saddam Hussein. If we resolve this issue diplomatically, we can show our strength as a great country, as a great country. Let us show our greatness. Vote no on this resolution.[43]

Next up was Representative Tom DeLay of Texas, the Majority Whip, known as "the Hammer" for enforcing party discipline in the House, and for retribution against any Republican who did not support the program of the House Republicans or the policies of President George W. Bush.

I once saw DeLay chase Representative Jim Leach, a highly regarded Republican moderate, across the floor of the House during a roll call vote to the far edge of the Democratic side beyond the back railing, and whisper violently into Leach's ear, leaving the well-respected Leach hanging onto the railing, visibly shaken. I had no idea what that confrontation was about or what was said, except that DeLay obviously wanted Leach's vote on the matter at hand. But knowing Tom DeLay, I was positive Leach was on the correct side of the controversy.

Tom DeLay once described the triumvirate of Republican leaders of a previous Congress as follows: Speaker Newt Gingrich was "the visionary," Majority Leader Dick Armey was "the policy wonk," and Majority Whip DeLay himself was "the ditch digger who makes it all happen."[44] During final debate on the Iraq war resolution, DeLay was digging his ditch furiously:

Americans have always had to summon courage to disregard the timid counsel of those who would mortgage our security to the false promises of wishful thinking and appeasement . . . we have to defeat dangers before they ripen. The war on terrorism will be fought here at home, unless we summon the will to confront evil before it attacks . . . regime change in Iraq is a central goal of the war on terror. It is vital because a war on terrorism that leaves the world's leading purveyor and practitioner of terror in power would be a bald failure . . . today, the free world chooses strength over temporizing and timidity. . . . in the fullness of time, America will be proud that in our hour of testing we chose the bold path of action, not the hollow comfort of appeasement.[45]

There was nothing timid, temporizing or appeasing about the message from the Hammer that day. The Minority Leader, Representative Dick Gephardt of Missouri, the hard-working, popular leader of the House Democrats, who also supported the war resolution although with more temperate rhetoric, followed DeLay in the debate.

Dick Gephardt was a great leader of the Democratic caucus. He and his excellent staff worked hard to help members, particularly new members, to win their favored committee assignments, achieve their legislative goals, raise money for re-election, and get re-elected. He travelled the country ceaselessly, as all caucus leaders must, to recruit candidates and help Democratic challengers and incumbents alike. He met regularly with members in the Capitol to discuss legislation, and always understood if a Democrat from a tough district had to cast a vote that was contrary to the party's position. He preached to new members the importance of helping constituents and staying on message. He held the allegiance of virtually every Democrat in the House.

The night I was elected to Congress in November of 1998, I received a late-night call from Gephardt who shouted into the phone, "You did it! You did it!" I was thrilled, both by the victory and by the phone call. In the fall of 2003, when Gephardt was seeking the Democratic nomination for President in 2004, he visited our home in suburban Philadelphia to meet some local political leaders I had gathered. In a moment of exuberance, in front of the assembled guests, I found myself standing in the front hall, holding the same telephone, recreating that Election Night phone call, acting out both parts of the conversation for the benefit of all. Lost in the moment, I suddenly realized that my friends were staring at me in wonder, my wife Francesca was rolling her eyes and Gephardt was looking at me as if I had lost my mind.

Leader Gephardt spoke last for the Democrats on the Iraq war resolution, and said:

> September 11 has made all the difference. The events of that tragic day jolted us to the enduring reality that terrorists not only seek to attack our interests abroad but also to strike us here at home. We have clear evidence now that they even desire to use weapons of mass destruction against us . . .
>
> Saddam Hussein's track record is too compelling to ignore, and we know that he continues to develop weapons of mass destruction, including nuclear devices, and he may soon have the ability to use nuclear weapons against other nations . . .[46]

Clearly, Leader Gephardt believed the recurring, adamant message of the Bush Administration, which was Saddam Hussein had weapons of mass destruction, was acquiring more, and was willing to use them. But Gephardt also understood the benefits of a multinational approach:

> At the insistence of many of us, the resolution includes a provision urging President Bush to continue his efforts to get the U.N. to effectively enforce its own resolutions against Iraq . . . Exhausting all efforts at the U.N. is essential . . . Completely bypassing the U.N. would set a dangerous precedent that would undoubtedly be used by other countries in the future to our and the world's detriment. It is too high a price to pay.[47]

The last leader to speak was the Majority Leader, Representative Dick Armey of Texas, first elected in the Reagan landslide year of 1984 as one of six freshmen Republican congressmen from Texas elected that year that were dubbed the Texas Six Pack.[48] Armey never lost his allegiance to conservative principles or his loyalty to Republican presidents, and his support for the Iraq war resolution was offered in stark terms:

> Is Saddam evil? Who could doubt it? . . . Saddam is evil. That is a fact . . . Can he strike our interests, our citizens, our land, and our responsibilities with them? Irrefutably, yes . . . Saddam will strike . . . Will he do so? Who can doubt that? He has a record of

having done so that is deplorable in the most evil and insidious ways. The question is when will he do so, not will he do so . . .[49]

Even though the "final hour" of debate on the resolution had concluded, one final parliamentary motion was in order under the House rule that was controlling legislative action on the Iraq war resolution, and that was a motion to recommit. Usually permitted by the House Rules Committee for all controversial legislation, a motion to recommit a bill or resolution to the committee that had approved it for floor action was considered the last opportunity for the opponents of the legislation to try to stop passage. Such motions rarely passed but were considered an important and time-honored procedure to allow minority views to be heard. But debate time on the motion to recommit was usually limited to just ten minutes.

Representative Dennis Kucinich, Democrat of Ohio, introduced the motion to recommit H.J. Res. 114 to the Committee on International Relations with instructions to report the resolution back to the full House with amended language.[50] Kucinich, dubbed the "boy mayor of Cleveland" when he was elected to that office in 1977 at the age of 31, was probably the most progressive member of the House of Representatives, and did not seem to fear anything in politics. Dennis always had the courage of his convictions. Later, he would file articles of impeachment against Vice President Dick Cheney in 2007 and President George W. Bush in 2008. But on this day, Kucinich was attempting to add language to the Iraq war resolution by way of a recommittal motion that would require a whole lot of transparency from the Bush administration.

The Kucinich motion did not propose any changes to the existing provisions of H.J. Res. 114, which encouraged the President to continue to use diplomacy and seek international agreement to disarm Hussein, and granted the President immediate authority to use American military force at his discretion. The Kucinich motion proposed additional language, to be added to the resolution by the committee, which required the President, prior to using the authorized force, to issue an unclassified report to Congress that addressed the impact of such use of force on our national security. The presidential report was to include an estimate of the costs and impact of military action, a plan to provide for humanitarian, economic and political stabilization assistance in Iraq, an estimate of military and civilian casualties, a statement of the international support for military action, an analysis of the Intelligence Community's assertions about Iraq's weapons of mass destruction, and an analysis of the long-term impact of a preemptive first strike on the stability of the world.

Representative Kucinich pointed out in defense of his motion to recommit that it was "neutral" on the central point of giving the President the authority to use all necessary force at his disposal. Rather, he was seeking information and transparency from the Bush administration:

> But with power comes responsibility, and in a democracy the responsibility is to the people. This motion to recommit would assign the administration with the responsibility to inform the American people on key questions raised by a use of force in Iraq, questions that Members on both sides of this proposition have raised.[51]

Representative Henry Hyde spoke against the Kucinich motion, saying it would create "insurmountable" roadblocks for the President.[52] Hyde was certainly correct that the Bush administration would have hotly resisted such reporting requirements, which was probably what Kucinich had in mind in the first place. But looking back, Kucinich was right on the merits. That requested information should have been provided to Congress and the American people before we started a preemptive war of choice. A great deal of American life, treasure and prestige would have been preserved had Congress insisted on such information from the Bush administration before we voted to authorize a first strike against Iraq.

But I didn't see it that way then. I had decided to support H. J. Res. 114, and the Kucinich motion seemed designed to gum up the works, which is the intention of most motions to recommit. So I voted against the Kucinich motion, and it failed by a margin of 101 in favor and 325 opposed.[53]

Now, after months of public deliberations and private consideration, after soul-searching and speech-making, after twenty-six hours of floor debate, after votes on two amendments and a motion to recommit, a majority of the members of the House of Representatives were prepared to give the President the military authority he requested to disarm Saddam Hussein of weapons of mass destruction.

It was a difficult decision for me. I did not fully trust the Bush administration, including the President, and I was troubled that many of my friends in the progressive wing of the House Democratic caucus were voting against the Iraq war resolution. My wife and daughter were outraged that I was about to support the President's request to authorize the use of military force. Many of my Democratic colleagues and my family simply did not trust George W. Bush to tell the truth about Iraq. I thought they were paranoid and overly partisan to distrust the President so much. I wasn't sure I was right, in fact, I was about 60% in favor of the war resolution and 40% opposed. But a member of Congress cannot cast a split vote based on percentages. When the vote would be called, I had to vote yes or no.

The Democratic Leader, Dick Gephardt, believed that Saddam Hussein possessed weapons of mass destruction, called on the President to continue his diplomatic efforts, and supported the Iraq war resolution that Gephardt himself has helped to negotiate on a bipartisan basis with the White House.

The second ranking Democrat in the House, Nancy Pelosi, also believed that Hussein had dangerous weapons, and Pelosi also favored continued diplomacy, but she opposed the war resolution. She was not allowed under the intelligence law to tell us why. I remember Pelosi remarking during a Democratic caucus meeting shortly before the vote that although she could not tell us what she had seen, "The intelligence does not match the threat. I am very comfortable voting against this resolution."

The different conclusions reached by the two Democratic leaders were much discussed privately by members of the Democratic caucus. I thought Nancy Pelosi was too adamant in her opposition to the war resolution, but she turned out to be correct. None of us, supporters of the resolution and opponents alike, realized at the time just how badly we were being misled by the President and his top aides about the actual threat posed by Iraq. Nobody knew just how false the pretenses really were that George W. Bush and his administration were using to lead us into war.

House Joint Resolution 114, Authorization for Use of Military Force Against Iraq Resolution of 2002, passed the House of Representatives on October 10, 2002 by a vote of 296 in favor and 133 opposed.[54] The Republican members supported the resolution by a margin of 215 in favor and 6 opposed. The Democratic members opposed the resolution by a margin of 81 in favor and 126 opposed. Majority Leader Armey had asked the House to give our trust to the President, to say as a body, "we trust you and we rely on you in a dangerous time to be our Commander-in-Chief."[55] 81 Democrats gave that "great trust" as Armey described it to our Commander-in-Chief. Nobody in the House knew how badly that trust was being abused.

I voted yes. I was wrong. Of all the public actions I have taken in twenty-five years in elected office, of all the votes I have cast, speeches I have made and policies I have advocated, that vote is the one I most deeply regret.

If I knew then what I know now, I would have voted no on the Iraq war resolution. But I didn't know it then. Perhaps I should have. I was convinced then that Saddam Hussein had weapons of mass destruction, and he needed to be disarmed. I also knew that voting for the war would be popular in my district and would be a benefit to my re-election campaign.

House Joint Resolution 114 passed the Senate on the following day, October 11, by a vote of 77 in favor and 23 opposed, and was signed into law by President Bush on October 16, 2002 as Public Law 107-243. President Bush had received the congressional authority he requested to use military force against Iraq.

Congress recessed shortly after the votes on the Iraq War resolution, and members of the House and Senate returned to their home districts for the November 2002 congressional elections. A few of my Democratic and progressive supporters back home expressed displeasure to me about my vote authorizing war. But most of my constituents regardless of their party registration seemed to support the President's position that the United States, with or without the United Nations, needed to stop the threat posed by Saddam Hussein. The majority of the people in my congressional district believed that Hussein had weapons of mass destruction, was acquiring more, and needed to be stopped before he could use them. My constituents believed what the White House and officials throughout the Bush Administration were saying about the imminent threat posed by the Iraqi weapons of mass destruction controlled by Saddam Hussein.

My Republican opponent in the general election, Dr. Melissa Brown, agreed with my support for the Iraq War resolution, and accordingly Iraq did not become a divisive issue in the campaign. Frankly, it was politically beneficial for me that Brown couldn't attack my loyalty or patriotism as a result of my vote on the war resolution. In light of her sharp attacks on other issues and the general GOP grandstanding on national security and terrorism since the attacks of 9/11, I am positive that Melissa Brown and the Republican campaign committees would have made a huge election issue out of the war resolution if I had opposed the President and voted no. As expected, President Bush supported Brown in the election, and appeared in one of her television commercials, but on November 5, 2002 I was re-elected to my third term in Congress.

Of course, the conclusion of the congressional elections did not stop the politicking or advocacy on the issue of Iraq from the Bush team. The President scored an important and impressive diplomatic victory when the United Nations Security Council on November 8, 2002 passed Resolution 1441[56] giving Iraq "a final opportunity to comply with its disarmament obligations" as set forth eleven years before in Resolution 687. However, Resolution 1441 did not authorize international military action against Iraq.

As a result of the passage of Resolution 1441, weapons inspections by the United Nations resumed in Iraq on November 27, 2002, with Saddam Hussein's compliance. I remember feeling some vindication that my vote in favor of the Iraq war resolution, which authorized unilateral and first-strike use of American military force if Iraq failed to cooperate with the U.N. or if the U.N. failed to act, had played a part in causing Saddam Hussein to realize it was time for him to comply with the demands of the international community, or else. Perhaps Hussein was finally feeling that Sword of Damocles hanging over his head that Congressman Tom Lantos had envisioned.

Whatever Hussein's private thoughts were, I knew that the resumption of international weapons inspections in Iraq was a very good thing. I was looking forward to learning from the inspectors just how big Hussein's stockpiles of weapons of mass destruction actually were. I didn't know then about the doubts in the intelligence community about the threats from Iraq. It never occurred to me in the fall of 2002 that Saddam Hussein actually did not have any weapons of mass destruction.

FIVE

Preparing For War

As the New Year arrived in January 2003, and as Congress and the American people waited for definitive word from the U.N. inspectors about Hussein's weapons, the Bush administration continued to advocate for war.

On January 7, 2003, Secretary of Defense Donald Rumsfeld said:

> With respect to chemical weapons, we know they not only have hid them but that they've used them. And with respect to biological weapons, we have clearly—the Central Intelligence Agency has said what it has said, and there's no doubt in my mind that they currently have chemical and biological weapons.[1]

The Secretary of Defense had "no doubt" that Saddam Hussein currently possessed chemical and biological weapons, citing the CIA as his source. But Secretary Rumsfeld did not share or acknowledge the doubts, reservations and dissenting agency opinions about Hussein's weapons contained in the October 1, 2002 classified National Intelligence Estimate on Iraq weapons.

Not to be outdone, White House Press Secretary Ari Fleischer got into the act two days later at the White House when he stated on the subject of Iraq:

> We know for a fact that there are weapons there.[2]

Mr. Fleischer did not provide his source.

As January wore on, more voices were raised expressing doubts about the Bush administration's policies toward Iraq. Some of my constituents were upset by what they saw as a rush to war, and were unhappy over my vote for the war resolution the previous October.

On January 21, when I was in Harrisburg attending the inauguration of our new governor Ed Rendell, 15 local members of the internet activist group MoveOn.org met with my district office staff to express their concerns about Iraq, accompanied by local reporters. In a series of meetings around the country with congressional offices, MoveOn was advocating the message: "Let the inspectors do their job," referring to the United Nations weapons inspectors currently searching for weapons in Iraq. MoveOn wanted Congress to pressure the President to give the inspections a chance to work before considering the unilateral use of force.

According to press coverage of the meeting,[3] Joe Heyer of Lansdale, serving as spokesman for the group, said, "Why is it so urgent we get this done so quickly? We don't feel Saddam Hussein is an immediate threat to the United States. There's no Iraqis on the Canadian border about to attack . . . there's no Iraqi airplanes about to bomb us."

Philip Marquis of Ambler said I should not have voted for a resolution that granted the President unlimited power to declare war on Iraq. He was unimpressed with the language in House Joint Resolution 114 that called upon the President to continue diplomatic approaches. Marquis said, "Joe seems to want it both ways. I need him to lead the opposition to this war."

Reached later by telephone by the reporter, I said that I voted for the resolution authorizing force because Hussein was a dangerous man:

> He is a threat to regional and world peace and he must be disarmed. But the way to do that is a multilateral approach . . . Now [the President] has to be patient. As long as the inspectors are in there, we're winning.

I repeated the argument about the value of having the inspectors at work in Iraq a few days later in a local newspaper article about the different views of area congressmen. I said:

> As long as inspectors are in Iraq, the international community is winning—since Hussein can cause no mischief in his

own country or the region while the inspectors are there. I'd be happy if they stayed there for ten years . . . we should never take unilateral action unless it's under the gravest circumstances.[4]

Two of my Republican colleagues from neighboring districts in suburban Philadelphia disagreed in the article that weapons inspectors were effective. Both said the United States must be prepared to push ahead against Iraq without approval from the United Nations, and both offered familiar Republican chestnuts. Congressman Pat Toomey said, "We never ceded our responsibility to protect our citizens to the United Nations," and Congressman Jim Greenwood said that the United States "can't be governed by France."[5]

The country awaited with great anticipation President Bush's State of the Union speech on January 28. Congress and the American people expected to hear directly from the President the latest news concerning Iraq, including the status of the international weapons inspections, an update on diplomatic efforts and, perhaps, an indication of the likelihood of war. The President's report to the people would be unfiltered by staff or media—we would hear directly from our President and Commander-in-Chief.

During my six years in Congress, I came to dread the State of the Union speech. I always wished I were back in my office watching the speech on television, or better yet home with my wife.

But there I was, on January 28, 2003, listening to my fifth State of the Union speech from the floor of the House, the last three delivered by George W. Bush.

Don't misunderstand. I always felt it was a great honor to sit there as a Member of Congress, with my fellow House members and our colleagues from the Senate, with the President's Cabinet, the Joint Chiefs of Staff, the Supreme Court and the Diplomatic Corps, listening while the President made his annual report to the Congress and the nation.

And I certainly was thrilled to be starting my third term in office. I had worked hard in my first two terms in Congress, learning the ropes on Capitol Hill and getting better known back home. The re-election campaign the previous fall had been a tough fight and I was glad it was over. I had cast some difficult votes in the last term, notably against the President's tax cut in 2001 and for the Iraq war authority last fall, and the long-term impact of those votes was still unclear. But I was very glad to be back, glad to still be a U.S. congressman.

But what a show this annual speech had become. What a spectacle. The distinguished members of the audience, who were crowded into the House chamber that was bathed in intense lighting for the television cameras, had become nothing much more than a swank studio audience, there to stand and cheer and applaud on cue for the benefit of the star of the show, the President of the United States.

One of the things I disliked about the State of the Union was all of the mindless standing ovations the Congress gave to the President. It was a fine thing to stand and applaud when the President first entered the chamber, to the ringing cry of "Mr. Speaker! The President of the United States!" And it was fitting and proper to stand and applaud again when the President was re-introduced on the rostrum by the Speaker of the House, and at the conclusion of his speech as he slowly made his way out of the chamber, shaking hands and slapping backs.

But was it really necessary to stand and applaud every time the President made a forceful point? Sometimes it seemed that all any President had to do was smile at his adoring audience and they would all leap to their feet, cheering madly. I had always thought that all the adulation was over the top when I had been a private citizen watching from home, and now that I was in the audience my frustration was only worse.

What I really hated was how partisan the whole exercise had become. In recent years it had become commonplace for the President's party members to jump up and cheer wildly every time he made a partisan point, while the other party representatives sat glumly on their hands. It didn't matter who the President was. The members would follow the remarks on their printed copies of the speech, scanning for applause lines. When seniors or veterans were mentioned, everybody stood and cheered. But when the subject was taxes or fiscal policy or health care or the role of government, when the President addressed any divisive issue at all, one side stood cheering, flushed with excitement and glee, while the other side sat slumped in their seats, sadly looking around, pretending to wonder what was causing all the fuss.

The whole thing made me feel like a jackass. There ought to be more seriousness of purpose here, this evening of all evenings, and a greater display of dignity.

But here I was, for the fifth time, waiting for the President to arrive in the House chamber to deliver his State of the Union address, because I felt it was the right thing to do. There was nothing wrong, in fact there was everything right, in the various representatives of the federal government, elected and appointed, coming together once a year to hear from their President. I just wished we would stand and applaud less and listen and consider more.

Something else always got my attention as I sat on the House floor waiting for the State of the Union to begin. I could never believe how many of my colleagues crowded both sides of the center aisle. At first I thought that some of them must have been sitting there all afternoon to secure those prime seats. Then I learned they send some poor staffer over to sit there all day holding the seat. Veteran members told me that traditionally staffers could put their Member's name on a piece of paper to reserve an aisle seat, but recently other Members started just crumpling up the paper and sitting in the "reserved" seat, so now they sent their staff to hold a seat all afternoon.

When I used to watch the State of the Union at home before my election to Congress, I always thought that the Congressmen reaching out to chat and touch the President on his shoulder must be his close friends and supporters. But I soon realized that the Democrats who crowded our side of the aisle generally opposed Bush's policies by day and badmouthed him by night. But not this night. They wanted to be there on national television, grinning and cheesing with the President. It was all about face time with the President, wanting the folks back home to see how important they were.

Suddenly, the familiar cry from the House Doorkeeper, "Mistah Speakah! The President of the United States!"

I rose to my feet and joined the standing ovation for President Bush, who was preceded down the aisle by the bipartisan leadership and the appointed congressional escort committee. Bush took his time, shaking hands, sharing a word, laughing and smiling, pointing to members who couldn't quite reach him. Both sides of the aisle were crowded now, and the President basked in the attention while the members along the aisle got their precious face time on television. I rolled my eyes as some of George Bush's severest Democratic critics along the aisle grasped for their chance to shake his hand or whisper in his ear.

In due course, the President reached the rostrum and gave copies of his speech to the House Clerk, the Vice President and the Speaker. Then the Speaker introduced the President again, and another standing ovation resulted. Finally, the members and the rest of the audience settled down and President Bush began:[6]

"Our faith is sure; our resolve is firm; and our Union is strong." Everybody was on their feet applauding, with the Republican side of the aisle cheering.

"We achieved historic education reform . . ." Members on both sides were standing and applauding.

"We reorganized our government and created the Department of Homeland Security . . ." There was widespread standing and applauding, but liberal Democrats and conservative Republicans were looking unhappy about the new security bureaucracy.

"We delivered the largest tax relief in a generation . . ." The Republican side was standing and cheering, but only a few moderate Democrats in swing districts were offering tepid applause.

The President continued:

The economy grows when Americans have more money to spend and invest, and the best and fairest way to make sure Americans have that money is not to tax it away in the first place . . .

Republicans were on their feet and cheering loudly, while most Democrats, including all the leaders, were sitting on their hands.

The President pushed forward:

I am proposing that all the income-tax reductions set for 2004 and 2006 be made permanent and effective this year . . . the tax relief is for everyone who pays income taxes . . . you, the Congress, have already passed all these reductions and promised them for future years. If this tax relief is good for Americans three, or five, or seven years from now, it is even better for Americans today.

The Republicans were deliriously happy, slapping each other on the back, while the Democrats were looking vacantly around, silent and glum.

Good grief, I thought, what about fiscal discipline and balancing the budget? I was proud that I had opposed George Bush's excessive tax cut in 2001, and since then the need for more federal revenue was even greater following 9/11 and the war in Afghanistan and all the defense and homeland security increases. How could we pay for all that and hope to balance the budget while cutting taxes even more? What was Bush thinking? The United States had never before declared war and cut taxes at the same time. It made no sense.

The President was continuing to cite domestic accomplishments and objectives about Social Security, private retirement accounts, affordable health care, medical liability reform and energy independence.

Not much new here, I thought. Same old stuff. My colleagues in the chamber were popping up and down depending on the individual points President Bush was making. My mind was wandering.

Then the President made a plug for the environment, proposing $1.2 billion in research funding to develop clean, hydrogen-powered automobiles.

Whoa, that was something new, I realized. I listened as President Bush continued to present new spending proposals to bring mentors to disadvantaged junior high school students, to help an additional 300,000 Americans get drug treatment, to implement AIDS Relief in Africa and the Caribbean. The Democratic side greeted each new spending proposal with enthusiasm, the Republicans much less so, with some conservatives looking very glum.

Suspense was building in the House chamber as members waited for President Bush to address the subject on everyone's mind: Iraq. At last, the President turned to foreign affairs and addressed America's role in the war on terror:

> We have arrested or otherwise dealt with many key commanders of Al Qaeda . . . more than 3,000 suspected terrorists have been arrested in many countries. Many others have met a different fate. Let's put it this way: they are no longer a problem to the United States and our friends and allies . . . we have the terrorists on the run. We're keeping them on the run. One by one, the terrorists are learning the meaning of American justice.

Every member was applauding and many on both sides of the aisle were on their feet. But I felt it was the wrong tone and too boastful, too much of the Texas cowboy.

The President finally focused on Iraq.

> Today, the gravest danger in the war on terror, the gravest danger facing America and the world, is outlaw regimes that seek and possess nuclear, chemical, and biological weapons. These regimes could use such weapons for blackmail, terror, and mass murder . . . we have called on the United Nations to fulfill its charter and stand by its demand that Iraq disarm . . . almost three months ago, the United Nations Security Council gave Saddam

Hussein his final chance to disarm. He has shown utter contempt for the United Nations and for the opinion of the world . . .

Final chance? I was surprised. What about the ongoing diplomacy Bush had promised to conduct, and letting the weapons inspectors finish their work? I didn't think that the U.S. had reached the point of declaring a "final chance". Was this just more Bush bluster?

The President continued:

The International Atomic Energy Agency confirmed in the 1990s that Saddam Hussein had an advanced nuclear weapons development program, had a design for a nuclear weapon, and was working on five different methods of enriching uranium for a bomb.

Old news, I thought. Then:

The British government has learned that Saddam Hussein recently sought significant quantities of uranium from Africa . . .

Wait a minute. That was something new! That sounds like proof that Iraq is continuing to build a nuclear capability. The President continued:

Our intelligence sources tell us that he has attempted to purchase high-strength aluminum tubes suitable for nuclear weapons production . . .

There were Condi Rice's aluminum tubes again, I thought. These statements seemed likely to bolster Bush's push for war. But were they true?

The President continued to pound on Saddam Hussein:

The dictator of Iraq is not disarming. To the contrary, he is deceiving . . . the only possible explanation, the only possible use he could have for those weapons, is to dominate, intimidate, or attack . . . Saddam Hussein aids and protects terrorists, including members of Al Qaeda. Secretly and without fingerprints, he could provide one of his hidden weapons to terrorists or help them develop their own.

George W. Bush finished with a flourish:

America will not accept a serious and mounting threat to our country and our friends and allies. The United States will ask the U.N. Security Council to convene on February 5 to consider the facts of Iraq's ongoing defiance of the world. Secretary of State Powell will present information and intelligence about Iraq's illegal weapons programs, its attempt to hide those programs from inspectors, and its links to terrorists groups. We will consult. But let there be no misunderstanding: If Saddam Hussein does not fully disarm, for the safety of our people and for the peace of the world, we will lead a coalition to disarm him . . .

As the members of Congress and the other dignitaries stood to applaud the President during his slow exit from the chamber, I thought the speech was another powerful message calling the nation to almost certain military action against Iraq. The President was forceful, focused and unforgiving. But what about his promises to exhaust diplomatic options and allow weapons inspectors to complete their tasks before using the military authority that I had voted to give him? President Bush sounded like his mind was already made up.

I scurried out the back door of the chamber and made my way to Statuary Hall where hundreds of reporters and TV cameras awaited for congressional responses to the President's State of the Union message. National Statuary Hall was the meeting place of the House of Representatives from 1807 until 1857, when the House moved into the current chamber. The old House became the repository for the sculptures of prominent Americans, two per state, authorized by Congress. First placed there in 1870, the statue collection outgrew the Hall by 1933, and Congress directed that the memorial sculptures be spread about the Capitol building, for both aesthetic and structural reasons. Now just 38 statues ringed the perimeter of the semicircular Statuary Hall, leaving a fine open space visited by hundreds of tourists daily and used for ceremonial events and dinners. Tonight, Statuary Hall was jammed with reporters, cameras, lights, cables—and most of the members of the House and Senate who were anxious to share their opinions of the President's address with their constituents back home.

I found the camera crew for a television station in Philadelphia, where a couple of my colleagues from Southeastern Pennsylvania and South Jersey had already gathered. I waited for my turn before the camera, listening to snatches of conversation and interviews near by. Camera stands were set up all around me, and there was barely room to maneuver around all the tripods, interviewers and interviewees. The news team that was sending video back to Philadelphia was comprised of just a cameraman and a lighting assistant. When I was positioned in front of the camera, the cameraman simply said, "Look at me, not the camera. What did you think of the President's speech?"

I never liked this interview format, talking to a cameraman who was paying more attention to his equipment than to what I was saying. It was hard to sound fully engaged and to look your best on TV when you were addressing someone off camera who wasn't listening to you. But that's the way it was when the TV station didn't want to spend the money to send a local reporter to Washington for the evening. So I did my best to act the part of an important congressman giving an interview to a spellbound reporter, while looking at the cameraman's left ear, the only part of his head that was visible behind the camera.

"Thanks, Congressman. Whose next?" asked the cameraman. Short but sweet. I knew I would be lucky if any part of my comments or any footage of my talking head actually got aired back home on the 11 o'clock news.

A print reporter from a local daily in my district reached me that night by telephone, and his story the next day contained my comments about President Bush:

> I think he should be patient about Iraq. While Saddam Hussein is a dangerous tyrant, as long as the weapons inspectors are there, he can be up to no mischief . . . [The President] is pursuing a fiscal policy that is exploding the deficit and robbing us of the resources we need for our domestic agenda.[7]

The following week, on February 5, 2003, Secretary of State Colin L. Powell made the presentation to the United Nations Security Council promised by President Bush in the State of the Union speech, outlining the American case against Saddam Hussein and Iraq's weapons of mass destruction.

Colin Powell was the only one of George W. Bush's top advisers who I thought was worth a damn. A retired four-star Army General and former National Security Advisor and Chairman of the Joint Chiefs of Staff, Powell served President George W. Bush as Secretary of State from 2001–2005.

Colin Powell was the best witness ever to appear before the House International Relations Committee during my six years of service on that committee. He would testify before us as Secretary of State every year and would provide a sweeping overview of American foreign policy, then would answer every member's specific questions. His appearances usually lasted about three hours, and he would sit alone at the witness table with no papers in front of him, which was very unusual for committee witnesses. His staff would sit nervously behind him, ready to spring to his aid, but he rarely needed to consult them. He would summarize his written testimony without looking at it and then take on all of our questions. Sometimes the backbenchers would try to stump him with some obscure foreign policy question we cooked up, but it never worked. He always knew what he was talking about. Colin Powell was awesome.

On the television screen in my congressional office on February 5, 2003, Secretary of State Colin Powell was settling in behind the marked United States location in the nearly circular dais in the Security Council Chamber in the United Nations Headquarters. Secretary Powell was dressed in a dark suit, white shirt and light reddish tie, sported an American flag pin in his left lapel, and CIA Director George Tenet loomed behind his right shoulder.

Powell was about to begin his presentation to the fifteen member Security Council. I knew that the five permanent members were China, France, Russia, the United Kingdom and the United States, based on the great powers that were victors in World War II, but I had no clue which nations were currently serving as the ten non-permanent members for two year terms elected by the General Assembly. It turned out that those ten were Angola, Bulgaria, Cameroon, Chile, Germany, Guinea, Mexico, Pakistan, Spain and Syria.[8]

Powell was his usual calm, forceful and well-prepared self as he began his presentation, entitled "Iraq: Failing to Disarm".[9] Using tapes of intercepted telephone conversations between Iraq army officers, satellite photos and summaries of intelligence gathered from anonymous Iraqi defectors, Powell built his case that Saddam Hussein was a dangerous dictator possessing dangerous weapons who must be stopped.

Powell's assurances were sincerely and convincingly offered:

The material I will present to you comes from a variety of sources . . .
I cannot tell you everything we know. But what I can share with you, when combined with what all of us have learned over the years,

is deeply troubling . . . every statement I make today is backed up by sources, solid sources. These are not assertions. What we are giving you are facts and conclusions based on solid intelligence.

And later:

These are not assertions. These are facts, corroborated by many sources, some of them sources of the intelligence services of other countries.

Powell's facts were methodically and compellingly delivered, piling up in the Security Council Chamber as "irrefutable and undeniable" accusations against Saddam Hussein. Powell pounded away:

The Iraqis are moving, not just documents and hard drives, but weapons of mass destruction to keep them from being found by inspectors . . . Most of the launchers and warheads have been hidden in large groves of palm trees and were to be moved every one to four weeks to escape detection . . . we have firsthand descriptions of biological weapons factories on wheels and on rails . . . we know that Iraq has at least seven of these mobile biological agent factories . . . there can be no doubt that Saddam Hussein has biological weapons and the capacity to produce more . . . and the ability to dispense these lethal poisons and diseases in ways that can cause massive death and destruction . . .

I knew I never heard before such specifics about mobile weapons factories. This level of detail gave great weight to Powell's presentation. He then turned his attention to chemical weapons:

Our conservative estimate is that Iraq today has a stockpile of between 100 and 500 tons of chemical weapons agent . . . Saddam Hussein has chemical weapons. Saddam Hussein has used such weapons. And Saddam Hussein has no compunction about using them again, against his neighbors and against his own people. And we have sources who tell us that he has recently authorized his field commanders to use them.

This was an astonishing and frightening presentation. Powell was absolutely certain about Hussein's stockpile of chemical weapons, and was providing new information about the Iraqi dictator's authorization for their use by field commanders. Such authorization would allow Iraqi military officers in scattered commands to disperse chemical weapons at their own discretion.

The Secretary of State turned to nuclear weapons:

We have no indication that Saddam Hussein has ever abandoned his nuclear weapons program . . . Saddam Hussein already possesses two out of the three key components needed to build a nuclear bomb . . . he has made repeated covert attempts to acquire high-specification aluminum tubes from 11 different countries . . . Saddam Hussein is very much focused on putting in place the key missing piece from his nuclear weapons program, the ability to produce fissile material.

There were Condi Rice's aluminum tubes again. They sure weren't letting those go, I thought. But there was no mention of the State of the Union claim about buying uranium in Africa, and no hype about a mushroom cloud. I wondered if Powell was walking back from the claims that George Tenet and Condoleezza Rice had made regarding nuclear weapons last fall.

Powell was displaying maps and photos, and said:

What I want you to know today is that Iraq has programs that are intended to produce ballistic missiles that fly 1,000 kilometers . . . you can see from this map . . . who will be in danger . . . notice the test stand . . . notice the large exhaust vent . . . these are missiles that Iraq wants in order to project power, to threaten, and to deliver chemical, biological and . . . nuclear warheads.

Secretary Powell was presenting some new material and new claims, backed up by apparent photographic proof. He continued on screen:

Now, unmanned aerial vehicles . . . UAVs are well suited for dispensing chemical and biological weapons . . . Iraq has dedicated much effort to developing and testing spray devices that could be adapted for UAVs . . . Iraq could use these small UAVs which have a wingspan of only a few meters to deliver biological agents to its neighbors or, if transported, to other countries including the United States.

I was trying to digest the new claims in this speech to the Security Council, trying to anticipate how this would play both at home and on the world stage.

Powell was already on to a new subject—terrorism:

Iraq and terrorism go back decades ... But what I want to bring to your attention today is the potentially much more sinister nexus between Iraq and the Al Qaeda terrorist network.

Powell spoke for several minutes about a number of "clear" links between Iraq and specific terrorist groups, and summed up:

With this track record, Iraqi denials of supporting terrorism take the place alongside the other Iraqi denials of weapons of mass destruction. It is all a web of lies.

Finally, after speaking for well over an hour, Powell's conclusions were presented with a direct forcefulness that I was sure the Security Council would find compelling:

How much longer are we willing to put up with Iraq's noncompliance before we, as a council, we, as the United Nations, say: "Enough. Enough" ... unless we act, we are confronting an even more frightening future ... Clearly, Saddam Hussein and his regime will stop at nothing until something stops him ... should we take the risk that he will not someday use these weapons at a time and the place and in the manner of his own choosing at a time when the world is in a much weaker position to respond? The United States will not and cannot run that risk to the American people. Leaving Saddam Hussein in possession of weapons of mass destruction for a few more months or years is not an option, not in a post-September 11th world.

After Powell finished, I leaned back in my chair and realized that was quite a show. The American Secretary of State had been forceful and persuasive, and even waved around what looked like a vial of anthrax. There was a lot of detail, new detail, things I hadn't heard before. Powell made it sound like we knew what weapons of mass destruction Hussein had, where they were, and how much they weighed. He even suggested that some of them were over there underneath the palm trees.

I wondered what George Tenet was doing there, lurking over Powell's shoulder? Presumably, the CIA Director was present to add weight and credibility to the presentation. After all, Powell was presenting the work product of the intelligence community. I wondered if Tenet was there as Powell's minder, to make sure the Secretary of State didn't go off script. But I couldn't believe that Colin Powell needed, or would tolerate, a minder.

But Secretary Powell did not address some fundamental questions that were becoming important to me. Why act right now? Why rush into war? Why not give the international weapons inspectors more time?

It turns out that Colin Powell screwed up on Iraq. He did not take an active role in promoting our involvement during 2002 when the Congress authorized our military intervention. But he did take on the assignment of being the primary salesman of our policy to the international community, and told the Security Council that there was "no doubt" that Saddam Hussein had biological and chemical weapons and the capacity to rapidly produce many more, and was certainly working to obtain the key components to produce nuclear weapons. Powell said he was relying on information he received in briefings from the Central Intelligence Agency, information he had carefully reviewed.

Colin Powell's presentation to the U.N. Security Council on February 5, 2003 was powerful, specific and convincing. While he did not answer every question in my mind, I found his speech impressive in its detail and compelling in its delivery.

Secretary Powell did not overcome the opposition from France, Russia and China to a military strike against Iraq, and the United Nations did not pass a resolution authorizing the use of a multinational force to disarm Saddam Hussein. But Powell made a strong pitch to America that we needed to take action to stop Hussein, even if we had to act alone.

Then, in quick succession, three key agencies issued public reports regarding the search for weapons of mass destruction in Iraq that cast serious doubt on the Bush administration claims that Saddam Hussein had amassed stockpiles of dangerous weapons.

First, on February 14, 2003, one week after Secretary Powell's presentation to the United Nations, two reports were presented to the U.N.

Security Council from their weapons inspectors regarding their search since inspections resumed in Iraq in November 2002. The head of the international weapons inspectors, Executive Chairman Dr. Hans Blix of the United Nations Monitoring, Verification and Inspection Commission (UNMOVIC) stated regarding weapons of mass destruction in Iraq:

"So far, UNMOVIC has not found any such weapons."[10]

Blix asked for more time for international weapons inspections to complete their work in Iraq.

I was very surprised by press reports of the Blix testimony.[11] I thought by now that the UN inspectors would have found some weapons of mass destruction in Iraq, if Hussein had the stockpiles of biological and chemical weapons that the Bush administration had asserted. Maybe this confirmed what Secretary Powell was claiming, that Hussein was a master of deceit and deception. Maybe Hussein was smarter than Hans Blix and was hiding his weapons from the international weapons inspectors.

But how can all these weapons just go missing? We were supposed to know where they were located and how much they weighed. Why didn't Secretary Powell just tell Chief Inspector Blix which palm tree to look under?

Second, at the same meeting of the Security Council on February14, the head of the International Atomic Energy Agency (IAEA), Director General Dr. Mohamed ElBaradei, reported regarding the agency's nuclear verification activities in Iraq:

We have to date found no evidence of ongoing prohibited nuclear or nuclear-related activities in Iraq.[12]

I found this news report troubling as well. The IAEA reviewed the 2,000 pages of documents found at the home of an Iraqi scientist in January that had been cited as proof that the Iraqi regime was hiding government documents in private homes. But now Mohamed ElBaradei, a world-renowned legal scholar and Egyptian diplomat, was stating those documents were just the scientist's personal files, and the IAEA was confirming that they had found nothing to indicate Hussein had made any progress on developing or reconstituting nuclear weapons.

The third doubt-producing report came from our own Central Intelligence Agency on February 24 in its semi-annual report on weapons proliferation. The report admitted that the intelligence

community had no "direct evidence" that Saddam Hussein had succeeded in reconstituting its biological, chemical, nuclear or long-range
missile programs since international weapons inspectors had left Iraq
in 1998. The report stated:

> We do not have any direct evidence that Iraq has used the
> period since Desert Fox to reconstitute its Weapons of Mass
> Destruction programs, although given its past behavior, this
> type of activity must be regarded as likely.[13]

Likely? Hussein's reconstitution of his deadly weapons was now
considered by the CIA to be merely "likely?" What about all the positive statements, the virtual guarantees, by President Bush and all the
key players in his administration that Hussein definitely had weapons
of mass destruction, was securing more and was willing to use them?
Now the CIA did not have "any direct evidence" of Hussein's weapons
programs?

What about the adamant conclusions offered in the October 4,
2002 CIA White Paper on Iraqi weapons, assuring the public and the
Congress that Saddam Hussein had large stockpiles of dangerous,
deadly weapons? What about the public speeches by President Bush
and the United Nations presentation by Secretary Powell, insisting
that Iraq possessed weapons of mass destruction?

What about the White House briefing on October 2, 2002 when
CIA Director George Tenet and National Security Adviser Condoleezza
Rice stated that Hussein had weapons of mass destruction and must
be stopped, and when Tenet assured Congressman Adam Schiff and
the rest of us that his level of confidence in the intelligence that Iraq
had an ongoing nuclear weapons program was "ten" on a scale of one
to ten?

As a result of these three expert agency reports in the space of ten
days, my level of confidence in the truthfulness of the Bush administration about Iraq was plummeting off the charts, no matter what
numerical scale was used.

By the end of February 2003, I was seriously questioning the
wisdom of my vote to give President Bush the authority to wage unilateral and preemptive war in Iraq. I was wondering, with a sinking
feeling, whether I had been wrong to accept the claims of the Bush
administration that Saddam Hussein posed an imminent threat to
the United States. I was frustrated that the President and his top

advisers seemed to be giving only lip service to diplomacy, and seemed increasingly committed to going to war against Iraq whether or not the United Nations agreed or gave support. I did not know who or what to believe about the presence of weapons of mass destruction in Iraq. I was thinking that my wife and daughter had been right when they told me you couldn't trust George Bush. I decided it was time to speak up regarding my concerns over the President's approach to the challenges posed by Iraq, expressing my support for the presence of weapons inspectors in the country and urging the President not to take unilateral military action.

I was frustrated that there was no opportunity to debate any of the challenges posed by Iraq during the normal course of business on the House floor, or under "regular order" as it was known. That was because all bills and resolutions that came to the floor for debate and voting came with a "rule" from the Rules Committee that established the amount of time for debate and the allowable amendments for each legislative proposal. Any attempt to bring up a new subject that was not permitted in a specific rule, such as the recent reports that no weapons were being found in Iraq, would simply be ruled out of order by the Speaker. The rigid House rules of procedure did not permit anything like the freewheeling and unlimited debate permitted in the Senate.

During the debate the previous October, every member of the House had the opportunity, however brief, to speak on the Iraq war resolution. But since then the House had virtually ignored the entire subject. All sorts of routine proposals were working their way through the legislative process since the beginning of the new Congress in January, and some were now reaching the floor for consideration by the full House. But as the nation was bracing for a war in a far-off land, based upon representations from the executive branch of a clear and present danger posed by a murderous tyrant, representations that were now suspected by some of being untrue, the House was paying no attention at all. Regular order did not permit a debate on the fundamental issue of war and peace.

So I began to use the period of time at the end of the regular legislative day, known as "Special Orders", to present statements and ask questions about the situation in Iraq, and was soon joined by several like-minded colleagues. Special Order time had to be requested and scheduled through the party leadership offices, and it was strictly doled out in one minute, five minute, and one hour chunks of time, evenly divided between the parties. Members used Special Orders regularly to address all sorts of issues, some national in scope, some affecting only their districts back home. Of course, the only members present were those who were offering their own statements, and the party leaders were long since gone to their cocktail parties and fund-raisers. A first or second term member of the majority party was dragooned into serving as the Speaker pro tempore, and only a skeleton staff remained. Special Orders were usually boring and lacked passion, and seldom received coverage in the press.

But one aspect of the House was the same during Special Orders as during the regular order of business. The television cameras were still rolling, broadcasting the "debate" live across the nation on cable television. This made the after-hour sessions very attractive to many members of the House.

I had a colleague from Colorado, Scott McInnis, who would regularly use an entire Special Order hour to read out loud some mail from his rural constituents and offer what appeared to be off-the-cuff responses right on the television from the floor of the House. I guessed it was easier than typing and sending a letter.

So my staff put in the request for a Special Orders speaking slot a day ahead of time, and I prepared five minutes worth of remarks on Iraq to deliver sometime after regular business ended the next day.

The following evening, March 4, I was in the House chamber as the last votes for the day were completed and the Majority and Minority leaders duly made the final announcements. As I waited for the House to empty out and the Special Orders time to begin, I was glad to have a few moments to sit down and relax. It had been a hectic day, with committee meetings in the morning and floor votes spread throughout the day, requiring a number of walks over to the House floor from my office to cast my votes. I recall I also had a family from my district visiting the Capitol, and I had hosted them in the Members' Dining Room for lunch.

Early on I had discovered how much my constituents liked to have lunch in the Members' Dining Room on the first floor of the Capitol. The food and service was pretty good, and people seemed to get a kick out of the special access, knowing that the general public can only dine there if they are with a member of the House.

I had started offering "Lunch for Your Family at the Capitol as the Guest of Your Congressman" as my donation to the endless number of charity fundraisers I was asked to support. Surprisingly, people seemed to really value the opportunity, and would routinely bid several hundred dollars or more at charitable silent auctions for the opportunity to pack up their family, travel to the Capitol, get a tour and eat lunch with, and on, their Congressman.

Actually, I really enjoyed the visits. It was a pleasant way to meet visitors from back home, who were always awed by their surroundings. It didn't cost much to pick up the tab at the House restaurant, and there was always the chance that my constituents would get the thrill of recognizing a colleague famous from the Sunday talk shows or a visiting celebrity from Hollywood. I remember Goldie Hawn made a big splash in the dining room one day. And the charity back home was always grateful for my gesture, since it usually resulted in a hefty contribution to their cause.

The challenge was having something intelligent to say to my visitors, particularly in the middle of a busy day when I was distracted by the press of business. A lot of my attention was devoted to remembering the full names of my guests, so I could make proper introductions to colleagues whom my guests recognized, and so I wouldn't totally screw up by forgetting names in the middle of a conversation. That was never good politics.

I found that most visitors enjoyed hearing about the issues and events I was dealing with that day. It was always easy to give my guests a summary of my activities, and to ask their opinions on some of the prominent issues of the day. However, some of the adults, and most of the kids, couldn't care less what was happening in the House that day, or any other day. For those folks, I would assume the role of tour guide.

I was awed by the majesty of the Capitol building, and loved the beauty and atmosphere of the House Chamber. So I brushed up on the history of some of the artwork, and the basic facts and figures of the architecture, and trotted out this information whenever someone asked or the conversation lagged.

I would relay the basic information that the footprint of the Capitol covered 4 acres and its floor space equaled 16.5 acres. The building had 540 rooms and 658 windows, and was 751 feet long, 350 feet wide, and 288 feet tall, to the top of the Statue of Freedom. I would summarize by saying the Capitol is almost as tall as it is wide, and twice as long, and the dome weighs four and a half thousand tons! The weight of the dome always got the best reaction.

During lunch, I could always talk about the Members' Dining Room itself. Actually three rooms plus the kitchen, it had been in continuous operation as the House restaurant since 1858, one year after the South wing of the Capitol was expanded and the current House Chamber first put into use. I discovered there were two things about the dining room that constituents always liked.

First, bean soup is offered every day. Speaker Joe Cannon complained one day in 1904 that there was no bean soup available, and it has been on the menu every day since. I always ordered it, since it was quite good, and encouraged my guests to do the same. People liked taking part in the tradition, and children were awed that one man had so much power. The young ones had trouble understanding the concepts of legislation and budgets, but they had no trouble appreciating the clout needed to put bean soup on the menu every day.

My second surefire topic was the beautiful fresco dominating the vast north wall of the dining room that portrayed British General Cornwallis surrendering to George Washington at Yorktown in 1781. Painted originally on wet plaster in the new House Chamber in 1857 by Italian-born Constantino Brumidi, the fresco had been hidden behind wood paneling during House renovations in 1946. Hidden, but not forgotten, the one inch layer of plaster on which the fresco was painted was painstakingly removed from the brick wall behind it in 1972, and the artwork was moved by crane out of the second story House Chamber and down the House steps to the first floor Members' Dining Room and re-installed. Brumidi emigrated from Italy in 1852 and became a proud U.S. citizen on November 12, 1857. He seldom signed the hundreds of frescos and paintings he created throughout the U.S. Capitol from 1855 until his death in 1880, but this one he signed. The late 1850s had seen the growth of anti-immigrant feelings in the U.S., including the rise of the nativist party known as the Know-Nothings, and Brumidi decided to take a stand. He declared his new citizenship status on the strap of the bag in the lower right corner of Cornwallis Sues for Cessation of Hostilities, signing his work as "C. Brumidi, Artist, Citizen of the U.S."[14]

Everyone, particularly children, loved the story. I would send the young ones over to the fresco to confirm the signature in the lower right corner. They would come back to the lunch table, eyes shining, and faces bright, as if they were the first to discover the historic relic.

I don't remember the name of the family I met for lunch on March 4, 2002, but that evening during Special Orders on the House floor I gave the following speech and also issued a press release. I said:

. . . Unilateral military action by the United States against Iraq at this time is not in our best national interest. Certainly, Saddam Hussein must be disarmed and Iraq must be rid of weapons of mass destruction . . . the question is not whether we will prevail against Iraq. We will, with or without help . . . but we will need help the day after that war is won . . . we need our friends to help with peacekeeping, rebuilding and international credibility, and that support will be absent if we take unilateral action . . .

President Bush very skillfully won unanimous Security Council support last fall to restart arms inspections and he deserves great credit for that. After the initial success, however, the Administration has not been able to maintain that unity . . .

What is the problem here? We are talking about an isolated country with a fourth rate military, and a leader who is a murderous tyrant that has no support and no friends in the United Nations. Yet the Security Council is split. Why is that? I believe it is because of the inept, bungled, cowboy diplomacy of the President of the United States and his senior advisers . . .

The inspections were restarted . . . the inspectors' presence in Iraq has made Saddam Hussein less dangerous for the time being . . .

It is dangerous to conduct a unilateral invasion of Iraq . . . I call on the Bush administration to renew its efforts to secure a broad multinational coalition or U.N. mandate to disarm Iraq.[15]

The news media seemed interested in my statement, perhaps because it was, apparently, the first critical commentary about the Bush approach in Iraq from a member of Congress who had voted in favor of the war authorization.

The lead paragraph in the Associated Press story was:

A House Democrat who voted last fall to let the White House use military force in Iraq accused the administration Wednesday of bungling diplomatic relations and said the United States should not go to war without international backing.[16]

The *New York Times* picked up the AP story and ran it with this headline:

"Pa. Democrat Backs Away From Iraq Vote."[17]

But not everyone was impressed with my statement. The AP story included this information:

"The White House did not immediately return calls seeking comment."

A local reporter from a daily newspaper in my home district interviewed me over the phone and wrote in her story about my speech:

> Hoeffel . . . refused to label his current position as a flip-flop or change of heart. And he refused to attribute this position to polls showing a decrease in support for a war or a response to growing peace movements throughout the world.[18]

There is nothing, absolutely nothing, in the whole wide world that a reporter likes better than covering a flip-flop, or a possible flip-flop, or an inkling of a flip-flop, by a politician. They can have a field day reporting and speculating about the contradictions once a politician changes a position or retracts a statement, which is why politicians are so reluctant to do so or to ever admit making a mistake. The resulting bad press tends to magnify and disparage the change of heart.

I honestly didn't think I had changed my position or flip-flopped on my vote, although I was privately worried that the Bush team had fooled me about weapons of mass destruction. I actually thought it was the President who had changed positions, and I told the reporter so. She wrote:

> Hoeffel said Congress had received assurances from the Bush administration that it would work through the United Nations and exhaust all diplomatic solutions before turning to the military . . .
>
> However, he said, since that time the president and his advisers have engaged in "cowboy diplomacy" . . .
>
> "They have denigrated the United Nations, insulted our allies, promoted a go-it-alone policy, and acted with arrogance and high-handedness," said Hoeffel.[19]

Well, not everyone back home agreed with my criticism of President Bush, and we were off to the races.

A local daily suburban paper wrote an editorial on March 7 that, while fair, had enough of an edge to it to help fire up some folks back in the district. The editorial was entitled "Congressman vs. Cowboy" and started with:

> Whether from a tug of conscience, a pang of guilt or a scan of the latest public opinion polls, some Democrats in Congress are starting to speak out and against the Bush administration's go-it-alone adventurism in the Middle East . . .
>
> This week Hoeffel took aim at Bush's "cowboy diplomacy" and said the president's inclination to invade Iraq with or without the blessing of the United Nations is the reason why many world leaders are lining up against U.S. policy . . .
>
> This represents a marked change for Hoeffel, one of 81 House Democrats who last fall voted to give Bush the option for military action against Iraq—with U.N. backing if possible or alone if necessary. In effect, they and 215 Republicans told the "cowboy" he could saddle up and head on out . . .[20]

Frankly, the editorial hit close to the truth with all three of their first-paragraph musings about my motivations for my floor speech that week. I would have added a fourth reason: a growing sense of outrage that the Bush team had exaggerated, hyped and lied about the threat posed by Hussein's weapons of mass destruction.

On March 9, a letter appeared in another local daily from Eric Seymour of Lansdale, who suggested that my "moderate" costume had finally worn out:

> The partisan liberal within has been exposed . . . for a sitting congressman to join with the pro-Saddam protesters and call our president a "cowboy" is simply shameful.[21]

On March 12, the *Philadelphia Daily News* published a letter from Christian P. Marrone of Lafayette Hill, which said:

> As a constituent of Rep. Joe Hoeffel, I find his comments about the president utterly contemptible. The only cowboy is Joe and his inept statement . . . he is a liberal in moderate clothing . . . it is clear the congressman cares more about what the French and others think than his own constituents and president.[22]

Again, the French!

Also on March 12 came an editorial in a Philadelphia weekly, entitled "Sorry, Joe, we'll ride with the cowboy," that noted I was "leading the charge" of Democrats blasting the President for being diplomatically "inept" and a "cowboy":

> The only thing harsher than their bombast was the timing of their remarks. They chose the eve of war . . .
>
> Hoeffel has it backward . . . France and Germany—or at least their leaders—will come out of this more isolated . . .
>
> Hoeffel also brandishes this canard . . . that unilateral military action at this time in not in our best interest . . . only in some Orwellian nightmare does allying yourself with dozens of nations . . . constitute unilateralism.
>
> To Hoeffel, it's the U.N. or tragedy . . .
>
> . . . the U.N. can be manipulated, stalled and compromised . . . [S]hould we link our security to these people?
>
> We'll ride with the cowboy.[23]

I was particularly popular on March 12, for that same day another Philadelphia newspaper published a story on our United States Senator, Rick Santorum, with the headline "Santorum weighs in on Iraq, France, Hoeffel." I thought the headline was an interesting coupling of people and places. When asked about my statement on the President and Iraq, Senator Santorum authoritatively intoned:

"[It] simply isn't worth the paper it's printed on."[24]

Another critical letter to the editor appeared locally on March 14. Walt Scott of Richlandtown criticized my "headline-grabbing, despicable remark about 'cowboy diplomacy'" and said:

"Presidents have a tough enough job without being second-guessed by amateurs like Congressman Hoeffel."[25]

By this time it was fairly obvious to me that not everyone back home was pleased with my criticism of President Bush, or my view that we ought to give the U.N. weapons inspectors more time to do their job. I wanted the President to be patient and continue to seek international consensus regarding Iraq, while the President and his many supporters seemed anxious to take action to stop Saddam Hussein, and the sooner the better.

While the editorials and letters to the editor gave voice to several opponents regarding my stand on Iraq, no media outlet could compare with the preeminent Philadelphia talk radio station, WPHT 1210, as the loudest megaphone and biggest stage for conservative, pro-Bush opinion in Southeastern Pennsylvania. And no talk radio host on that station could compare with Dom Giordano for savvy political talk, staunch conservative views, good-natured brashness (his show's slogan was "It's Dom Time!"), or fundamental fairness to those few liberal Democratic politicians who would cautiously venture onto his airwaves from time to time when his producers would extend an invitation to call in. Dom Giordano always treated me with respect and fairness when I was on his show.

But Giordano sure didn't mind having some on-air fun at my expense, particularly when I was accusing the President of "cowboy diplomacy." The talk show host placed me in his contest for his listeners to vote for the Top Blowhard of 2003. As callers lit up the phone lines, I advanced past the likes of Martin Sheen, Dixie Chick Natalie Maines and Barbara Streisand to make it into the Final Four,[26] where my competition included Jacques Chirac and Michael Moore. Pretty elite company for a simple suburban congressman.

Dom Giordano told me recently: "You were in the final four of a field of 64. You really inflamed them over Bush. I had to exercise my one challenge to stop you from winning."[27]

It sounds like Dom's exercise of his challenge was an act of mercy. Unfortunately, nobody remembers who won.

While all this was going on back home, the Bush administration was receiving more bad news in the form of the most recent reports to the United Nations from their weapons inspectors. On March 7, 2003, the heads of the U.N. Monitoring, Verification and Inspection Commission and the International Atomic Energy Agency again reported no evidence of proscribed activities or weapons of mass destruction in Iraq. As the start of the war loomed near, the weapons inspectors were finding no evidence of the Bush administration's chief rationale for the war—Saddam Hussein's stockpile of weapons of mass destruction in Iraq.

Dr. Hans Blix, the chief U.N. weapons inspector, testified on March 7 to the Security Council as follows:

Inspections in Iraq resumed on the 27th of November 2002. In matters relating to process, notably prompt access to sites, we have faced relatively few difficulties . . . at this juncture we are able to perform professional, no-notice inspections all over Iraq . . .

As I noted on the 14th of February, intelligence authorities have claimed that weapons of mass destruction are moved around Iraq by trucks, in particular that there are mobile production units for biological weapons . . . Several inspections have taken place at declared and undeclared sites in relation to mobile production facilities . . . No evidence of proscribed activities have so far been found.

. . . No underground facilities for chemical or biological production or storage were found so far.

How much time would it take to resolve the key remaining disarmament tasks? It will not take years, nor weeks, but months.[28]

So here was the chief weapons inspector in front of the Security Council in open session reporting three main points: his international team was conducting unfettered inspections all over Iraq, they had still not found evidence of proscribed weapons, and there was no evidence that mobile facilities were trucking weapons around the country to avoid detection. All three findings debunked major claims that were being made by the Bush administration to justify moving forward with a military invasion of Iraq to disarm Saddam Hussein.

Dr. Mohamed ElBaradei of the International Atomic Energy Agency also testified to the Security Council as follows:

The IAEA has now conducted a total of 218 nuclear inspections at 141 sites, including 21 that have not been inspected before. In addition, the agency experts have taken part in many joint U.N.-IAEA inspections . . .

With regard to the aluminum tubes, the IAEA has conducted a thorough investigation of Iraq's attempt to purchase large quantities of high-strength aluminum tubes . . . extensive field investigation and document analysis have failed to uncover any evidence that Iraq intended to use these . . . tubes for any project other than the reverse engineering of rockets . . . based on available evidence, the IAEA team has concluded that Iraq efforts to import these aluminum tubes were not likely to have been related to the manufacture of centrifuge . . .

With regard to uranium acquisition, the IAEA has made progress in its investigation into reports that Iraq sought to buy uranium from Niger in recent years . . . [B]ased on thorough analysis, the IAEA has concluded with the concurrence of outside experts that these documents which formed the basis for the report of recent uranium transaction between Iraq and Niger are in fact not authentic. We have therefore concluded that these specific allegations are unfounded . . .

. . . there is no indication of resumed nuclear activities . . .

. . . there is no indication that Iraq has attempted to import uranium since 1990.

. . . there is no indication that Iraq has attempted to import aluminum tubes for use in centrifuge enrichment . . .

After three months of intrusive inspections, we have found no evidence or plausible indication of the revival of a nuclear weapon program in Iraq.[29]

So here was the director of the international team of nuclear inspectors reporting the following four points to the Security Council: his team had conducted hundreds of inspections, there was no evidence that Iraq had used aluminum tubes for a centrifuge enrichment program, reports that Iraq bought uranium from Niger were false and based on forged documents, and there was no evidence that Iraq had revived a nuclear weapons program. As we saw with the weapons inspectors, all these findings by the nuclear experts debunked major claims currently being made by the Bush administration to justify moving forward with a military invasion of Iraq to disarm Saddam Hussein.

This was the moment of truth for George W. Bush. The American invasion of Iraq was fast approaching, and in fact President Bush would give the order to invade in less than two weeks. Yet the international weapons and nuclear experts were reporting publicly that they could find no weapons of mass destruction in Iraq.

George Bush could have asked his own experts and top advisers one basic question: what the hell was going on? How could he rely on what his intelligence agencies thought and presumed and guessed about Hussein's weapons of mass destruction when the international weapons inspectors on the ground in Iraq couldn't find any weapons or any evidence of them?

Bush himself had just made the claims in his recent State of the Union speech that Iraq had bought aluminum tubes to enrich uranium, and had bought uranium from Niger, and now the International Atomic Energy Agency said those claims were false, and the one about Niger was based on forgeries. Bush could have asked his staff and intelligence advisers how it was even possible that such bogus claims got into his speech. He could have called the international inspectors to the White House to meet with his team to get to the bottom of these fundamental differences.

This was George Bush's chance to make an historic decision. His entire rationale for invading Iraq—Saddam Hussein was an imminent threat to America because of his weapons of mass destruction—was totally undercut by the failure of the weapons inspectors to find any weapons.

This was George Bush's chance to postpone the invasion and give the inspectors the time they wanted to complete their work. It would have been a tough decision. It is very hard to keep an invasion force already deployed in the Middle East cooped up while inspectors continue to inspect and diplomats seek to avoid war.

What if President Bush, upon learning that the international weapons and nuclear inspectors were finding no weapons after three months of looking, had postponed his order to invade Iraq until the question of weapons was clarified? What if George Bush had given the international inspectors the time they wanted, "not . . . years, nor weeks, but months," to complete their work in Iraq? What would he have learned?

President Bush would have learned that Saddam Hussein had no weapons of mass destruction. He would have learned that Hussein had been effectively disarmed back in the 1990s by international sanctions and inspections. He would have learned that what his Vice President Dick Cheney said on Meet The Press on September 16, 2001, "Saddam Hussein's bottled up, at this point," was still correct. President Bush would have learned it was not necessary to take unilateral, preemptive military action against Saddam Hussein in order to safeguard America and our allies.

After months and months of beating the drums of war, it would have been a very tough decision for George W. Bush to postpone the American invasion of Iraq that was ready to go. But that is what the American people expect of our president—tough decisions that are in the best interests of America.

Of course, George W. Bush failed to make that decision to delay the invasion to make sure about the actual status of Hussein's weapons. He may not have even considered it. By that failure to delay, President Bush failed America.

Instead, ten days later, on March 17, 2003, President Bush in a nationally televised speech gave Saddam Hussein 48 hours to leave Iraq, or else.

As a warm-up act for the President's primetime speech scheduled for the following day, Vice President Dick Cheney went on NBC's Meet the Press with Tim Russert and on CBS's Face the Nation with Bob Schieffer on Sunday, March 16. In the space of just an hour or so, Dick Cheney spouted three of the most spectacularly incorrect statements anyone on the Bush team ever uttered about Iraq.

First, on NBC, during a discussion on Hussein's pursuit of nuclear weapons:

Mr. Russert: "And even though the International Atomic Energy Commission said he does not have a nuclear program, we disagree?"

Vice Pres. Cheney: "I disagree, yes . . . we know he has been absolutely devoted to trying to acquire nuclear weapons. And we believe he has, in fact, reconstituted nuclear weapons. I think Mr. ElBaradei frankly is wrong."[30]

Of course, it was Mr. Cheney who was wrong. No nuclear weapons were found in Iraq. It is staggering to realize that when faced with expert, on-site findings that no nuclear weapons could be found, Dick Cheney simply said the experts were wrong and he was right.

Second, Tim Russert then asked whether the international community would perceive the United States as an "imperialist power" if we invaded:

Vice Pres. Cheney: "Well, I hope not, Tim . . . Now, I think things have gotten so bad inside Iraq, from the standpoint of the Iraqi people, my belief is we will, in fact, be greeted as liberators."[31]

Of course, the American invasion, while militarily successful, quickly bogged down into a long, bitter, deadly nine-year occupation that took the lives of over 4,500 American soldiers through suicide bombings, sniper shootings, roadside explosions and armed insurgency by a variety of militia and rebel forces. Given those tragic developments, it is obvious we were not greeted as liberators.

Third, on CBS, Bob Schieffer asked about the length of the pending war:

Schieffer: "If we do have to take action, do you think it will be a long war or a short war?"

Vice Pres. Cheney: "My own judgment based on my time as Secretary of Defense, and having operated in this area in the past, I'm confident that our troops will be successful, and I think it'll go relatively quickly, but we can't . . ."

Schieffer: "Weeks?"

Vice Pres. Cheney: ". . . we can't count on that."

Schieffer: "Months?"

Vice President Cheney: "Weeks, not months."[32]

Of course, the American involvement in the Iraq War lasted not weeks or months, but for nine years until United States military forces were removed in December 2011.

Dick Cheney seemed to enjoy his image as the experienced old hand who was advising the President on foreign policy and national defense matters. But these must be the three most incorrect and arrogant statements regarding our national security ever uttered in the history of the American vice presidency.

The following evening, March 17, I was back in my Capitol Hill office watching, once again, a Presidential speech regarding Iraq. This time the President was broadcasting to the nation from the White House, standing behind a podium adorned with the presidential seal in the central hallway.

As before, I heard the President speak with absolute assurance about the presence of weapons of mass destruction in Iraq.

Early in the speech the President said:[33]

Intelligence gathered by this and other governments leaves no doubt that the Iraq regime continues to possess and conceal some of the most lethal weapons ever devised. This regime has already used weapons of mass destruction against Iraq's neighbors and against Iraq's people. The regime has a history of reckless aggression in the Middle East. It has a deep hatred of America and our friends and it has aided, trained and harbored terrorists, including operatives of Al Qaeda. The danger is clear: using chemical, biological or, one day,

nuclear weapons obtained with the help of Iraq, the terrorists could fulfill their stated ambitions and kill thousands or
hundreds of thousands of innocent people in our country or
any other.

Frankly, I thought that was as good a summary of the President's
argument for war that I had heard: Hussein's got deadly weapons, he
is willing to use them, he has used them before, and he would even
give them to the terrorists. But these presidential statements were
contradicted by the findings of the international weapons inspectors
presently at work in Iraq.

The President reviewed the history of America's efforts to work
with the U.N. Security Council to disarm Saddam Hussein. He said:
"Today, no nation can possibly claim that Iraq has disarmed. And it
will not disarm so long as Saddam Hussein holds power."

Yet that was exactly the conclusion that could be reasonably drawn
from the failure of the weapons inspectors to find any evidence of
weapons, despite three months of unfettered, "no-notice" inspections.

The President continued:

All the decades of deceit and cruelty have now reached an end.
Saddam Hussein and his sons must leave Iraq within 48 hours.
Their refusal to do so will result in military conflict com-
menced at a time of our choosing.

The President spoke with his usual forcefulness. He even gave
Hussein and his sons an ultimatum! Modern wars didn't often start
with rhetoric reminiscent of a cowboy movie. The Cowboy was riding
again tonight.

But what if the Cowboy was wrong about the weapons of mass
destruction, and the international weapons inspectors were right? It
seemed we needed more time to determine whether the weapons actually existed, and to seek more international support for an invasion.

But forty-eight hours later, on March 19, 2003, at 9:34 p.m. EST,
America went to war against Iraq.

SIX

War

On March 19 the invasion of Iraq began. U.S. Army General Tommy Franks commanded the invasion force of about 200,000 military personnel: approximately 150,000 American soldiers, 46,000 British soldiers, 2,000 Australian soldiers and 200 Polish soldiers. General Franks stated the coalition objectives: to end the regime of Saddam Hussein, eliminate Iraq's weapons of mass destruction, drive out terrorists, collect intelligence about terrorists and weapons of mass destruction, deliver humanitarian support, secure Iraq's oil fields and start the transition to a representative self-government.[1]

Coalition forces launched massive air strikes and amphibious assaults using heavy armor, infantry, marines and airborne commandos. I was proud of the outstanding performance of American armed forces. The invasion was decisive and fast, meeting spirited, courageous but short-lived resistance. On April 9, Baghdad fell to coalition forces, ending major combat operations twenty-one days after the war started. In Baghdad, American armed forces seized deserted government ministries and tore down a huge statue of Saddam Hussein.[2] The fall of Baghdad generated an outpouring of public gratitude for the invading coalition forces, but also sparked vast civil disorder, looting and crime.[3] Tens of thousands of Iraqi soldiers and civilians were killed during the invasion. Coalition forces reported the death in combat of 140 American soldiers and 33 British soldiers.[4] No weapons of mass destruction were found.

The missing weapons were a cause of huge concern to all of us in Congress. Since before the invasion, both supporters and opponents of the military action had worried privately about the existence of weapons of mass destruction and whether Hussein, if he had them, would use them against invading American troops. We knew the Pentagon was assuring the public that all necessary steps were being taken to protect our soldiers from chemical and biological weapons, but I was very worried that my vote to authorize the war might result in the death and disfigurement of thousands of brave, young Americans if Hussein unleashed his terrible weapons. The reports as recently as two weeks before the invasion that the nuclear and weapons inspectors had found no evidence of weapons of mass destruction were reassuring, but no guarantee. Those weapons could be found, or used, tomorrow. But equally disquieting was the nagging uncertainty of why the President started the war in the first place if the international inspectors were not finding Hussein's weapons.

On March 21, two days after the invasion, Press Secretary Ari Fleischer gave a briefing at the White House, which did little to clarify the discrepancies between the Bush administration and the international inspectors regarding the status of Hussein's weapons of mass destruction. Speaking for the President, Fleischer said:

> Well, there is no question that we have evidence and information that Iraq has weapons of mass destruction, biological and chemical particularly . . . [W]e have said that Saddam Hussein possesses biological and chemical weapons, and all this will be made clear in the course of the operation, for whatever duration it takes.[5]

This stubborn refusal by top officials in the Bush administration to admit the obvious, that no weapons of mass destruction were being found in Iraq, calling into question the basic rationale for the war, would be repeated over and over again in the months ahead.

Defense Secretary Donald Rumsfeld got into the act in a big way twice before March was over. On March 24 on CBS, Mr. Rumsfeld said:

> We have seen intelligence over many months that they have chemical and biological weapons, and that they have dispersed them and that they're weaponized and that, in one case at least, the command and control arrangements have been established.[6]

It was true that Mr. Rumsfeld had seen such intelligence over many months. But he didn't tell us about all the caveats and reservations contained in that intelligence that was given on a classified basis to the Bush administration. He didn't acknowledge the discrepancies between his claims about weapons in Iraq and what the international inspectors and now his own troops were finding, or not finding, on the ground in Iraq.

Donald Rumsfeld wasn't done yet. On March 30, ten days after the invasion, he appeared on ABC and said the following:

> The area in the south and the west and the north that coalition control is substantial. It happens not to be the area where weapons of mass destruction were dispersed. We know where they [weapons of mass destruction] are. They're in the area around Tikrit and Baghdad and east, west, south and north somewhat.[7]

"We know where they are." This was a remarkable statement. Although Rumsfeld's sense of direction seemed a little vague, he certainly was positive about the location of the weapons of mass destruction. If he was right, if we knew where they were, it could only be a matter of time until American and coalition forces found them.

Back home, I held three town meetings on Saturday, March 22, 2003 throughout my district to meet with my constituents and discuss the major issues of the day. As the next day's coverage in *The Intelligencer* newspaper indicates, there was no shortage of opinion about the war among the 50 constituents who attended my meeting in the Abington Township municipal building.

The paper quoted Beth Gallagher of Glenside:

> I'm horrified by the idea of it [the war]. When I put my children to bed at night, I just think about the horror of it for Iraqi mothers. It's only going to make things more unsafe for our children.[8]

An unidentified man was quoted:

> Now we've alienated our friends in the U.N. We are turning into the policemen of the world. What's next, North Korea, Iran? Congress has got to do something to reel this administration in.[9]

When I explained that I had wanted the President to wait to achieve a U.N. consensus before taking military action, another man challenged how long I would have remained patient:

How long would you have been willing to wait for France and Cameroon and all those countries to get on board with our interests? We're waiting for Cameroon to get on board for my kid's safety? Come on![10]

Walter Collins of Upper Dublin put it succinctly: "I'm against pre-emptive war. I was last week and I am this week."[11]

I was struck at all three meetings by the strong groundswell of opposition to the war that I was hearing from a number of constituents. Opinion on the war seemed more evenly divided now, unlike the large majority support I had heard the previous fall at similar town meetings and campaign events.

During my six years in Congress I frequently scheduled town meetings back home on Saturdays to meet with local residents to hear their comments about current events, and to receive their requests for help with the bureaucracy of the federal government. The town meeting I remember most fondly occurred during my first year in office at the Lansdale Borough Hall, and involved an earlier war.

Toward the end of that 1999 meeting, a middle-aged woman tentatively put up her hand in the back of the room. I had noticed her earlier when she wheeled in an elderly gentleman and took a seat in the back row next to the man's wheelchair.

She said she came today to ask me to help her father, Samuel Cavoti of North Wales, get his medals from his service in the Army during World War II. She said her father and his entire family was proud of his service during the war, and they believed he was entitled to service medals that he had never received. But the Army paperwork seemed daunting, and she was hoping I could help.

I loved moments like this, when a deserving constituent would ask for help with the federal government regarding a problem that I was sure my staff could resolve. My staff was excellent, and they helped my constituents, and made me look good, every day that I was in office. I told her my staff and I would be happy to help.

People throughout the room were smiling and craning their necks to see the father and daughter in the back row. Mr. Cavoti looked happy but a bit befuddled. I wasn't sure how much of all this the old veteran was taking in.

To keep this feel-good moment going, I asked the daughter where her father had served.

In Europe, under General Omar Bradley, was the reply.

I acknowledged that he must have seen a lot of action, and I asked her when his service in Europe started.

The woman suddenly turned to the man in the wheelchair and rubbed his shoulder. "Tell him, Daddy."

"What?" said the man, in a surprisingly loud voice.

"The Congressman wants to know when you landed in Europe. Tell him."

"The first wave of the first division on the beach in Normandy," said Samuel Cavoti crisply, suddenly sitting ramrod straight in his wheelchair.[12]

I looked dumbly at the daughter, and back at Mr. Cavoti.

The beach at Normandy, I thought. The site of the bloodiest, most desperate combat on the first day of the Allied invasion of occupied France in June 1944.

The entire room was looking at the veteran now, and there was total silence. I paused for a moment, not quite sure what to say, and then blurted, "Ladies and gentlemen, we are in the presence of an authentic American hero."

Applause started, then quickly swelled in the room, and the audience soon was on its feet. Cavoti and his daughter looked shy and emotional. The crowd was nodding and smiling, and those nearest to the veteran reached out to shake his hand or just to touch him. I found myself struggling to keep my composure. The applause continued for a long time.

Back in Washington after the March 2003 town meetings, I gave my second speech focused on Iraq during Special Orders on April 8 in the House, entitled "Will We Win the Peace?" I was alarmed that the resounding victory our brave troops were about to win could be jeopardized if we followed it with antagonistic diplomacy, continued unilateralism, or an American military colonial government in Iraq. I said:

> The morning after our military victory over Saddam, we will wake up to four challenges in Iraq: peacekeeping, humanitarian relief, reconstruction and governance. How we face those challenges will determine whether we win the peace, win the battle for the hearts and minds of the people of Iraq, enhance our status in the Muslim world, and maintain our credibility as the leader of free and democratic nations.[13]

I suggested that we take eight steps to meet the four challenges:

1. Place State, not Defense, in charge in Iraq after the military victory.
2. Internationalize stabilization and reconstruction operations.
3. Put NATO forces in charge of peacekeeping.
4. Establish United Nations administration of the humanitarian relief.
5. Finance reconstruction through the World Bank and IMF.
6. Convene a donors' conference, a funding opportunity for the Arab League.
7. Establish corruption-free control by Iraqis over Iraq oil.
8. Arrange a U.N. conference to boost a transitional Iraqi-based government.

Needless to say, none of these suggestions were implemented by the Bush administration. I did not expect the White House to hang on my every word and carry out all my wishes. These ideas were my summary of a lot of smart, thoughtful commentary in the public arena in the spring of 2003. This body of expert opinion was readily available to the Bush administration. It appears that the Bush team listened to none of it, content in their myopic, go-it-alone belief that they knew best.

A few days later on April 14, after Baghdad had fallen to the coalition forces and all members of Congress were expressing our gratitude over the victory and our support for the troops, a letter to the editor was published back home from Wayne Lutz of Glenside, who wrote:

> . . . our own Rep. Joseph Hoeffel . . . responded to the glorious news by embarrassing this constituent with yet another display of hypocrisy . . . Mr. Hoeffel said these things even after voting to give President Bush the option for military action against Iraq. When he sensed that things were going awry, he struggled to distance himself from that vote. Now, when asked by your paper for his feelings on the stunning coalition victory in Baghdad, "Janus" Hoeffel is once again supportive and congratulatory.[14]

I looked up that last part to be sure I understood the insult. "Janus" means two faced.

Mr. Lutz helped illustrate a problem a number of us who had voted for the war were having at this time. We believed that Saddam Hussein needed to be disarmed, but we were increasingly concerned about the failure to find any weapons of mass destruction in Iraq. We supported the U.S. diplomacy that had restored weapons inspections in Iraq in November 2002, but we were alarmed that President Bush had brushed aside the inspectors before they could finish and ordered the invasion. I wanted to continue to raise my voice in opposition to those Bush policies I thought were wrong, but now the troops were in the field and in harm's way and deserved unified support on the home front. Criticism of the administration could sound like a lack of support for the troops and the war effort. My efforts so far to balance criticism of the President with support for the war fighters had sounded like hypocrisy to Mr. Lentz, and maybe to many others as well.

I was stunned on May 1 when President Bush donned a flight suit and flew out in a Navy warplane to the aircraft carrier USS *Abraham Lincoln*, which was just 30 miles off the coast of California. The carrier was well within the reach of the President's helicopter, which would have been the conventional way of transporting the Commander in Chief from shore to ship and back. I thought the trip was an expensive and unnecessary publicity stunt.

I watched George Bush's subsequent speech from the flight deck of the Abraham Lincoln, with the President more traditionally attired in the standard blue suit, white shirt and red tie. I found the President's remarks an odd mixture of cautious leadership and boastful bravado:

> We have difficult work to do in Iraq. We are bringing order to parts of that country that remain dangerous . . . Major combat operations in Iraq have ended. In the Battle of Iraq, the United States and our allies have prevailed . . . our nation and our coalition are proud of this accomplishment . . . the tyrant has fallen, and Iraq is free.[15]

Most of all, I recognized that there was nothing mixed about the message sent by the huge banner hung from the superstructure of the carrier, displayed on television prominently in the background high above the presidential podium: "Mission Accomplished." True, Baghdad had fallen and Saddam Hussein was out of power, but could the mission actually be accomplished unless we found and destroyed the weapons of mass destruction? After all, disarming Hussein had been the main mission all along.

The President got a lot of coverage and attention for his statement that major combat operations were over in Iraq. Surely, the country was gratified by the swift military victory by our brave soldiers. But George Bush ran the risk of appearing like a fool, strutting around under a boastful banner on an aircraft carrier in his flight suit, as if he had landed the fighter plane by himself. The Navy probably should have shut down the flight deck to anything but the regular Presidential helicopter. But they couldn't say no to their Commander in Chief.

SEVEN

The Aftermath of War, 2003

On May 13, 2003, I gave another speech during Special Orders in the House of Representatives pointing out the failure to find any weapons of mass destruction in Iraq, raising questions about post-invasion challenges and suggesting a new American effort, a modern-day Marshall Plan, to help economic development in the Middle East. I said:

> In Iraq there are some major challenges today. Security remains a huge challenge. There has been looting, lawlessness, car-jackings, break-ins. Humanitarian aid is lagging. There is a great need for medicine, for clean water, electricity. Relief workers are reporting it hard to do their jobs because of the lack of their own personal safety in Iraq. The much-needed reconstruction has not started yet. The demands of religious and ethnic groups are loud and unresolved, and the advent of pluralism and self-government seems to be a very long way off.[1]

Clearly, things were not going as planned two weeks after the President had announced the end of combat operations. In fact, it was beginning to appear that there had been very little, or very bad, American planning for the aftermath of our military operations. How were we going to get Iraq back on its feet, how much was it going to cost, and how long was it going to take? The Bush administration never provided accurate answers to those questions.

I thought I had part of the solution, and I presented it at the end of my speech:

> . . . in Iraq and in the rest of the Middle East and throughout many areas of Europe there is a great need for economic assistance, and I would suggest this House consider the establishment of a modern-day Marshall Plan, a plan modeled after our great success in Western Europe after World War II in which over 4 years we helped 14 countries with $13 billion of assistance to get those allies and former enemies of ours in World War II back on their feet economically. That $13 billion in the 1940s would be the equivalent of $100 billion today. That is a great deal of money, but that is an amount of money over several budget years, and with the help of our allies around the world, that is certainly achievable.[2]

Nothing much ever happened with this idea. It received some discussion among a few of my colleagues but never got much traction. Senator John McCain was said to be interested in the concept and I wrote to him about it, but nothing came of it. People were worried about the expense of $100 billion for this economic development plan, and they thought the high price tag made the proposal a non-starter. Of course, now that our nine-year involvement in Iraq is over, to the tune of some $800 billion, perhaps the cost of the modern-day Marshall Plan seems more reasonable.

By the end of May, a month after the President's announcement of the end of combat operations, no weapons of mass destruction had been found. The controversy over the missing weapons was getting louder, and the actions and claims of the Bush team were growing more extreme. Nothing illustrated these developments more clearly than the bizarre dispute over mobile weapons labs.

On May 28, the Central Intelligence Agency issued another of their public White Papers, this one issued jointly with the Defense Intelligence Agency, the intelligence branch of the Defense Department. The Bush administration had long argued that Saddam Hussein was hiding his biological weapons by developing and hiding them in mobile biological weapons laboratories, and here was the apparent proof. Entitled, "Iraqi Mobile Biological Warfare Agent Production Plants," the White Paper breathlessly announced:

Coalition forces have uncovered the strongest evidence to date that Iraq was hiding a biological warfare program.[3]

After detailing the discovery and capture of "a specialized tractor-trailer" near Mosul in late April, the discovery of "a second mobile facility equipped to produce BW agent" in Mosul in early May, and the discovery of a third "mobile laboratory truck" in Baghdad in late April, the White Paper reported:

> The design, equipment, and layout of the trailer found in late April are strikingly similar to descriptions provided by a source who was a chemical engineer that managed one of the mobile plants. Secretary of State Powell's description of the mobile plants in his speech to the United Nations was based primarily on reporting from this source.[4]

Some source that turned out to be.

After four pages of analysis and discussion trying to make the case that these vehicles were mobile biological labs, the White Paper tried to preempt any naysayers by identifying a possible "cover story" for the discovery:

> Senior Iraqi officials of the al-Kindi Research, Testing, Development, and Engineering facility in Mosul were shown pictures of the mobile production trailers, and they claimed that the trailers were used to chemically produce hydrogen for artillery weather balloons. Hydrogen production would be a plausible cover story for the mobile production units.[5]

Plausible indeed, for it turns out that the vehicles and trailers were actually used to produce hydrogen for Iraqi weather balloons. According to stories published in the *New York Times* and *The Observer*, senior engineers and experts from the Defense Intelligence Agency and State Department concluded upon further examination that the vehicles had been used merely to service artillery weather balloons, and British defense officers and intelligence and technical experts who conducted their own inspections reached the same conclusion. In fact, the British experts concluded that the mobile units they inspected were part of a system to manage artillery observation balloons originally sold to Saddam Hussein by the British themselves in 1987.[6]

Apparently, in a desperate attempt to justify administration assertions about mobile weapons labs, and in an unprofessional rush to judgment regarding discoveries in the field, junior intelligence analysts at the Central Intelligence Agency and Defense Intelligence Agency reached incorrect conclusions about these vehicles in a publicly released White Paper that senior American and British intelligence officers could not support and easily debunked within a matter of days.

Unfortunately, the president was taken in by the blunder. On May 29, 2003, at the start of a trip through Europe and the Middle East, President Bush said in an interview on Polish television:

> We have found the weapons of mass destruction. We found biological laboratories . . . but for those who say we haven't found the banned manufacturing devices or banned weapons, they're wrong, we found them.[7]

The President continued to make similar claims throughout his trip through Europe and the Middle East. But within a few days senior intelligence officials were backing off the claim of discovering mobile weapons labs, leaving the President stranded high and dry. It was George Bush's false and almost ridiculous claims on Polish television about finding weapons of mass destruction that seemed to trigger a backlash of disclosures and criticisms about his team's abuse of prewar intelligence, as we shall see.

Suddenly, senior administration officials were hedging their claims about Iraqi weapons, and few of his top people were vociferously defending the President's handling of intelligence matters in Iraq. Except for John Bolton.

On June 4, 2003, in the week between the release of the White Paper claiming the discovery of mobile weapons labs, with George Bush's accompanying announcement, and the press reports debunking those claims, I participated in a public hearing of the House International Relations Committee. The topic of the hearing was "U.S. Nonproliferation Policy After Iraq", and the purpose was to examine the challenges posed by the worldwide proliferation of nuclear weapons and other weapons of mass destruction. The Bush administration's star witness was John R. Bolton, Under Secretary for Arms Control and International Security, U.S. Department of State.

Nobody exemplified more clearly the aggressive, go-it-alone diplomatic style of the Bush administration than John Bolton, who served George Bush for many years, finally as the United States Ambassador to the United Nations from August 2005 until December 2006.

Ambassador Bolton never pulled his punches, although he often swung wildly. He once suggested that it wouldn't make "a bit of difference"[8] if the United Nations building in New York lost its top 10 stories—which was an interesting diplomatic approach by the US ambassador to the UN.

In an NPR radio interview on November 12, 2007 John Bolton blamed liberals for his decision not to fight in Vietnam even though he was a supporter of the war at the time, saying, "it was clear to me that opponents of the Vietnam War had made it certain we could not prevail, and that I had no great interest in going there to have Teddy Kennedy give it back to the people I might die to take it away from."[9] So it seemed that his refusal to put on the nation's uniform was all Senator Kennedy's fault.

John Bolton also staunchly defended the Bush administration's positions that Iraq could fabricate a nuclear weapon within one year of acquiring fissile material (which it couldn't), and that Iraq had a vibrant chemical and biological warfare program (which it didn't), which justified the President's decision to go to war. Like a baseball umpire, he was often wrong but never in doubt.

On June 4, five weeks after the end of combat operations and with still no sign of weapons of mass destruction, I was questioning Under Secretary John Bolton after his testimony to the House International Relations Committee.

My frustrations were coming to a boil, and I said: "Like millions of Americans, I am wondering where the hell the weapons of mass destruction are."[10]

I believe I was the first member of the House of Representatives to ask that question in public. I continued:

I think the administration faces a growing credibility gap regarding the weapons of mass destruction. Could these weapons have been successfully hidden? Could they have been secretly destroyed? Could they have been transported to another country? Was our intelligence faulty? Was the intelligence misused? . . . we all thought they would have been found, eliminated and verified long before today.

John Bolton was glaring at me, his face reddening. I knew I was taking a chance by going public with questions and taunts about the missing weapons. After all, they could be discovered tomorrow, and my public rant would look very foolish. But I was really fed up and just kept going:

> And please understand the Administration's efforts to deal with this . . . will depend upon facing the facts in Iraq and not just trying to paper over the fact that we have not found what the Administration said . . .

Bolton looked like he was about to explode. Word was already out in Washington that there was great disagreement in the intelligence agencies about the accuracy of the May 28 CIA/DIA report claiming the discovery of mobile weapons labs, and I prodded:

> And we cannot seem to find anything now except mobile laboratories that apparently do not have any traces of weapons of mass destruction in them.

John Bolton said through gritted teeth: "That is right. They are some of the cleanest laboratories in Iraq."

I responded: "What do we need to [close] what is, I am afraid, a growing credibility gap?"

I could see the Under Secretary's facial muscles twitching as he responded:

> Well, I think that the question of how long it takes to uncover the total Iraqi WMD capability is not one I can answer now. I wish that it had been easier to find the WMD capabilities, although I must say the mobile biological weapons laboratories maybe are not a smoking gun but they are certainly a very hot pistol.

I couldn't resist: "They are not smoking."

John Bolton, eyes bulging, veins popping, neck muscles flexing, shouted: "They were wiped clean! They were wiped clean!"

I admit I was pleased that I had agitated the administration's key witness, but the moment passed quickly. John Bolton regained his composure and described the "very prudent way" that the administration planned to proceed trying to find the missing weapons in Iraq.

Bolton ended his response to my questions with a mixture of surprising candor . . .

We do believe that the credibility of what we said before the onset of military action and the credibility of what we find in Iraq now does have an important consequence for us as we talk about the WMD program in other countries . . . you know, if you were to ask me do I feel impatient that we do not have more information, do I wish there was more that we could discuss here publicly, absolutely.

. . . as well as the familiar stubbornness of the top Bush advisers:

But I am confident that that information is coming . . . and as that information comes out people will see that the case that Secretary Powell made before the Security Council is accurate indeed.[11]

It was increasingly obvious to me that Colin Powell, knowingly or not, had presented false information to the United Nations and the world about weapons of mass destruction in Iraq. No amount of bluster from Powell's underling in front of the committee could change that astonishing revelation.

President Bush himself tried to make the case that Powell's testimony to the U.N. had been accurate, but the President's premature assertions that we had found the weapons of mass destruction in mobile weapons labs were quickly debunked by senior American and British intelligence officials.

By the beginning of June 2003, the major rationale for the American-led war against Iraq—Saddam Hussein must be disarmed—was being undermined by the failure to find any evidence of weapons of mass destruction in Iraq. Four months of international inspections from December 2002 to March 2003 and two months of American and coalition searches in April and May had come up empty. Many Americans were asking themselves and their political leaders the question I asked John Bolton: where the hell were the weapons of mass destruction?

In the weeks that followed President Bush's bogus claim that we had found the weapons of mass destruction, developments turned against the President and his top officials. News reports, document releases, interviews on and off the record and the deafening silence from the weapons inspectors all served to discredit the administration's prior claims about weapons in Iraq.

It turned out that George W. Bush's last big moment regarding Iraq was his victory lap on the flight deck of the *Abraham Lincoln* under the banner "Mission Accomplished" on May 1. He was correct to announce the impressive military victory, but his triumphalism was badly undercut by the facts on the ground. The continuing failure to discover anything about weapons of mass destruction in Iraq–which was good news for American soldiers there but bad news for the President's credibility—was now being augmented by a slow, steady surge of undermining information about the administration's use and misuse of pre-war intelligence. Numerous examples in the late spring and summer of 2003 of critical comments and damaging disclosures regarding the manipulation of intelligence served to challenge the integrity of the Bush administration, and led me to the conclusion that George Bush had led us to war in Iraq under false pretenses.

On May 31, Reuters reported that a growing number of U.S. national security professionals were accusing the Bush administration of slanting the facts and "cherry-picking" the intelligence to justify its rush to war.[12]

Reuters quoted Patrick Lang, former head of human intelligence gathering for the Defense Intelligence Agency:

> [The DIA] was exploited and abused and bypassed in the process of making the case for war in Iraq based on the presence of weapons of mass destruction.

The story also quoted Vince Cannistraro, a former chief of CIA counterterrorist operations, who said he knew of serving intelligence officers who were blaming the Pentagon for playing up "fraudulent intelligence":

> There are current intelligence officials who believe it is a scandal . . . [the administration had a] moral obligation to use the best information available, not just information that fits your preconceived ideas.

Also quoted by Reuters was Greg Thielmann, former head of weapons intelligence at the State Department's Bureau of Intelligence and

Research, who said it appeared that the Iraqi intelligence had been shaped: ". . . from the top down."

The Reuters story also quoted David Albright, a former U.N. weapons inspector, saying that in the run-up to invading Iraq: "The normal process of establishing accurate intelligence was sidestepped."

Finally, Reuters concluded the story by reporting the letter sent to President Bush on May 1 from a group primarily made up of CIA intelligence analysts calling themselves Veteran Intelligence Professionals for Sanity, which criticized the administration for: "A policy and intelligence fiasco of monumental proportions."

The floodgates of criticisms and damaging disclosures about the use and misuse of pre-war intelligence were now open, and the Bush administration could not merely ride out the torrent of harmful revelations. The unfavorable news eventually swamped the credibility of George Bush and his administration.

On June 6, someone leaked to the press a classified Defense Intelligence Agency report from September 2002 entitled, "Iraq—Key WMD Facilities—An Operational Support Study."[13] The report expressed doubts whether Saddam Hussein was producing chemical and biological weapons. The caveats, reservations and overall lack of certainty expressed in the classified report by military intelligence experts were staggering, particularly in light of the positive, totally certain statements being made in the fall of 2002 by the Bush administration team about Iraq's weapons of mass destruction.

The DIA September 2002 classified report said of Iraq's chemical warfare program:

> . . . we believe Iraq retained production equipment, expertise and chemical precursors and can reconstitute a chemical warfare program in the absence of an international inspection regime.

This statement assessing the ability of Iraq to develop chemical weapons ("we believe Iraq . . . can reconstitute a chemical warfare program . . .") in no way supported the positive statements in September and October 2002 by the President and his top people that Iraq already had chemical weapons, and in fact had large stockpiles of them.

The DIA report continued:

There is no reliable information on whether Iraq is producing and stockpiling chemical weapons, or where Iraq has—or
will—establish its chemical warfare agent production facilities.

This was an astonishing revelation. The Defense Intelligence
Agency had "no reliable information" whether Iraq was even producing, let alone stockpiling, chemical weapons. Yet the Bush team had
been publicly claiming since the time this report was issued on a classified basis that Iraq indeed had an active chemical warfare program
and large stockpiles of chemical weapons.

The DIA classified report from September 2002 went on:

Although we lack any direct information, Iraq probably possesses CW agent in chemical munitions, probably including
artillery rockets, artillery shells, aerial bombs and ballistic
missile warheads. Baghdad also probably possesses bulk chemical stockpiles, primarily containing precursors, but that also
could consist of some mustard agent or stabilized VX [nerve
agent].

This was a terrifying list of possible chemical weapons, to be sure.
But the list of caveats was equally eye-catching: "we lack any direct
information," "Iraq probably possesses," "probably including," "Baghdad also probably possesses," "could consist of." The DIA intelligence
analysts were very clear about their caveats and doubts.

The *Philadelphia Inquirer*, the major daily in my district, published
a story on June 7 stating:

Senior defense officials confirmed yesterday that a report
by the Pentagon's Defense Intelligence Agency in September expressed doubts about whether Saddam Hussein was
producing chemical and biological weapons . . . while Iraq
had biological weapons stockpiles, "the size of those stockpiles is uncertain and is subject to debate," said the classified
report . . .[14]

Clearly, the President and his top advisers in the White House
and the key executive departments had made, and were still making,
positive claims about Iraqi weapons that were not supported, and
were even contradicted, by this classified intelligence report from

the Defense Department. How could anybody read this report, or be briefed on its contents, and conclude in good faith that Iraq had stockpiles of chemical weapons? To paraphrase Vice President Cheney, somebody was lying—big time.

As I read these press accounts in June 2003, I recalled the absolute certainty about Iraqi weapons expressed in both the CIA White Paper I had read the previous October and my White House briefing on October 2. I was amazed and angered how the White House and CIA could issue a public paper and brief a congressional delegation that they were positive Hussein had chemical and biological weapons when the Defense Intelligence Agency told them the month before that there was no reliable information about those weapons.

As I saw it, it called into question the truthfulness of all the statements made by the President and his top people last September. They all said with complete confidence that Hussein had these weapons.

I wondered if it was possible that the White House could have missed this September 2002 report admitting the Defense Department had no reliable information regarding chemical weapons.

It is hard to know what documents reach a President's desk. It is also hard to know if George W. Bush ever read the reports that did reach his desk.

But Donald Rumsfeld, Secretary of Defense, surely knew about his own agency's report. Condoleezza Rice, National Security Adviser, should have known about the DIA report. And George Tenet had to know. The National Intelligence Estimate on Iraqi weapons had been circulated secretly on October 1, and George Tenet's CIA was the principal agency responsible for the preparation of that document. The September report of the Defense Intelligence Agency was surely used by the CIA to prepare the Estimate on Iraqi weapons.

I reached the inescapable conclusion that George Tenet and Condoleezza Rice had deliberately misled my congressional colleagues and me on October 2 when they briefed us with such certainty and assurance regarding the presence in Iraq of stockpiles of chemical and biological weapons. They had lied to my face—big time.

This same day, June 7, CBS News in cooperation with the Associated Press published a story about Greg Thielmann, the former director of the Office of Strategic, Proliferation and Military Affairs in the State Department's Bureau of Intelligence and Research. Thielmann was quoted as saying:

What disturbs me deeply is what I think are the disingenuous statements made from the very top about what the intelligence did say. The area of distortion was greatest in the nuclear field . . . when the administration did talk about specific evidence . . . it did it in a way that was also not entirely honest.[15]

Thielmann's office in the Bureau of Intelligence and Research was privy to classified intelligence gathered by the CIA, DIA and other agencies about Iraq's chemical, biological and nuclear programs. After retiring in September 2002 after 25 years in the State Department, he was now frequently speaking out about what he saw as abuse of the Iraqi intelligence by the Bush administration.

The final June 7 bad news report for the Bush administration came from Reuters, which reported the conclusion of a leading national security historian that the CIA bowed to Bush administration pressure to hype the threat from Saddam Hussein's weapons programs. After a detailed study of CIA public pronouncements, John Prados, the acclaimed author of eleven books on national security issues, concluded:

What is clear from intelligence reporting is that until about 1998 the CIA was fairly comfortable with its assessments on Iraq. But from that time on the agency gradually buckled under the weight of pressure to adopt alarmist views. After mid-2001, the rush to judgment on Iraq became a stampede.[16]

Not surprisingly, a CIA spokesman disputed Prados' conclusion as "utter nonsense", and CIA Director George Tenet said: "The integrity of our process was maintained throughout, and any suggestion to the contrary is simply wrong."[17]

Reuters then quoted Mel Goodman, a professor at the Pentagon's National War College and the director of the Intelligence Reform Project at the Center for International Policy in Washington, D.C. Goodman, who resigned as a CIA analyst over alleged skewing of intelligence in 1990, said: "To deny that there was any pressure on the intelligence community is just absurd."[18]

The national press corps was finally, and belatedly, in full cry over the increasing evidence that the Bush administration had misused prewar intelligence about Iraqi weapons of mass destruction. And the Bush team began to desperately defend themselves and turn on each other as they realized their personal credibility was under severe attack.

The June 9 *Washington Post* reported that the President's two top foreign policy advisers said it was the intelligence community, not them, who judged that Saddam Hussein had weapons of mass destruction, and that no prewar exaggeration had occurred.

The *Post* quoted National Security Adviser Condoleezza Rice describing as "revisionist history" the recent criticism that the President and senior officials may have overstated what was known about Iraqi weapons. The newspaper quoted her appearance on NBC's *Meet the Press*:

> The truth of the matter is that repeated directors of central intelligence, repeated reports by intelligence agencies around the world, repeated reports by United Nations inspectors asking hard questions of Saddam Hussein, and tremendous efforts by this regime to conceal and hide what it was doing, clearly give a picture of a regime that had weapons of mass destruction and was determined to conceal them.[19]

That statement by Condoleezza Rice wasn't "the truth of the matter" at all. Her statement was quite misleading and untrue. The classified reports from the intelligence community, most notably the National Intelligence Estimate on Iraqi weapons, did not "clearly give a picture of a regime that had weapons of mass destruction." Those reports were full of caveats, reservations and written dissents. Nor had UN weapons inspectors reported that Hussein had weapons. Their prewar reports said they couldn't find any evidence of weapons of mass destruction in Iraq. Condoleezza Rice wasn't even close to the truth of the matter.

Secretary of State Colin Powell also appeared on the Sunday talk shows and, according to the *Washington Post*, defended the administration's prewar statements, and particularly his own presentation to the UN Security Council the previous February 5, as "good, solid assessments" of Iraq's weapons programs, and carefully added that the determination that Hussein had weapons was:

> The official judgment of the director of central intelligence who is the one responsible for gathering all of this information . . . I'm sure more evidence and more proof will come forward as we go down the road.[20]

Colin Powell might have felt sure about more evidence and more proof appearing about weapons of mass destruction, but he was wrong. Those weapons never did appear, but cracks began appearing within the administration about who was responsible for the false and misleading claims about Iraqi weapons.

The morning of Monday, June 9, before heading to Washington, I held a press conference in the Montgomery County Courthouse in Norristown in my district. I was quoted in the local press on the subject of the missing weapons in Iraq:

> There is a growing credibility gap . . . one of the jobs Congress should do is to continue to ask reasonable and rational questions about this . . . these weapons may be found next week, who knows? What is important is accountability . . .
>
> Like millions of Americans, I am wondering where the hell these weapons of mass destruction are . . . If Iraq did not have them there has to be an accounting why our political leadership was so insistent that it did.[21]

That same evening of June 9 was the first time some colleagues and I spoke together on the floor of the House during Special Orders in what we came to call "Iraq Watch." We were reading about the damaging disclosures concerning the apparent misuse of intelligence by the Bush administration, and we had a lot of doubts and a lot of questions. Jay Inslee of Washington, Bill Delahunt of Massachusetts, Ted Strickland of Ohio, Neil Abercrombie of Hawaii and Rahm Emanuel of Illinois joined me on a regular basis. Inslee, Strickland and Abercrombie went on to become governors of their states, and Emanuel would become White House Chief of Staff and mayor of Chicago. Obviously, they owe it all to the spellbinding debate and public fame of Iraq Watch.

We met once a week in the House during Special Orders for after-hours colloquies to publicly discuss and debate in an almost empty chamber, but in front of the C-SPAN cameras, what was happening, and often not happening, in Iraq in the name of the American people.

As the months wore on, and the quick military victory that was won in a couple of weeks by our brave troops morphed into a long, unhappy and dangerous occupation, we asked a lot of questions of the Bush administration.

We asked that while we were winning the war, were we also winning the peace? If Vice President Cheney was correct that we would be greeted as liberators, why did it appear that we were considered occupiers instead? And why were we unable to protect our own courageous troops from being killed by snipers and roadside bombs?

We asked whether the Bush administration had misled the Congress and the American people regarding the presence in Iraq of weapons of mass destruction. We asked about all the discrepancies coming to light between the equivocal intelligence findings and the certainty of the Bush statements about Iraqi weapons.

We wondered how it was possible for the President to make an allegation in the January 2003 State of the Union speech that Iraq was trying to buy uranium in Niger, when the CIA had warned the White House ten months earlier that the claim was bogus. We asked for an accounting from the Bush administration for all its statements, assertions and promises that never came true.

We asked why looting became rampant, humanitarian aid lagged, and little reconstruction was underway. We asked why our post-invasion planning seemed so poor. We asked how good things could ever start happening in Iraq without first establishing fundamental security in the country.

We wondered why the Bush administration had sought and won from the United Nations Security Council on May 22, 2003 approval for Resolution 1483 designating the United States and Great Britain as the occupying powers in Iraq under international law. We questioned why we became occupiers rather than liberators. We wondered why our national policy was to occupy rather than internationalize and "Iraqitize" the situation.

We asked how long the military occupation would last, and how much it would cost. We asked how long the reconstruction of the country would take, and how much would it cost. We asked how long it would take to build international support and to put the Iraqis back in charge of their own country.

My colleagues and I asked all these questions and made all these arguments during Iraq Watch on the floor of the House month after month. I made thirty such statements in the House by the time I left Congress in late November 2004. We never got answers, we never heard the truth, and we never heard the Bush team ever acknowledge how badly they screwed up in Iraq.

Years later I asked Bill Delahunt whether he thought Iraq Watch made much of a difference. He laughed and said:

Iraq Watch was a big pain in the administration's ass! . . . It took some courage to do Iraq Watch. We were asking essential questions when there was total silence. We were a band of lonely warriors.[22]

Ted Strickland also remains proud of his efforts in Iraq Watch, and still feels "a quiet rage" over the "planful deceptions" and "manipulation of intelligence" by George Bush, Dick Cheney and Donald Rumsfeld. When he was governor, Strickland sponsored an annual event at the Governor's Mansion in Columbus for the families of Ohio soldiers lost in Iraq. He would meet with the families for private talks before the public ceremony honoring the fallen heroes. He asked me recently:

Have those that led us into this unnecessary war ever interacted with the families? They wouldn't even allow us to see and honor the coffins when they returned to this country.[23]

On June 9, 2003, during Iraq Watch, I asked the following questions:

Fundamentally, did the Bush administration overstate its case for war against Iraq, based upon weapons of mass destruction? Did the administration mislead the Congress and the American people intentionally, or not, about Iraq's weapons of mass destruction program? Did the Bush administration misuse the intelligence gathered by our national security agencies? Did they hear only what they wanted to hear? Did they believe only what they wanted to believe? Or did they tell us only what they wanted us to hear about the weapons of mass destruction?[24]

Bill Delahunt then added during the debate:

I think it is important to note that the top Marine officer in Iraq, Lieutenant General Jim Conway . . . from a report in the *Washington Post* . . . said in a press conference that U.S. intelligence was simply wrong in leading the military to believe that the invading troops were likely to be attacked with chemical weapons . . . he is making a statement that deserves an answer.[25]

I responded by quoting the comments made two days earlier by former State Department intelligence expert Greg Thielmann accusing the administration of distorting intelligence and presenting conjecture as fact. I then described the confusion regarding what the intelligence had actually said:

> The certainty that was used by the Bush administration to present this information in the fall of 2002 I think is a critical issue here. It is not completely clear at this point what all of the intelligence agencies were saying. Their information is becoming declassified and is beginning to be made public, but it is very clear what administration leaders were saying . . . yet a national intelligence estimate of October 2002, which was reputed to have said that Iraq had weapons of mass destruction, when we look at the backup material that is just being declassified, it is much more equivocal.[26]

My comment about "the backup material" is a clear reference to the DIA report from September 2002, declassified two days earlier, stating "there is no reliable information" and "we lack any direct information" about chemical weapons in Iraq. It is also clear from my comments that my colleagues and I had not seen "a national intelligence estimate of October 2002" that "reputed" to say that Iraq had weapons of mass destruction. We did not know yet that the still classified Estimate of October 1, 2002 was filled with caveats and reservations about Iraqi weapons. All we saw before we cast our votes on the war resolution in October 2002 until well after that June evening in 2003 was the whitewashed public White Paper of the CIA that concluded with absolute certainty that Saddam Hussein had weapons of mass destruction.

While few Republican congressmen were willing to publicly stand up to the White House during the spring and early summer of 2003, and no Republicans ever joined us during Iraq Watch in the House to question the war strategy, a handful of GOP members seemed increasingly disenchanted with the Bush administration concerning the war. None showed more personal fortitude than Walter Jones, Republican of North Carolina.

Walter Jones is one of the fine Southern gentlemen in Congress, soft spoken, courtly and unfailingly polite. In 2003–04, I was fortunate that my office was located next to Walter's office in the Cannon

House Office Building on Capitol Hill. Walter is a conservative Republican who was a strong supporter of President George W. Bush and his Iraq war policy, at least at the beginning. Walter was so mad at the French for their perceived opposition to American policy leading up to the invasion of Iraq that he successfully advocated for the famous renaming of French fries in the House cafeteria as "Freedom Fries".

But Walter lost faith in the President and came to view our invasion of Iraq as a tragic mistake. Soon after the war started Walter began to place poster boards on tripods in the hall outside of our adjacent offices with the names and photos of the American soldiers who were dying in Iraq. As the casualties mounted the poster boards became more numerous, soon filling the spacious hallway with a grim, sad and very moving reminder of the human toll being exacted by our policy in Iraq. People would just stand in the hallway, gazing quietly and reverently at the posters. Walter received a lot of criticism for his respectful but jarring display of the American soldiers killed in Iraq, particularly from some Republicans and Bush supporters who were riding high in the spring of 2003 on a wave of patriotic support for America's military. Walter and I would talk about the war and his personal protest as we walked back and forth to the House chamber for votes. But in the face of some considerable pressure from the Bush team, Walter never wavered. He didn't grandstand or lose his courtly composure. He just let the names and photos of the war dead speak for themselves.

On Friday, June 13, the *Philadelphia Inquirer* reported that President Bush had made the now-discredited claim in his January 2003 State of the Union speech about Saddam Hussein trying to buy uranium in Niger even though the CIA had previously warned the White House that the story did not check out. The story contained these two paragraphs:

A senior CIA official, who spoke on condition of anonymity, said the intelligence agency informed the White House on March 9, 2002—ten months before Bush's nationally televised speech—that an agency source who had traveled to Niger could not confirm European intelligence reports that Iraq was attempting to buy uranium from the West African country . . .

Three senior administration officials said Vice President Cheney and some officials on the National Security Council staff and at the Pentagon ignored the CIA's reservations and argued that the President and others should include the allegation in their case against Hussein.[27]

Of course, we already knew that the claims about Hussein purchasing uranium in Niger were false and were based upon forged documents, according to the findings of the International Atomic Energy Agency. But these leaks and off-the-record statements by anonymous government officials were a clear indication that the Bush administration was beginning to turn on itself and point fingers of blame as the lies and distortions about prewar intelligence became more apparent.

On June 25 I spoke in the House in support of a resolution to award the Congressional Gold Medal to British Prime Minister Tony Blair, whom I called "a great ally of ours." But I contrasted the forthright manner in which England was dealing with the weapons controversy, with public hearings in Parliament, two Cabinet resignations, and Blair subjecting himself to public questions, with the refusal of the Bush administration to account for their misleading public statements and assurances about Hussein's weapons of mass destruction. I said that an accounting of how our intelligence was used was critical for the future of the Bush doctrine of preemption:

> Our credibility is at stake. If we are ever again to embrace the notion of preemptive use of military force which may be necessary in an age of terror . . . we must know our intelligence is accurate; otherwise, the doctrine of preemption is unusable. If we are going to keep this country safe, we have to know . . . how well or how poorly our intelligence operation functioned.[28]

At the end of my remarks on June 25, I said there was a "document dump at the intelligence committee" that I was going to review. This referred to the effort of the House leadership in June 2003 to give all members of the House, not just the leaders themselves and the members of the Intelligence Committee, access to the classified intelligence documents about Iraqi weapons. I saw the classified documents for the first time either that day or the next. They were made available only to members of the House in a secure room in the Capitol, and we were not allowed to bring any telephones or electronic devices into the room, nor could we take any notes or make copies of the documents. We were not allowed to talk about what we read to anyone without security clearance.

I saw the September 2002 DIA report stating there was "no reliable information" about Iraq's chemical weapons, which had been leaked to the press three weeks before. I saw the October 4, 2002 CIA White Paper that stated so adamantly that Hussein had weapons of mass destruction, which I had read the previous October. And I saw for the first time the still-classified National Intelligence Estimate on Iraqi weapons, which contained so many caveats and reservations. I was astounded to see the differences between the certainties expressed by the Bush administration about Iraqi weapons compared to the doubts expressed by the intelligence analysts in the Estimate. But I did not yet fully realize how large the discrepancy was, and I wasn't allowed to talk to anyone about the specifics I had read.

I knew it was time for the Bush administration to explain what had happened with its use of prewar intelligence. It was time to give an accounting of statements made and action taken. It was time to acknowledge mistakes and explain how they would be corrected.

Fundamentally, it was time for George W. Bush to own up to the reality that the facts on the ground in Iraq by the end of June 2003 were far different from his promises and statements made in the fall of 2002. The country needed to hear an explanation from their President about what had gone wrong, and a plan for correcting the problems and moving forward to success in Iraq.

But the President of the United States saw it differently. On July 2, 2003, the President was asked why American troops were still in danger and were still being killed in Iraq even though two months had passed since the President had announced the successful end of combat operations. Inexplicably, the Cowboy went riding again, feeling tall in the saddle. George Bush said:

> Anybody who wants to harm American troops will be found and brought to justice. There are some that feel like if they attack us that we may decide to leave prematurely. They don't understand what they are talking about if that is the case . . . there are some who feel like the conditions are such that they can attack us there. My answer is, bring 'em on.[29]

Nobody knows what prompted George Bush to use this juvenile and provocative phrase. At the time he made it, 25 American soldiers had been killed during the occupation of Iraq since his May 1 declaration of the end of combat activities. Before that, 140 American soldiers were killed during the military invasion stage of our operations in Iraq. After President Bush's taunt, over 4,000 American troops would die in Iraq until combat troops were removed in December 2011. Indeed, the insurgents brought it on, with deadly results.

George W. Bush's taunt "Bring 'em on!" may be the stupidest public comment ever made by an American president. At the time, I was appalled. Now, I believe it was that comment that caused most Americans to begin to lose faith in this president's leadership in Iraq.

The *Philadelphia Inquirer* ripped the President in their lead editorial on Sunday, July 6:

> "Bring 'em on"?
>
> U.S. soldiers are dying and dodging guerilla bullets in a hot and hostile country and their commander-in-chief says, "Bring 'em on"?
>
> Mr. President, do you live in a play house or the White House?
>
> . . . childish taunts such as that are not the calibrated words demanded of the United States president at this turn of history's wheel.[30]

The Washington Post on July 17 published a story about the growing controversy over the use of Iraq intelligence that included the following:

> Minnesota Public Radio this week quoted Mary Kewatt, the aunt of a soldier killed in Iraq, saying: 'President Bush made a comment a week ago, and he said "bring it on". Well, they brought it on, and now my nephew is dead.[31]

It is unlikely that George W. Bush will ever live down his senseless, arrogant taunt.

On July 8 the *Washington Post* published a report on the White House admission that the President should not have claimed that Iraq tried to buy uranium in Niger:

> The Bush administration acknowledged for the first time yesterday that President Bush should not have alleged in his State of the Union address in January that Iraq had sought to buy uranium in Africa to reconstitute its nuclear weapons program . . .

"Knowing all that we now know, the reference to Iraq's attempt to acquire uranium from Africa should not have been included in the State of the Union speech," a senior Bush administration official said last night in a statement authorized by the White House.[32]

Of course, this belated admission by the White House, confirmed on the record by CIA Director George Tenet on July 11,[33] was six months after the President's speech, five months after Secretary of State Powell had refused to use the same claim in his presentation to the United Nations Security Council, and a full four months after the International Atomic Energy Agency had reported to the Security Council that the uranium story was untrue and based upon forged documents.

The participants in Iraq Watch that evening, July 8, were not impressed. When I asked Bill Delahunt about the White House admission, he responded:

The latest information is that today, today, the White House announced that when the President made the statement regarding the sale of highly enriched uranium to the Iraqi regime by a country in Africa, they made a mistake. Better late than never.[34]

Later in that evening's Iraq Watch, Neil Abercrombie asked Rahm Emanuel, in light of Emanuel's prior service as a White House staffer, if he could give "an educated, speculative assessment" of what would have happened if the Clinton White House would have put such bogus information in the President's State of the Union address. Emanuel responded:

Well, heads would have rolled. You cannot allow the President of the United States to have gone up on any speech, let alone a State of the Union, to address the nation and . . . the world with information that was clearly . . . not up to snuff. Heads would have rolled. There would have been an accounting . . .[35]

We all agreed during that evening's Iraq Watch that such an accounting was sadly missing from the Administration's response and from the indifference of the majority Republicans in the House of Representatives.

The following day, July 9, during a remarkable press conference sponsored by the Arms Control Association at the National Press Club in Washington, the retired State Department official Greg Thielmann gave his most extensive remarks to date about the misuse of Iraq intelligence by the Bush administration. Describing the office in the Bureau of Intelligence and Research that he had directed as responsible for monitoring, reporting on, and analyzing all-source intelligence on political-military subjects for the senior leadership of the State Department, Thielmann said:

> From my perspective, as a mid-level official in the U.S. Intelligence Community and the Department of State, the Bush administration did not provide an accurate picture to the American people of the military threat posed by Iraq before the nation went to war. Some of the fault lies with the performance of the Intelligence Community. But most of it lies with the way senior officials misused the information they were provided.
>   . . . as of March 2003, Iraq posed no imminent threat to its neighbors or to the United States . . . its nuclear weapons program . . . was essentially dormant . . . its chemical and biological weapons programs . . . were apparently directed at reestablishing contingent rapid production capabilities rather than maintaining ready stockpiles . . . Iraq probably had no ballistic missiles capable of delivering weapons payloads to population centers [in the Middle East] . . . there was no significant pattern of cooperation between Iraq and the al Qaeda terrorist organization . . .

Thielmann analyzed for his audience at the National Press Club the differences he saw in intelligence assessments between "honest errors" and "malfeasance," and reached the following conclusion:

> [The] principal reason Americans did not understand the nature of the Iraqi threat was the failure of senior Administration officials to speak honestly about what the intelligence showed.[36]

Greg Thielmann became the Bush administration's most effective and determined critic regarding what he considered to be the intentional misuse of the prewar Iraq intelligence. He spoke out repeatedly and made himself readily available to reporters and commentators.

On July 13 Thielmann was quoted by the Associated Press stating that intelligence agencies agreed on the "lack of meaningful connection to al Qaeda,"[37] and on July 14 by the *Washington Post* saying, "What disturbs me deeply is what I think are the disingenuous statements made from the very top about what the intelligence did say."[38] On July 20, the Associated Press quoted Thielmann saying, "There was no solid evidence that indicated Iraq's top nuclear scientists were rejuvenating Iraq's nuclear weapons program."[39]

Some questioned why Greg Thielmann had not spoken out sooner, while he still worked at the State Department in September 2002, or shortly after his retirement, when his objections might have changed congressional opinion before the October 2002 votes to authorize the war in Iraq.

Unfortunately, nobody was speaking out in the Intelligence Community in the fall of 2002 about the Bush administration's distortions and outright lies about the Iraq intelligence reports that the analysts were producing. The analysts had to know that the White House was distorting their work product, and they could have publicly objected. It was not the Intelligence Community's finest hour.

But I was glad Greg Thielmann had the courage to speak out when he did, and more intelligence insiders should have followed his brave example. Thielmann's comments were referred to frequently during Iraq Watch throughout the summer of 2003.

The most damaging disclosure to the White House during all of 2003 regarding the growing controversy over the misuse of prewar intelligence came at its own hands on Friday, July 18, when unnamed officials partially declassified the October 1, 2002 National Intelligence Estimate on Iraqi weapons at an off the record White House briefing.

As reported on the front page of the July 19 edition of the *Philadelphia Inquirer*:

> Hoping to quell the controversy over President Bush's use of questionable intelligence to help make the case for war with Iraq, White House officials yesterday released portions of a top-secret report from last year that concluded that Saddam Hussein was actively seeking nuclear weapons.[40]

If White House officials were hoping to "quell the controversy" over the President's use of intelligence, they failed miserably in what must be the biggest public relations gaffe in White House history. When the White House partially declassified the National Intelligence Estimate on Iraqi weapons, they disclosed the very evidence that made the case against George Bush and his administration for hyping and distorting intelligence and leading the country to war under false pretenses. The White House didn't just shoot itself in the foot; it completely blew away its own credibility.

The *Inquirer's* news coverage on July 19 spelled out the discrepancies between the reservations and caveats about Iraqi weapons in the Estimate and the certainty expressed in the president's public statements about Saddam Hussein in the fall of 2002:

> The classified National Intelligence Estimate, prepared for the White House in October, came loaded with reservations that reflected deep divisions in the intelligence community over Iraq's weapons program, and was at odds with the certainty expressed by Bush and his top aides.[41]

The *Inquirer* quoted directly from the declassified portions of the National Intelligence Estimate to demonstrate the doubts and reservations it contained:

> We lack specific information on many key aspects of Iraq's weapons of mass destruction programs . . . we have low confidence in our ability to assess when Saddam would use WMD.

The *Inquirer* also reported that the intelligence experts stated in their classified report they had "low confidence" in their ability to predict whether Hussein would attack the United States or whether he was willing to share weapons of mass destruction with al Qaeda terrorists, although the newspaper pointed out that President had repeatedly raised concerns about those threats in making the case for war.

The White House disclosures of parts of the National Intelligence Estimate on Iraqi weapons severely undercut the credibility of the White House itself, as well as the President. There was such commotion in the media in the days following the off the record briefing that Counselor to the President Dan Bartlett had to identify himself on the record July 22, in what he called "today's update to Friday's briefing", as the senior White House official who gave the off the record briefing the week before. I have marveled ever since that it was the Bush White House staffer responsible for President Bush's strategic communications who released portions of the classified document that communicated so clearly to the nation that his boss and other top officials had hyped and exaggerated the intelligence on Iraqi weapons.

Congress, the media and the public were stunned by these revelations about the doubts and reservations of intelligence experts which had never seen the light of day, and which were so contrary to the certainty of all the public comments by the President and his top people.

On July 20, a *Philadelphia Inquirer* article reviewed the "seven-month campaign" by the President and his senior aides to convince Americans and the rest of the world that Saddam Hussein was an imminent threat that could only be stopped by war. The story stated:

> Nearly a year later, that case appears to be coming apart, with some key pieces of evidence in doubt and others disproved outright . . . Hussein may not have been an imminent threat to the world at all, but a regional bully whose weapons programs weren't nearly as advanced as widely believed . . . critics and even nonpartisan analysts say the White House took what the United States' spy agencies knew about the Iraqi threat and pushed it to the limits of credibility, and perhaps beyond.[42]

These were not opinions in an editorial, but rather were statements, albeit cautious ones, in a news article. The White House partial declassification two days earlier of the October 2002 Estimate on Iraqi weapons, intended to "quell the controversy" over the President's use of intelligence, had fanned the flames of that controversy even higher. The media and the public were concluding that the Bush administration had misused the intelligence and misled the country.

In the July 21, 2003 Iraq Watch I said:

> It is becoming more and more clear as time goes by that last fall there were those in the White House . . . and the President himself who . . . exaggerated the threat of the weapons of mass destruction in order to win support in Congress and in the country for the invasion of Iraq.

It is now known that our intelligence agencies were reporting to the White House and to the Pentagon with significant
uncertainty and with serious doubts about certain aspects of
the weapons of mass destruction program in Iraq . . .[43]

The Bush White House never regained its footing on the subject of
its use of prewar intelligence after its own disclosure of portions of the
National Intelligence Estimate that expressed so many doubts about
Iraq's weapons of mass destruction.

But not for lack of trying. After the self-defeating White House disclosures on July 18 of classified material from the Estimate on Iraqi
weapons that ended up backfiring on the credibility of the White House,
CIA Director George Tenet stepped up on August 11, 2003 with a spirited defense of the National Intelligence Estimate itself. Tenet said:

We stand by the judgments in the NIE as well as our analy-
ses on Iraq's programs over the past decade. Those outside the
process over the past ten years and many of those commenting today do not know, or are misrepresenting, the facts. We
have a solid, well-analyzed and carefully written account in the
NIE and the numerous products before it.

After David Kay and others finish their efforts—after we
have exploited all the documents, people and sites in Iraq—we
should and will stand back to professionally review where we
are—but not before.[44]

David Kay was the head of the Iraq Survey Group, a 1,400 member
international team of military experts and weapons inspectors organized by the Pentagon and the Central Intelligence Agency and sent
to Iraq following the end of combat operations to find the weapons
of mass destruction. As we shall see, on January 23, 2004, David Kay
would resign his position, saying that stockpiles of weapons of mass
destruction were not in Iraq, and did not exist before the war.

The Iraq Watch of September 9, 2003 proved to be interesting. An
admonishment of one of my colleagues from the Speaker pro tempore set
me off into a bit of a rant about the misuse of prewar intelligence. It all
started with Ted Strickland's comments about President Bush's deceptions:

I am here tonight to say something that for me is kind of difficult to say. I believe the President has deceived us, that he has

distorted the truth, and that he has engaged in false claims which has taken us into a war which is daily claiming the lives of our soldiers . . .[45]

At the conclusion of Ted Strickland's remarks, the Speaker pro tempore, who that evening was archconservative Steve King of Iowa, interjected:

The Chair would remind all Members to refrain from improper references to the President, such as accusing him of deception.[46]

The Speaker pro tempore's admonition was appropriate under House procedures. Steve King was just doing his job that evening, certainly under the tutelage of the House Parliamentarian. But it ticked me off, and after a few minutes of further debate I returned to the subject and got myself worked up:

A suggestion was made by one of us this evening that the President was deceitful and we were admonished by the Chair that was not appropriate language. None of us are here to challenge the Chair. We are here to ask for the truth and ask questions about our policies in Iraq.

I would like to review the bidding a little, to set this question in some context, whether or not the President has been deceitful . . .

I then "reviewed the bidding" by recounting the President's positive, certain comments about Iraqi weapons in the fall of 2002, the equally adamant White House briefing I attended on October 2, 2002, and the revelations in recently declassified documents of the substantial doubts and written dissents in the fall of 2002 by intelligence experts about the actual status of Saddam Hussein's weapons programs.

I summed up:

It is my belief that the President exaggerated the threat of weapons of mass destruction in the fall of 2002, in the buildup to the war, in order to secure public support and congressional support for an authorization of war.

One of my colleagues at this point must have sought my recognition to make a comment, for the transcript of my remarks then states:

I will yield when I have unloaded my frustrations, which will be in just a moment.

It is my belief that the President misled Congress, and . . . the White House was well instructed about the doubts and the uncertainty from the CIA, the FBI, and the rest of the intelligence agencies.

Now, if it is objectionable to say that on the floor of the House, if the Republican leadership does not want to hear that on the floor of the House, bring it on. Let us bring it on right here, because this is the nub of the argument. This is what we are here to ask about.[47]

So there I was, red in the face, using the President's ill-advised taunt in my own mini-rant at the Republicans and the Bush administration. I must say that Speaker pro tempore King had nothing further to say to the Iraq Watchers that evening. And I must also admit that the Bush administration never "brought it on" to its congressional critics about Iraq. The Bush team never responded to Iraq Watch in any fashion.

I wasn't finished with rants in the fall of 2003. On October 20 I held a press conference at the Montgomery County Courthouse in Norristown in my district. I was defending my no vote the week before on the President's request for an additional $87 billion for military operations and reconstruction work in Iraq and Afghanistan. I said the Congress had missed an opportunity to use "the power of the purse" to force the Bush administration to work more closely with Congress about what to do in Iraq, and how to do it.

The National Republican Congressional Committee had put out a statement saying that I sided with the "far left wing of the Democratic Party" and that I had "abandoned soldiers in the field" with my no vote. I angrily responded at the press conference that nothing could be further from the truth, and a local paper published my remarks:

The troops are about the only thing in our operation in Iraq that are working well. The troops have fought brilliantly and the performance of our military has been outstanding.

Everything else about our operations in Iraq stunk. The planning stunk. The unilateral approach stunk. The misleading comments about the extent of the threat of weapons of mass destruction stunk. The arrogant and stubborn approach of the Bush administration stunk. The way we are conducting the reconstruction stinks.[48]

Not very elegant or eloquent words. I could have done a better job with my choice of language. But in October of 2003, just one year after I had voted to give President Bush authority to go to war against Iraq, it was exactly the way I felt.

EIGHT

The Aftermath of War, 2004

Respectful applause rose from the audience as we all stood on our feet. Across the center aisle, the crowd was louder and more raucous, with lots of cheering. President George W. Bush was slowly making his way down the center aisle of the House Chamber, with members pressing in from both sides to greet him and slap him on the back. The President, looking strong and confident, was basking in all the adulation, and the Republican side of the chamber was whooping it up.

It was Monday evening, January 20, 2004, the beginning of a presidential election year, and the congressional Republican majorities were feeling good about their President and their own chances for re-election the following November. It was State of the Union night once again, George W. Bush's fourth opportunity as President to address Congress and the nation in this constitutionally mandated annual report, and nobody in the chamber doubted that President Bush would proclaim the state of the union "confident and strong".

I was only mildly interested in what the President would have to say this evening. I had a pretty good idea what was going to be in the speech before it was delivered. There would be some chest thumping over the capture of Saddam Hussein, well-deserved accolades for America's armed forces, and some dire warnings about the continuing threat of terrorism. Certainly, optimistic words about the economy, salutes to school children and seniors, and demands for more tax cuts. Always, more tax cuts.

I wasn't so sure how Bush would describe the continuing challenges in Iraq. Far from being greeted as liberators, American diplomats, bureaucrats and contractors were bogged down in a tough, unfinished and dangerous effort to establish physical security, economic opportunity and democratic institutions for the people of Iraq. While American and coalition forces had performed brilliantly the past spring and made short work of the Iraqi army, the days and months following the end of combat operations and the proclamation of "Mission Accomplished" had proven frustrating as the joint American/British civil and military occupation struggled to bring order to the country. Things were not working out as promised before the war by the Bush team, and far too many Americans were still dying in Iraq many months after the proclaimed end of combat operations.

I could understand the confidence felt by my Republican colleagues regarding their re-election prospects this year. Despite the obvious failures in the nation-building effort in Iraq, the country was still pleased by the victory over Saddam Hussein, and by his capture, and the President still enjoyed strongly positive poll numbers because of his leadership in the Iraqi war and the war on terror. After all, Americans were still serving in harm's way, and some were paying the ultimate sacrifice. It did not seem to most Americans like a good time to challenge the Commander-in-Chief while troops were still serving in the field. People were still patriotically rallying around the flag.

But I also knew that a lot of Americans were asking where exactly were the weapons of mass destruction. Hundreds of Americans had already died in Iraq, and the death toll continued to mount, and yet no weapons had been found, weapons whose presence and threat had served as the rationale for the invasion of Iraq. What was the President going to say tonight, what could he say, about all that?

As the applause died down and the speech began, my mind wandered a little. I wondered if the confidence of the Republicans in their election prospects was well placed. Many folks were expressing a lot of concern and even outright anger to me over the nation's policies in Iraq, and in particular regarding the failure to find any weapons of mass destruction. I frequently found myself in the uncomfortable position of defending my vote for the war while criticizing the Administration's conduct of the occupation. I knew some of my most solid supporters were not happy with my vote, and I wondered if any of the Republicans were hearing negative reactions from people in their base of support. From the look and sound of the Republicans tonight, they seemed smug and satisfied with the state of political affairs.

The President himself looked and sounded very comfortable, and he moved smoothly through his speech,[1] touching on the themes and applause lines that I had anticipated. The President praised the hundreds of thousands of American service men and women deployed across the world in the war on terror . . . affirmed that the government's vigilance was protecting America . . . proclaimed Americans to be the "hardest working people in the world".

The President said the economy is growing stronger . . . tax relief is working . . . we are raising standards for public schools . . . we are giving seniors prescription drug coverage in Medicare . . . the American people are showing that the state of the Union "is confident and strong".

There it was! Every President said it, or something like it. No State of the Union would be complete without such a declaration that all was well.

The President urged Congress to give homeland security and law enforcement "every tool they need" and to renew the PATRIOT Act . . . the country was on the offense against the terrorists . . . America had ended the rule of Saddam Hussein and the people of Iraq were free.

Here we go, I thought. It was chest-thumping time.

The President continued:

Some in this Chamber and in our country did not support the liberation of Iraq. Objections to war often come from principled motives, but let us be candid about the consequences of leaving Saddam Hussein in power. We're seeking all the facts . . .

But you told us you already had all the facts, I thought.

The President went on:

Already, the Kay Report identified dozens of weapons-of-mass-destruction-related program activities and significant amounts of equipment that Iraq concealed from the United Nations. Had we failed to act, the dictator's weapons of mass destruction programs would continue to this day.

I couldn't believe what I had just heard. George Bush was still flogging the weapons issue, his Achilles heel.

I wondered what in the world was a "weapons-of-mass-destruction-related program activity?" I asked myself if you can set one of those off? Can you stockpile it? Can you give it to a terrorist?

I was incredulous. The United Nations inspectors a year ago had found no weapons before the war was started. The American armed forces had found no weapons in Iraq after the war was won. The Iraq Survey Group, led by David Kay, was finding no weapons at the present time. After a year of searching, it was increasingly obvious that there weren't large stocks of weapons of mass destruction in Iraq. Almost surely, there weren't any such weapons at all. And instead of admitting it, instead of facing the music, now the President was going to start talking about "weapons-of-mass-destruction-related program activities."

The following evening I spoke for five minutes during Special Orders in the House on the war in Iraq and the issue of weapons of mass destruction. With a considerably smaller audience than the President had enjoyed the night before, I said:

> Last night the President . . . brought up, rather surprisingly, weapons of mass destruction . . . and dozens of weapons of mass destruction-related program activities in Iraq. I do not know what a weapons of mass destruction-related program activity is. I would like to find out. I do know this: it is not weapons of mass destruction. We have not found weapons of mass destruction in Iraq. David Kay, the American inspector, has not found them. The international inspectors did not find them . . .
>
> The President, when he won his authority to go to war, made a number of commitments. He said that he would exhaust diplomatic options before going to war. He did not. He said he would allow the international inspectors the opportunity to complete their work in Iraq. He did not. He said he would go to the United Nations and build a coalition, and he did not. And now the President would still have us believe that we are on a successful hunt and are turning up weapons of mass destruction in Iraq as part of a broad-based coalition in that country, and neither of those statements is true.[2]

That same day, January 21, Vice President Dick Cheney asked for more time and patience in the hunt for the missing weapons of mass destruction. He insisted in an interview with National Public Radio that the administration had not given up looking for weapons in Iraq. Cheney said:

> It's going to take some additional considerable period of time in order to look in all the cubbyholes and ammo dumps and all the places in Iraq where you'd expect to find something like that.[3]

Two days later, David Kay resigned as the chief United States arms inspector in Iraq, saying weapons stockpiles in Iraq did not exist. Kay was the head of the Iraq Survey group of 1,400 experts and inspectors sent to Iraq by the Pentagon and the CIA to find the weapons of mass destruction. David Kay apparently did not agree with the Vice President that more time was needed to reach a conclusion about Hussein's missing weapons.

When Reuters asked Kay on January 23 what happened to the stockpiles of chemical and biological weapons expected to be in Iraq, Kay responded:

> I don't think they existed. I think there were stockpiles at the end of the first Gulf War [in 1991] and those were a combination of U.N. inspectors and unilateral Iraqi action got rid of them. I think the best evidence is that they did not resume large-scale production [of] large stockpiles of chemical and biological weapons in the period after '95 . . . the nuclear program was . . . rudimentary . . . there were a few little things going on, but it had not resumed in anything meaningful.[4]

On National Public Radio, on January 25, David Kay said when asked whether we ever would find clear evidence of weapons of mass destruction: "My summary view, based on what I've seen, is that we are very unlikely to find large stockpiles of weapons. I don't think they exist."[5]

David Kay was quoted in a January 26 *Slate* interview:

> I'm personally convinced that there were not large stockpiles of newly produced weapons of mass destruction. We don't find the people, the documents or the physical plants that you would expect to find if the production was going on.[6]

It was clear what the recently resigned chief U.S. weapons inspector was saying: there were no stockpiles of weapons of mass destruction in

Iraq since the mid-1990's. So when we went to war in March 2003 to disarm Saddam Hussein, he was already disarmed.

It was now all over for the Bush administration and their attempts to justify their advocacy for war based on weapons of mass destruction. They could no longer get away with lame suggestions that the weapons were really dangerous, and would some day be found and, therefore, the war had been a good idea.

The editorial writers had a field day.

On January 27, editorials in both the *Philadelphia Inquirer* and the *New York Times* ripped the administration over Iraqi weapons. The *Inquirer* wrote:

. . . will the White House keep desperately pretending that WMD were not the chief pretext by which the American public was sold on a swift, preemptive invasion of Iraq? . . .

[David] Kay did say he found evidence of Hussein's hunger for WMD and of a skeletal program for restarting production. Bush is making much of those points, but that's a far cry from the robust and imminent threat he cited to justify short-circuiting United Nations inspections. The rush to invade looks particularly culpable given how poorly Bush planned for the war's aftermath.[7]

The *New York Times* wrote, in an editorial entitled "Mr. Cheney, Meet Mr. Kay":

Vice President Dick Cheney continued to insist last week that Iraq had been trying to make weapons of mass destruction, apparently oblivious to the findings of the administration's own chief weapons inspector that Iraq had possessed only rudimentary capabilities and unrealized intentions. The vice president's myopia suggests a breathtaking unwillingness to accept a reality that conflicts with the administration's preconceived notions . . .

As for those trailers cited by Mr. Cheney, the consensus view, Mr. Kay told *The Times*, is that they were intended to produce hydrogen or perhaps rocket fuel, not biological weapons. Mr. Kay had earlier called the trailer assertions an embarrassing fiasco. So, too, with Iraq's nuclear weapons program. Mr. Cheney once famously declared that it had been reconstituted, but

Mr. Kay called it rudimentary—hardly capable of producing a bomb in a year or two, as the administration had implied.[8]

The truth was coming out about the misuse of intelligence, and the administration faced criticism from within and without its ranks. The Los Angeles Times covered George Tenet's speech on February 5 at Georgetown University in which the CIA Director acknowledged prewar intelligence failures. The story contained these paragraphs:

Despite his defiant posture and impassioned tone, Tenet retreated from the agency's prewar claims on nearly every front. He admitted that the CIA had few if any human sources in Iraq, acknowledged that it may have "overestimated" Hussein's nuclear weapons programs, and said that "we do not know" if Iraq produced biological weapons before the war.

The most damaging disclosure was Tenet's admission for the first time that the CIA had allowed "fabricated" information from an "unreliable" Iraqi defector about suspected mobile germ-weapons labs to appear in two key prewar assessments: Secretary of State Colin Powell's dramatic presentation to the United Nations Security Council one year ago Thursday, and the October 2002 National Intelligence Estimate provided to members of Congress shortly before they voted to approve the use of force in Iraq.[9]

The *LA Times* reported that Tenet's speech, including his claim that the CIA never warned President Bush that Saddam Hussein was an "imminent threat," sparked a "bitter new round" of finger-pointing on Capitol Hill about who bore the most responsibility for the "apparently exaggerated" prewar claims about Iraq's weapons, put new pressure on the White House to explain its decision to launch a preemptive war, and created a "potential division" between Tenet and the president.

President Bush tried to rise to the occasion and beat back the growing allegations that he had distorted the prewar intelligence and taken the country to war under false pretenses. On February 7, two days after Tenet's speech at Georgetown University, George Bush gave an Oval Office interview to NBC, which was broadcast on Sunday, February 8.

Early in the interview, George Bush grandiosely announced, "I am a war president." Under respectful but relentless questioning from host Tim Russert, the President tried to put the best face on David Kay's resignation of two weeks earlier and his assessment that no weapons stockpiles had existed in Iraq since the mid-1990s. The President said:

> For the parents of the soldiers who have fallen who are listening, David Kay, the weapons inspector, came back and said, "In many ways Iraq was more dangerous than we thought" . . .
>
> But again, I repeat to you, I don't want to sound like a broken record, but David Kay who is the man who led the Iraq Survey Group, who has now returned with an interim report, clearly said that the place was a dangerous place.[10]

The President's continuing refusal to acknowledge his hype about Iraqi weapons, his ongoing effort to spin the Kay resignation and findings into something positive about his administration's actions, was too much for me. In the next Iraq Watch on February 24, 2004, I started off with this: ". . . the last few weeks have been tough weeks for President Bush regarding his policies in Iraq . . ."[11]

After recounting the President's efforts in the State of the Union to suggest there were ongoing "weapons of mass destruction-related program activities" in Iraq, followed by his *Meet the Press* interview where he stated that David Kay came home to make "an interim report" which said, "In many ways Iraq was more dangerous than we thought," I continued:

> Well, in fact . . . Dr. Kay came back from Iraq not to make an interim report, but to quit. He said he has had enough. He is frustrated. He says he is not getting the support that he thinks the Iraq [Survey] Group should get in order to focus on the search for weapons of mass destruction. He believes those weapons do not exist. And far from saying things were worse over there than he thought, he said we could not find the things that we were told we would find.[12]

It was pathetic that George Bush tried to convince Americans that the David Kay resignation and inability to find any weapons was somehow validating for the administration. George W. Bush wasn't facing up to the reality that he hyped the existence of Iraqi weapons far beyond the uncertain, doubt-laced intelligence reports produced for him by the Intelligence Community. Bush just blamed the intelligence.

George J. Tenet deserves credit for his Georgetown University speech in which he finally, belatedly, admitted and took some responsibility for errors in the intelligence on Iraqi weapons. But he didn't acknowledge the discrepancies between his caveat-filled and uncertain classified National Intelligence Estimate on Iraqi weapons of October 1, 2002 and his staunchly adamant public White Paper of October 4, 2002 until he wrote his memoirs a few years later, as we will see in Chapter Ten.

As for that "potential division" between George Tenet and George Bush that the *Los Angeles Times* worried about after Tenet's George-town University speech, the President took action to heal any division or bruised feelings and to encourage Tenet's continued loyalty. On December 14, 2004, President Bush awarded recently retired CIA Director George J. Tenet the Presidential Medal of Freedom, the highest civilian award in the United States.[13]

NINE

Consequences

The January 2004 resignation of chief U.S. weapons inspector David Kay, and his announcement that no stockpiles of weapons had existed in Iraq since the mid 1990's, began an irreversible flow of bad news from Iraq about the missing weapons of mass destruction. The news never got any better for President Bush or his administration. The consequence was the end of George Bush's credibility regarding his chief rationale for going to war in Iraq.

Every subsequent study and report simply confirmed what had become painfully obvious: there were no weapons of mass destruction in Iraq, there had not been any stockpiles of such weapons in Iraq since the mid 1990's, and George Bush had led the nation into war under false pretenses.

Principal among these subsequent documents were three major reports from the Senate Intelligence Committee about the collection of Iraqi intelligence and its use and misuse by the Bush team, and the final report of the Iraq Survey Group.

On July 7, 2004, the Senate Select Committee on Intelligence issued their *Report on the Intelligence Community's Prewar Intelligence Assessments on Iraq*. The report was the result of an unprecedented, one-year investigation by the Senate Intelligence Committee and its staff concerning the U.S. Intelligence Community's assessments of Iraq and weapons of mass destruction during the period of time leading up to the invasion of Iraq in March 2003. The committee staff reviewed more than 30,000 pages of documentation and interviewed more than

200 people, including intelligence analysts and senior officials from the major federal agencies involved in intelligence gathering and analysis, and the full Committee held a series of hearings concerning the intelligence on Iraq. The 511-page report included 117 formal conclusions, copious discussion and background information. There was bipartisan agreement between the Committee's Republican majority and Democratic minority, and the members of the Committee unanimously endorsed its conclusions.

As we saw in Chapter Two, the 2004 Senate Report found many failures by the Intelligence Community in both the gathering of intelligence and its analysis regarding Iraq, failures that misled both government officials and the general public.

The Report's first and most damning conclusion was:

Most of the major key judgments in the Intelligence Community's October 2002 National Intelligence Estimate (NIE), Iraq's Continuing Programs for Weapons of Mass Destruction, either overstated, or were not supported by, the underlying intelligence reporting. A series of failures, particularly in analytic trade craft, led to the mischaracterization of the intelligence.[1]

The 2004 Senate Report contained 117 conclusions, most of them trying to amplify and explain the reasons for the failures identified in Conclusion One. The Senate Report reached the following fundamental conclusions:

- the Intelligence Community did not accurately explain the uncertainties behind the judgments in the October 1, 2002 National Intelligence Estimate on Iraqi weapons,
- the Intelligence Community suffered from a "group think" dynamic that led to a collective presumption that Iraq had a flourishing weapons program,
- the analysis in the October 2002 Estimate suffered from a "layering" effect where assessments were built on previous judgments without including previous-stated uncertainties,
- there were "significant short-comings" in the human intelligence collection efforts in Iraq, including no agency sources in Iraq after 1998,

- there was poor information sharing between the CIA and the rest of the Intelligence Community regarding prewar analysis of Iraqi weapons,
- the Intelligence Community relied too heavily on foreign government services and third party reporting,
- the language in the October 2002 Estimate that Iraq was trying to buy uranium and yellowcake from Niger "overstated" what the Intelligence Community actually knew about Iraq's possible procurement attempts,
- the judgment in the October 2002 Estimate that Iraq was reconstituting its nuclear program "was not supported by the intelligence."
- the available information indicated that the high-strength aluminum tubes were intended for an Iraqi conventional rocket program and "not a nuclear weapon."
- the statement in the October 2002 Estimate that Iraq was expanding its infrastructure to produce nuclear weapons was "not supported" by the available intelligence,
- the assessment in the October 2002 Estimate that "we judge that all aspects . . . of Iraq's biological weapons program are active . . . and more advanced" was not supported by the intelligence, and the key judgment that "Baghdad has biological weapons" overstated what was actually known,
- the key judgment of the October 2002 Estimate that "Baghdad has . . . chemical weapons" overstated what was actually known,
- the key judgment in the October 2002 Estimate that Iraq was developing an unmanned aerial vehicle "probably intended to deliver biological warfare agents" overstated what was actually known,
- much of the information provided or cleared by the CIA for inclusion in Secretary Powell's speech to the United Nations was "overstated, misleading, or incorrect."

The 2004 Senate Intelligence Committee Report found many errors and short-comings in the performance of the Intelligence Community, particularly "in analytic trade craft," that led to key judgments in the October 2002 Estimate that "either overstated, or were not supported by," the underlying intelligence reporting.

As the Committee Chairman, Senator Pat Roberts, said:

Today we know these assessments were wrong, and as our inquiry will show, they were also unreasonable and largely unsupported by the available intelligence . . . these are very emphatic statements. Simply put, they were not supported by the intelligence the community supplied to the committee, and they should not have been included in the National Intelligence Estimate.[2]

It was disappointing, to say the least, for Congress and the American people to learn that the comprehensive intelligence document designed to represent the Intelligence Community's best and considered judgment on the state of Iraqi weapons did not accurately reflect the underlying intelligence analysis of the experts in the various intelligence agencies.

But in addition to the flawed intelligence, as we also saw in Chapter Two, the Senate Intelligence Committee also found problems and discrepancies between the intelligence reports themselves. The 2004 Senate Report compared the classified October 1, 2002 National Intelligence Estimate on Iraqi weapons with the unclassified White Paper that followed three days later on October 4. The Senate Report stated:

The unclassified paper was substantially similar to, although not nearly as detailed as, the classified NIE. The key judgments were almost identical in layout and substance in both papers. The key judgments of the unclassified paper were missing many of the caveats and some references to alternative agency views that were used in the classified NIE, however. Removing caveats such as "we judge" or "we assess" changed many sentences in the unclassified paper to statements of fact rather than assessments.

The 2004 Senate Intelligence Committee Report reached three public Conclusions regarding the public White Paper:

- the elimination of the caveats and reservations from the unclassified White Paper misrepresented judgments of intelligence experts to the public that did not have access to the classified National Security Estimate.
- the exclusion of the dissenting opinions and the names of the agencies dissenting that were in the classified National Intelligence Estimate but not the unclassified White Paper provided readers with an incomplete picture of the

nature and extent of the debate within the Intelligence
Community.

• the key judgment in the unclassified October 4, 2002
White Paper on Iraq's potential to deliver biological agents
conveyed a level of threat to the United States homeland
inconsistent with the classified National Intelligence
Estimate.

The 2004 Senate Report clearly concluded that the White Paper that
George Tenet produced as a public summary of the classified Estimate
"misrepresented [experts'] judgments" to the public, provided readers
"with an incomplete picture" of the debate within the Intelligence Community, and "conveyed a level of threat" to the U.S. homeland that was
"inconsistent" with the judgments in the classified Estimate.

In effect, according to the Senate Select Committee on Intelligence, our Intelligence Community first produced a comprehensive
intelligence report that did not reflect the underlying intelligence
reporting of our experts. Then George Tenet and the CIA made a bad
situation immeasurably worse by releasing a public summary of that
flawed intelligence document which turned uncertain intelligence
opinion into positive statements of fact, thus misleading the Congress
and the country.

The final word on the missing Iraqi weapons of mass destruction
was supplied in the final report of the Iraq Survey Group, released on
September 30, 2004. The Iraq Survey Group was appointed by the
Defense Department and the CIA after the March 2003 invasion of Iraq,
and was comprised of 1,400 civilian and military intelligence and weapons experts. Their mission was clear: go to Iraq, inspect every potential weapons site, read every relevant scientific and military document,
interview military and civilian personnel involved with weapons, and
find the missing weapons of mass destruction.

The Iraq Survey Group came up empty. They never found weapons
of mass destruction in Iraq. Their final report became known as the
"Duelfer Report," after their Chair, Charles A. Duelfer, a former United
Nations weapons inspector who was appointed by George Tenet to head
the Group following David Kay's resignation in January 2004. Charles
Duelfer ended up in agreement with David Kay: there were no weapons
of mass destruction in Iraq.

The Duelfer Report[3] was a three volume document totaling 918
pages, and represented the largest and most authoritative attempt ever

made to find out what happened to the weapons that the Bush administration had claimed Saddam Hussein possessed.[4]

The Duelfer Report reached the following fundamental conclusions:

- There were no stockpiles of weapons of mass destruction in Iraq,
- Iraq destroyed its chemical weapons stockpiles in 1991, and only a few old, abandoned chemical munitions were discovered,
- Iraq abandoned its biological weapons program in 1995. While it could have re-established a rudimentary biological weapons program, there were no indications it was trying to do so.
- Iraq ended its nuclear program in 1991. There was no evidence of any serious effort to restart the program, and Iraq's ability to reconstitute a nuclear weapons program progressively decayed after 1991.
- Saddam Hussein personally controlled all of Iraq's strategic decisions, and he wanted to recreate Iraq's weapons capability if U.N. sanctions ever were lifted, and if Iraq's economy improved.
- Saddam Hussein's main objective of his public blustering was to fool his archenemy Iran into thinking that Hussein possessed weapons of mass destruction.

The *Washington Post* opened its coverage of Duelfer's Senate testimony with this paragraph:

The 1991 Persian Gulf War and subsequent U.N. inspections destroyed Iraq's illicit weapons capability and, for the most part, Saddam Hussein did not try to rebuild it, according to an extensive report by the chief U.S. weapons inspector in Iraq that contradicts nearly every prewar assertion made by top administration officials about Iraq.[5]

As a result of the Duelfer Report, it was clear to virtually everyone that Saddam Hussein had been disarmed by the 1991 Persian Gulf War and by the impact of U.N. sanctions and inspections in the mid-1990s, before Hussein had thrown the international inspectors out of Iraq in 1998. There was no question the U.S. Intelligence Community missed that basic development and delivered flawed intelligence to U.S. policymakers.

But there were plenty of questions remaining about the Bush administration's use, and by now obvious misuse, of intelligence, and the Senate Select Committee on Intelligence wanted to get to the bottom of the controversy. Partisan differences on the committee, and the pressures of the presidential election of 2004, complicated the search for common ground, but committee members, particularly the Democrats, wanted to fully investigate the collection, accuracy and potential abuse of prewar intelligence. Accordingly, the Senate Intelligence Committee would issue five more reports over the next four years, two of which warrant further discussion here.

On September 8, 2006, the Senate panel issued a report[6] comparing the prewar assessments about Iraq's weapons of mass destruction with postwar findings on the ground in Iraq. Not surprisingly, the Senate Intelligence Committee reached a number of sad and frustrating conclusions that postwar findings in Iraq did *not* support the prewar judgments in the October 2002 Estimate that:

- Iraq was reconstituting its nuclear weapons program,
- Iraq's acquisition of high-strength aluminum tubes was intended for a nuclear program,
- Iraq was trying to buy uranium from Niger,
- Iraq had biological weapons,
- Iraq possessed, or ever developed, mobile facilities for producing biological warfare agents,
- Iraq had chemical weapons,
- Iraq had a program for an unmanned aerial vehicle to deliver biological agents.

The 2006 Senate Report contained three important postwar findings indicating, first, that Saddam Hussein distrusted Al Qaeda and refused all requests from Al Qaeda to provide material or operational support. Second, postwar findings supported prewar assessments that there was no credible information that Iraq was complicit in or had foreknowledge of the September 11 attacks. Third, no postwar information indicated that Iraq intended to use Al Qaeda or any other terrorist group to strike the U.S. homeland before or during the war with Iraq.

Of course, these findings directly contradicted the prewar claims of the Bush administration regarding Saddam, Al Qaeda and the attacks of September 11. The work of the Senate Intelligence Committee identified the numerous large gaps between the repeated claims of the President and his top advisers, and many of the prewar assessments and most of the postwar findings about Hussein's missing weapons and the absence of a connection between Iraq and Al Qaeda.

The final major Senate Intelligence Committee report on Iraq was issued on June 5, 2008, and in many ways was the most damaging of all to the credibility of the President and other top officials. The report[7] investigated whether the prewar public statements about Iraq by the Bush administration were substantiated by the intelligence reports they were receiving. The Senate committee reviewed "hundreds of intelligence reports" produced before the start of hostilities on March 19, 2003, and compared the intelligence with five major prewar speeches by the leaders of the administration, specifically the speeches by President Bush before the United Nations General Assembly on September 12, 2002, in Cincinnati on October 7, 2002, and the State of the Union on January 28, 2003, Vice President Dick Cheney to the Veterans of Foreign Wars on August 26, 2002, and Secretary of State Colin Powell to the United Nations Security Council on February 5, 2003, as well as other public statements by administration leaders.

Senator Jay Rockefeller, chair of the Senate committee, reached the following conclusion in the 2008 report:

> Before taking the country to war, this Administration owed it to the American people to give them a 100 percent accurate picture of the threat we faced. Unfortunately, our Committee has concluded that the Administration made significant claims that were not supported by the intelligence. In making the case for war, the Administration repeatedly presented intelligence as fact when in reality it was unsubstantiated, contradicted, or even non-existent. As a result, the American people were led to believe that the threat from Iraq was much greater than actually existed.
>
> It is my belief that the Bush Administration was fixated on Iraq, and used the 9/11 attacks by Al Qaeda as justification for overthrowing Saddam Hussein. To accomplish this, top Administration officials made repeated statements that falsely linked Iraq and Al Qaeda as a single threat and insinuated that Iraq played a role in 9/11. Sadly, the Bush Administration led the nation into war under false pretenses.

There is no question we all relied on flawed intelligence. But, there is a fundamental difference between relying on incorrect intelligence and deliberately painting a picture to the American people that you know is not fully accurate.[8]

The 2008 report of the Senate committee cited several examples where the administration's public statements either contradicted, distorted, or were not supported by the intelligence reports the public officials were receiving at the time of their comments. While the committee acknowledged that many statements by the administration were substantiated by the flawed intelligence, some important statements were not substantiated, and other administration claims failed to acknowledge the underlying uncertainties in the intelligence reports on their desks.

For example, the Senate committee reached the following conclusions:

- many statements by President George Bush, Vice President Dick Cheney, Secretary of State Colin Powell and Secretary of Defense Donald Rumsfeld regarding Iraq's possession of weapons of mass destruction "reflected a higher level of certainty" than the intelligence judgments themselves,
- statements by Bush, Cheney and Powell that Iraq was developing unmanned aerial vehicles that could be used to deliver chemical or biological weapons did not convey the "substantial disagreements" that existed in the intelligence community,
- statements and implications by Bush and Powell suggesting that Iraq and Al Qaeda had a partnership, or that Iraq had provided weapons training to Al Qaeda, were "not substantiated" by the intelligence,
- statements by Bush and Cheney indicating that Saddam Hussein was prepared to give weapons of mass destruction to terrorist groups for attacks against the United States were "contradicted" by available intelligence information,
- statements by Bush, Cheney, Powell and National Security Adviser Condoleezza Rice regarding a possible Iraqi nuclear weapons program did not convey the "substantial disagreements" that existed in the intelligence community,
- statements by Bush and Cheney prior to the October 2002 National Intelligence Estimate regarding Iraq's chemical

weapons production capability did not reflect the intelligence community's "uncertainties" about whether such
production was ongoing,

- statements by Bush and Cheney regarding the postwar
  status in Iraq, in terms of the political, security and economic situation, did not reflect "the concerns and uncertainties" expressed in the intelligence products,
- Rumsfeld's statement that Iraq operated underground
  weapons facilities that were not vulnerable to conventional
  airstrikes was "not substantiated" by available intelligence
  information.

The Senate Select Committee on Intelligence concluded in September 2008, by a bipartisan but divided vote of 10–5, that the Bush administration on many occasions misrepresented the prewar intelligence on
Iraq, and overstated the threat from Iraq, and ultimately led the country
to war under false pretenses.

In 2002 and 2003, President George W. Bush and his top lieuten-
ants told Congress and the American people many times that Saddam
Hussein had weapons of mass destruction, was acquiring more, and was
willing to use them.

By 2008, as a result of the work of the Senate Select Committee on
Intelligence and the final Duelfer Report of the Iraq Survey Group, the
American people had convincing proof of what they had already figured
out by that time: the prewar intelligence on Iraqi weapons was faulty
from the start, then the intelligence was hyped and misrepresented by
high level officials and, finally, the President and the White House made
the case for war by repeatedly presenting uncertain intelligence as settled fact when it was often unsubstantiated, contradicted, or didn't exist
at all.

It is hard to believe that George Bush was reelected President in
2004. After all, by Election Day on November 2, 2004, the American
people knew that the Bush promises about Iraq had not come true.
There were no weapons of mass destruction to justify the invasion, we
were not greeted as liberators, our occupation was difficult and deadly,
we were spending unbudgeted billions and our international stature
was tarnished.

Months and months of press disclosures about faulty, misused and
manipulated prewar intelligence had shaken public confidence in the
honesty and competence of the architects of the war. Two damaging

reports had been released: the June 2004 Senate Intelligence Committee report that the key findings of the National Intelligence Estimate on Iraqi weapons were flawed and the public White Paper had further distorted those findings, and the September 2004 Iraq Survey Group conclusions that Hussein's weapons stockpiles were eliminated by the mid 1990s and Iraq was virtually disarmed before we invaded.

Why wasn't George W. Bush held to account by the voters on November 2, 2004? In part, because it is always hard to beat incumbents, particularly in the middle of a war when brave, young Americans are in harm's way and patriotic feelings among the voters are running high.

But I believe the primary reason for George Bush's reelection is the skillful, cynical way the President and his political operatives made the 2004 election more about John Kerry's performance in the Vietnam War than George Bush's performance leading the Iraq War.

Senator Kerry was a legitimate war hero in Vietnam and certainly earned his medals for bravery. He has served his country very well in war and peace, and continues to have my respect and admiration. But in the 2004 presidential election, Kerry failed to defend himself against the spurious attacks by the Swift Boat veterans and other Bush attack dogs. American voters were left wondering: if Kerry won't vigorously defend his own honor, how do we know he will fight for us? John Kerry would have made a fine president, but instead George W. Bush was reelected.

TEN

The Bush Team Memoirs

By 2008, after a failed campaign in 2004 for the U.S. Senate, I was back home serving once again as a Montgomery County Commissioner. My focus was on balancing county budgets, managing county operations, improving local and regional transportation and expanding economic development. The failures and disappointments over Iraq were in the back of my mind—until the Bush team started publishing their memoirs. I could not believe what I was reading.

Between 2010 and 2012, five of the six major players in the Bush administration published their memoirs and wrote about their role regarding the Iraq War, Saddam Hussein and weapons of mass destruction. The memoirs of George Bush, Dick Cheney, Donald Rumsfeld, Colin Powell and Condoleezza Rice are in this group. The sixth major player, George Tenet, first published his memoir earlier, in 2007.

As a body of work, these books must be the sorriest collection of apology-free, self-serving, fact-avoiding, finger-pointing memoirs in the history of the genre, at least as practiced by alumnae of presidential administrations.

President Bush, Vice President Cheney, Secretary of Defense Rumsfeld and National Security Adviser Rice take no responsibility and issue no apologies for their failed policies in Iraq or for their misuse and distortion of intelligence that led us to war under false pretenses. Their basic attitude in their memoirs toward Iraq and the missing weapons of mass destruction is, "Isn't it a shame that the intelligence was wrong. Who knew?" There is no acknowledgment in these books that the authors had all sold the war to the American people by intentionally turning uncertain intelligence opinions about weapons of mass destruction into adamant statements of fact. It is aggravating to read these clumsy attempts to avoid blame for failed policies and to justify, and even deny, misleading the country.

The memoirs of Secretary of State Powell and CIA Director George Tenet are considerably more honest. They both express sorrow and frustration for the failures regarding Iraq, some of which were their responsibility. They accept their share of the blame. Tenet admits the war was significantly oversold to the Congress and the American people. It is true that Powell and Tenet do some finger pointing and defend their own actions, but at least they both man up.

The attempts by Bush, Cheney, Rumsfeld and Rice to rewrite history and avoid accountability for their actions directly motivated me to write this account to try to set the record straight, at least as I saw and experienced that record. Let's review the memoirs of the Bush administration leadership to search for some truth and correct some lies about Iraq.

* * *

Former President George W. Bush published his memoir *Decision Points*[1] in 2010. To Bush's credit, he did write one of the truest statements to be found in any of the memoirs:

> In retrospect, of course, we all should have pushed harder on the intelligence and revisited our assumptions.[2]

Overall, George Bush has remarkably little to say in his memoir about the controversy over the use, or misuse, of intelligence to secure the congressional authorization for war. He allots just six paragraphs to the passage of the war authorization, and three of those are devoted to identifying and quoting prominent Democrats who supported the President and voted yes. The National Intelligence Estimate on Iraqi weapons, and its impact on the debate, is described in just three sentences,[3] and the CIA White Paper is never mentioned at all.

President Bush does acknowledge that he suffered a "massive blow" to his credibility once the public perceived he had sent American troops into combat based "on intelligence that proved false." He reports "a sickening feeling" every time he thinks about it.

But George Bush dismisses as "illogical" and "dishonest" the charge that his numerous assertive statements about Iraqi weapons were far more positive than the uncertain intelligence he was receiving, thus misleading the country. His defense:

Members of the previous administration . . . and the vast majority of members of Congress had all read the same intelligence that I had and concluded Iraq had weapons of mass destruction. So had intelligence agencies around the world. Nobody was lying. We were all wrong.[4]

However, Bush is wrong when he claims that "the vast majority" of members of Congress read the same intelligence reports he read. We did not. Only eight leaders of the House and Senate and members of the two intelligence committees even had access to classified documents like the National Intelligence Estimate on Iraqi weapons. Those members were not allowed by law to share any of the classified intelligence they saw or heard with staff or other members. The "vast majority" of members of Congress had access only to the unclassified White Paper published by the CIA as a public summary of the classified intelligence. As we have seen, that public White Paper whitewashed the intelligence, taking out the caveats and reservations expressed in the uncertain judgments and rendering the findings into positive statements of fact. Most of Congress and all of the American people were intentionally misled by the White Paper, and were not provided the same intelligence that George Bush saw.

The most troubling aspect of George Bush's memoir is his frequent use of misquotes and misleading, partial quotes from the official reports of American and international weapons inspectors in an apparent attempt to suggest that those inspection reports somehow backed up his claims about Iraqi weapons of mass destruction. In fact, those reports dealt hammer blows to George Bush's claims and credibility, because they consistently reported that they were not finding any stockpiles of weapons of mass destruction in Iraq, stockpiles that President Bush and his team stated with certainty that Hussein possessed.

For example, Bush writes that Hans Blix, the chief international weapons inspector, gave the following public report to the United Nations on January 27, 2003: ". . . the Iraqi regime was defying the inspections process."[5]

But Hans Blix did *not* report to the U.N. that Iraq was defying the inspections process. His January 27, 2003 report actually said:

It would appear from our experience so far that Iraq has decided in principle to provide cooperation on process, notably access . . . Iraq has on the whole cooperated rather well with [the United Nations inspectors] in this field. The most important point to make is that access has been provided to all sites we have wanted to inspect and with one exception it has been prompt.[6]

Further, the Bush memoir never refers at all to two subsequent Blix public reports to the United Nations in which the chief weapons inspector continues to report cooperation from Iraq regarding inspections. On February 14, 2003, Blix reported:

> Since we arrived in Iraq, we have conducted more than 400 inspections covering more than 300 sites. All inspections were performed without notice, and access was almost always provided promptly.[7]

And on March 7, Blix reported:

> Inspections in Iraq resumed on the 27th of November 2002, In matters relating to process, notably prompt access to sites, we have faced relatively few difficulties ... at this juncture we are able to perform professional, no-notice inspections all over Iraq ...[8]

Two other points should be made about these three Hans Blix reports to the United Nations. First, all three reported no stockpiles of weapons or important evidence of weapons were being found in Iraq. George Bush did not mention that when he quoted, inaccurately, from the January 27 Blix report.

Secondly, all three reports were given in public session of the U.N. Security Council before the invasion of Iraq started. George Bush had an opportunity to evaluate these reports, delay the invasion and give the inspectors more time to complete their work. Instead, he chose to misquote one of the reports in his memoirs.

George Bush did the same thing in his only memoir mention of Mohamed ElBaradei, director of the International Atomic Energy Agency, who was inspecting Iraq for possible nuclear weapons. Bush quotes a late January statement by ElBaradei:

> The ball is entirely in Iraq's court ... Iraq now has to prove that it is innocent ... They need to go out of their way to prove through whatever possible means that they have no weapons of mass destruction.[9]

But here is what ElBaradei said to the Security Council on January 27 during his update:

> Over these first two months of inspection, we have made good progress in our knowledge of Iraq's nuclear capabilities, with a total of 139 inspections at some 106 locations to date . . . the Iraqi authorities have provided access to all facilities visited—including presidential compounds and private residences—without conditions and without delay . . .[10]

Mohamed ElBaradei made similar favorable statements about Iraq's cooperation with inspections in his subsequent updates to the Security Council on February 14 and March 7, and every report by the International Atomic Energy Agency inspectors stated they had found no evidence of a nuclear program in Iraq.

George Bush, as he did with the Blix reports, ignored the substantive findings of the ElBaradei reports. Instead of responding before the invasion when international inspectors could find no weapons in Iraq, Bush chose to wait until he wrote his memoir to cite some of those reports in a vain effort to suggest that the weapons inspectors were somehow backing up the Bush program in Iraq.

George Bush tried the same sleight of hand regarding the September 2004 final report of the Iraq Survey Group, sent to Iraq by the administration after the invasion to find the missing weapons of mass destruction. He quotes the head inspector Charles Duelfer as reporting: "Saddam wanted to recreate Iraq's WMD capability . . . after sanctions were removed and Iraq's economy stabilized."[11]

That is an accurate quote. But George Bush failed to include Duelfer's other findings, such as Hussein had ended his nuclear program in 1991 and the inspectors found no evidence of concerted efforts to restart the program, and Iraq destroyed its chemical weapons stockpile in 1991, and abandoned its biological weapons program in 1995 with no indications of any attempt to re-establish the program. The Duelfer Report did far more to discredit George Bush's prewar claims that it did to support him.

President Bush never leveled with the American people, either in his distorted, hyped claims about weapons of mass destruction, or in his memoir.

* * *

Former Vice President Dick Cheney published his memoir *In My Time*[12] in 2011. Parts of it dealing with Iraq and weapons of mass destruction read like a work of fiction.

Cheney quotes extensively from his own August 26, 2002 speech to the Veterans of Foreign Wars national convention in Nashville, Tennessee. The stated purpose of the speech was to convince the veterans, and colleagues in the White House, that there was no sense in installing an "aggressive" inspection regime in Iraq since that might create a source of "false comfort," as we would think we were doing "something significant" about Hussein when we were not. Cheney quotes 200 of his own words from the speech to describe how Hussein could not be trusted and could fool the inspectors while rearming, and how we could help liberate Iraq.

But there is no mention in the former Vice President's memoir of the 34 words he also uttered in Nashville that made that speech so infamous:

> Simply stated, there is no doubt that Saddam Hussein now has weapons of mass destruction. There is no doubt he is amassing them to use against our friends, against our allies, and against us.[13]

The only thing people remember about Dick Cheney's August 26, 2002 speech to the Veterans of Foreign Wars is that it was the opening salvo of the Bush administration's public campaign to convince America that Saddam Hussein had weapons of mass destruction and was willing to use them. Back then, Dick Cheney was proud to be leading the charge against Hussein's weapons. But now, you would never know that from the Cheney memoir.

After misleadingly quoting himself, Cheney goes on to misleadingly quote from the October 1, 2002 National Intelligence Estimate on Iraqi weapons, and from the Blix report of January 27, 2003 to the United Nations. Just as we saw in President Bush's memoir, Vice President Cheney seems intent on using partial quotes from official reports to bolster his prewar statements and actions, when those reports actually shred the credibility of his prewar claims.

Cheney cites the 2002 National Intelligence Estimate as containing judgments that were "of a piece" with the briefings he had been receiving. He then quotes from the Estimate:

> Iraq has continued its weapons of mass destruction programs in defiance of U.N. resolutions and restrictions.[14]

But he omits from the quotation the important qualifier "we judge that" which actually proceeded those words in the Estimate. We have seen in the 2007 National Intelligence Estimate regarding Iraq's prospects for stability, discussed in Chapter 2, how qualifiers like "we judge" and "we assess" are intentionally used by the Intelligence Community to signify they are expressing an analytic judgment, not a fact or a proof, and to indicate they do not have evidence that shows something to be a fact. The Vice President surely knows that, and his omission of the critical qualifier also surely was intentional. In fact, Cheney's omission of the qualifier is identical to the numerous omissions of caveats and reservations in the public White Paper of October 4, 2002, which so badly misled the country. The Vice President does not want to admit to this day that he took uncertain intelligence opinions and turned them into positive statements of fact.

The Cheney memoir discusses at some length the January 27, 2003 Blix report[15] to the United Nations, to show how untrustworthy Saddam Hussein was and how his declarations about weapons were incomplete. But, just like President Bush, Cheney fails to mention the central findings of the January 27, February 14 and March 7 Blix reports to the Security Council: there were no stockpiles of weapons of mass destruction in Iraq, and no evidence that stockpiles had existed since the mid-1990s. Of course, we all know the United Nations weapons inspectors declared that those stockpiles didn't exist, and we know now those inspectors were correct, but Dick Cheney can't even bring himself to admit that in his memoir.

Dick Cheney is proud of his role as the tough guy of the Bush administration, the guy who asked the hard questions about terrorism and weapons, and demanded more and better information from the experts. Here he is playing up his role as chief inquisitor during the run up to war in Iraq:

> I asked tough questions, no doubt about that. And I asked a lot of them. I pushed hard to get information that would help us develop policies that would ensure America wasn't attacked again. If I had not been as thorough as I was, I would not have been fulfilling my obligations and responsibilities as a senior official. In light of subsequent revelations, such as the mistakes in the 2002 National Intelligence Estimate on Iraqi WMD, I wish I'd been tougher.[16]

This is an audacious bit of bluster. Cheney is suggesting that he might have fixed the intelligence "mistakes" in the 2002 Estimate had he only asked more questions, been even tougher. We now know that the classified intelligence about Iraq was flawed, but we also know it was full of caveats and doubts. Dick Cheney and other senior officials deleted the doubts when they made their case for war. Cheney himself was the first administration leader to baldly proclaim that Iraq had such weapons when he said on August 26, 2002:

> Simply stated, there is no doubt that Saddam Hussein now has weapons of mass destruction.[17]

Cheney's adamant statement was made five weeks before the National Intelligence Estimate was circulated on October 1, and about two weeks before the Estimate was even *ordered* by George Tenet. Cheney had made up his mind about Saddam Hussein and his weapons long before he read any "mistakes" in the Estimate. His tough questioning of intelligence analysts should have laid bare for him their uncertainties and doubts about the intelligence on Iraqi weapons. Instead, Cheney and his colleagues distorted that intelligence to fit their preconceived notions and make their case for war.

The Cheney memoir hits rock bottom on the subject of the infamous sixteen words in the President's 2003 State of the Union speech, "The British government has learned that Saddam Hussein recently sought significant quantities of uranium from Africa." The former Vice President argues that those words are actually true and the resulting controversy was a "ridiculous situation" which should not have led to several White House apologies. Despite findings by the International Atomic Energy Agency that the Niger-Iraq story was false and based on forgeries, despite a public apology from National Security Adviser Condoleezza Rice for the President's use of the phrase, despite public acknowledgments of blame from CIA Director George Tenet and Deputy National Security Adviser Steve Hadley, Dick Cheney is still beating the drum and defending the phrase because, he says, it is true. Here is what he wrote about the controversy:

> An apology would only fan the flames, and why apologize when the British had, in fact, reported that Iraq had sought a significant amount of uranium in Africa? *The sixteen words were true* [emphasis in the original].[18]

Talk about a "ridiculous situation." Dick Cheney wants us to believe that the Bush claim about Iraq and Niger was true and deserves no apology from the administration, even though the claim was thoroughly debunked by American and international intelligence and nuclear experts. Further, he offers no acknowledgment that the bogus claim was a significant part of the President's false assertion that Hussein was reconstituting a nuclear weapons program. Dick Cheney remains unashamed and unrepentant.

* * *

Former Secretary of Defense Donald Rumsfeld published his memoir *Known and Unknown*[19] in 2011. Rumsfeld is as unrepentant in his book as Dick Cheney, and his statements about Iraq are even more false.

To give the Secretary his due, he did understand before the war that the failure to find weapons of mass destruction in Iraq would be a serious matter. He quotes from his memo about possible problems that he submitted to President Bush and the members of the National Security Council in the autumn of 2002: "US could fail to find WMD on the ground in Iraq and be unpersuasive to the world."[20]

Rumsfeld writes in his book: "I understood that if WMD were not found, the administration's credibility would be undermined."[21]

He certainly got that right.

Rumsfeld also provides a vigorous defense of the Bush administration's honesty about weapons of mass destruction in Iraq. He contends:

> Powell was not duped or misled by anybody, nor did he lie about Saddam's suspected WMD stockpiles. The President did not lie. The Vice President did not lie. Tenet did not lie. Rice did not lie. I did not lie. The Congress did not lie. The far less dramatic truth is that we were wrong.[22]

However, Rumsfeld does not acknowledge that the administration in their private briefings, public papers and public statements removed all the caveats and reservations from the classified intelligence about Iraqi weapons. He does not discuss how the country was misled when the administration changed uncertain intelligence opinion into statements of fact. But he does want us to know that they did not lie.

Rumsfeld's memoir is filled with false and misleading statements about Iraq.

Rumsfeld writes a long passage about the difficulties intelligence agencies face in both uncovering the truth about hostile regimes and then communicating that information effectively to senior policy makers, then sums up the classified intelligence he was receiving that he used to make the case for war:

What was unique about Iraq was that the intelligence community reported near total confidence in their conclusions. Their assessments appeared to be unusually consistent.[23]

But we have seen that the 2002 National Intelligence Estimate on Iraqi weapons was replete with reservations and caveats. Four intelligence agencies dissented in the written report to portions of the findings. The findings themselves did not accurately reflect the underlying intelligence in the same document. Rumsfeld's own Defense Intelligence Agency stated in September 2002 there was "no reliable information" on Iraq's chemical warfare program or stockpiles. The classified intelligence Rumsfeld was seeing in the fall of 2002 was not expressed in "near total confidence" and was not "unusually consistent."

The former Defense Secretary is quick to blame the intelligence analysts for his mistakes. He writes:

In the run-up to the war in Iraq, we heard a great deal about what our intelligence community knew or thought they knew, but not enough about what they knew they didn't know.[24]

As we have seen, this charge simply isn't true. The intelligence analysts expressed numerous reservations about what they didn't know. The problem was that Donald Rumsfeld and his senior colleagues were not listening.

The Rumsfeld memoir's only mention of chief U.N. weapons inspector Hans Blix is a quote from Blix's January 27, 2003 report to the Security Council that comments on Hussein's lack of "genuine acceptance" of his obligations to disarm.[25] But there is no mention that the three reports filed by Blix on January 27, February 14 and March 7 reported the inability of the inspectors to find any stockpiles of weapons of mass destruction or evidence of stockpiles.

Similarly, Rumsfeld summarizes the final Duelfer Report of the Iraq Survey Group, the American weapons inspectors sent to Iraq to find the weapons, as if the report's main conclusion was that Hussein wanted to rearm if international sanctions were ever lifted.[26] There is no mention by Rumsfeld that the fundamental and most significant conclusion of the Duelfer Report was that Hussein had been disarmed by existing sanctions since the mid-1990s.

Like George Bush and Dick Cheney, Donald Rumsfeld refers in his memoirs to international and American inspection reports as if they bolster the Bush administration's credibility, instead of shredding it.

Rumsfeld believes the administration made a "substantial" error in judgment by not contesting more vigorously the critics who built "a deceitful narrative" about the administration's rationale for going to war. He writes:

> The Bush administration should have pointed out that, while Saddam Hussein did not have WMD stockpiles, he did in fact maintain dual-use facilities that could produce chemical and biological weapons . . . those facilities were effectively as dangerous as stockpiles.[27]

It is absurd to claim that dual-use facilities, which at the time of the invasion were not producing weapons of mass destruction due to the impact of sanctions and the presence of inspectors, were "effectively as dangerous as stockpiles" of such weapons. Rumsfeld won't admit to his readers that the Bush rationale for war was false: there were no weapons stockpiles.

Finally, Rumsfeld rejects any notion that the Bush administration misled the country into war in Iraq under false pretenses. Regarding the accuracy of his statements about Iraq and weapons of mass destruction, Rumsfeld wrote:

> While I made a few misstatements . . . they were not common and certainly not characteristic. Other senior administration officials also did a reasonably good job of representing the intelligence community's assessments accurately in their public comments about Iraqi WMD, despite some occasionally imperfect formulations.[28]

Donald Rumsfeld has got to be kidding. He cannot be serious. He wants us to believe that he and the administration did "a reasonably good job of representing the intelligence community's assessments accurately." That claim is stunning, arrogant. and false.

*　*　*

Former National Intelligence Adviser Condoleezza Rice published her memoir *No Higher Honor*[29] in 2011. She is more willing to acknowledge in her memoir the administration's errors than George Bush, Dick Cheney or Donald Rumsfeld. But she makes the same misguided effort as her colleagues to distort or even ignore the prewar reports of the international inspectors that should have given the Bush administration pause before starting the invasion. Rice also argues, incorrectly, that the United States had no options but to invade Iraq in the spring of 2003.

Rice plays the same trick deployed by Dick Cheney in his memoir of dropping the important qualifying phrase "we judge that" when she quotes from the National Intelligence Estimate regarding Iraq's continuing weapons programs.[30] Her failure to include that key caveat continues the efforts of the Bush administration to change uncertain intelligence assessments into positive statements of fact, as we saw in the public White Paper on Iraqi weapons that Rice never mentions in her book.

Condoleezza Rice continues the Bush mantra that nobody in the administration meant to mislead the country, despite that misleading White Paper. She writes about the controversy surrounding the United Nations presentation by Secretary of State Colin Powell:

> . . . Colin didn't seek to deceive anyone. None of us did. In retrospect, I wish I'd said over and over again that intelligence always carries uncertainties; that is the nature of the beast.[31]

Of course, the great failure of the Bush administration, and Condoleezza Rice, was not that they all were silent about the uncertainties of intelligence. Rather, it was their intentional effort to turn uncertain intelligence into statements of fact that the intelligence did not fully support. And, as we have seen, they continue this great failure in their memoirs.

The former National Security Adviser also distorts the findings of the international inspectors. She describes as "telling" the January 27, 2003 report to the United Nations Security Council by chief international inspector Hans Blix that Hussein had not yet accepted his obligations to disarm, as if this supported the Bush rush to war. She then adds dismissively: "The second [Blix] report, on February 14, was more ambiguous."[32]

More ambiguous? The February 14 Blix report stated that the U.N. inspectors had conducted 400 inspections, without notice to the Iraqis, and Iraq had decided in principle to cooperate and provide access to all sites. Most importantly, Blix reported that no weapons of mass destruction had been found. There were few problems with the inspections and no weapons were found. What was ambiguous about that report?

What about the final prewar Blix report, on March 7, that confirmed that his team was conducting "professional, no-notice inspections all over Iraq" and had still not found evidence of illegal weapons or activities? Condoleezza Rice does not mention these findings at all.

But Rice does mention that she simply didn't believe the head of the International Atomic Energy Agency, Mohamed ElBaradei, despite their "reasonably good relationship," when he told her personally that Saddam Hussein had not reconstituted his nuclear program.[33] She does not mention ElBaradei's three prewar reports to the Security Council that his inspectors had not found nuclear weapons or nuclear program activities in Iraq.

Despite the prewar inability of the international inspectors and nuclear experts to find illegal weapons or weapons programs in Iraq, despite the unfettered access to possible weapons sites reported by the inspectors, Rice nevertheless felt we had to go to war. She wrote:

> By the beginning of 2003, I was convinced that we would have to use military force . . . the fact is, we invaded Iraq because we believed we had run out of options. The sanctions were not working, the inspections were unsatisfactory, and we could not get Saddam to leave by other means.[34]

But according to the multiple reports from the international inspectors, the sanctions were working and the inspections were satisfactory. They were reporting, before the war started, that Saddam Hussein had no weapons of mass destruction.

Condoleezza Rice did have other options in the spring of 2003. She could have advised the President to give the international inspectors the extra time they were requesting to complete their assignment in Iraq. If Hussein truly had no weapons, then the Bush administration had lost its primary rationale for war. Presumably, the invasion would then have not been necessary.

Condoleezza Rice was not out of options. She was out of good ideas and common sense, and did not have the courage to stand up to the President and his rush to war.

* * *

Former Secretary of State Colin Powell published his memoir *It Worked For Me: In Life and Leadership*[35] in 2012. He devoted one full chapter, entitled "February 5, 2003: The United Nations" to the Iraq controversy, noting he had never before written his account of his U.N. speech and probably won't write another. More than anything, Powell seems deeply saddened by the experience.

Powell describes his U.N. speech as "one of my most momentous failures" and "a blot on my record." He admits there is nothing he can do about it, and writes: "What's done is done. It's over. I have to live with it."[36]

Powell writes that the National Intelligence Estimate on Iraqi weapons was "mostly circumstantial and inferential," and "persuasive."[37] He considers the intelligence community's failures in analysis and judgment "one of the worst intelligence failures in U.S. history."[38]

In one of the most honest and noteworthy assertions in all of the memoirs of the Bush team, Powell writes: "If we had known there was no WMDs, there would have been no war."[39]

After recounting his strenuous efforts to scrutinize the CIA's intelligence, Powell admits he is still "annoyed" by the failures that led to his flawed presentation to the United Nations. He writes:

> Yes, I get mad when bloggers accuse me of lying—of knowing the information was false. I didn't. And yes, a blot, a failure, will always be attached to me and my UN presentation. But I am mad mostly at myself for not having smelled the problem. My instincts failed me.[40]

Colin Powell blew it on February 5, 2003 in New York, and he knows it. In his memoir, he is willing to admit his failure and own up to his responsibility. It still amazes me that such an experienced and capable man as Colin Powell was so badly fooled by the hyped, inaccurate intelligence regarding Iraq, particularly in light of his inside access and the expressed doubts of the State Department's intelligence branch that reported directly to him. But Colin Powell was the best member of the Bush team, and I respect his willingness to face the truth and shoulder some blame.

* * *

Former CIA Director George Tenet published his memoir *At the Center of the Storm*[41] in 2008. It is by far the most informative and candid of all the memoirs written by the Bush team. Tenet writes openly about the intelligence failures at the CIA and does not deny his own failings. He is particularly honest about how the CIA and the Bush administration in their private briefings, public papers and public statements removed the reservations from the underlying intelligence reports and thus changed uncertain opinion into misleading statements of fact. Tenet's candor in his memoir is remarkable.

Tenet admits that he and his analysts made a lot of mistakes. He writes:

Yes, we at CIA had been wrong in believing that Saddam had weapons of mass destruction . . . the core of our judgments on Iraq's WMD programs turned out to be wrong.[42]

But Tenet insists that his motivation and integrity were sound:

Never did I give policy makers information that I knew to be bad. We said what we said about WMD because we believed it.[43]

Tenet takes the blame for the infamous sixteen words about Iraq looking for uranium in Niger that appeared in the President's 2003 State of the Union speech, although plenty of others in the White House share that blame. He writes:

Obviously, the process for vetting the speech at the Agency had broken down. We had warned the White House about the lack of reliability of the assertion when we had gotten them to remove similar language from the president's October Cincinnati speech, and we should have gotten that language out of the State of the Union as well. It was because of my failure to fully study the speech myself that I took responsibility.[44]

While Tenet gripes about the "garbage" in a White House memo that had to be removed to prepare the Powell U.N. speech, he shoulders his share of the responsibility for the intelligence failures in that presentation to the Security Council:

Despite our efforts, a lot of flawed information still made its way into the speech. No one involved regrets that more than I do . . . it was a great presentation, but unfortunately the substance didn't hold up.[45]

Tenet devotes considerable attention to the classified National Intelligence Estimate on Iraqi weapons and the public White Paper that the CIA was responsible for preparing. He is unflinching in his acknowledgment not only of mistakes in the underlying intelligence, but also of the "major error"[46] of taking the uncertainties out of the public discussion of the classified intelligence.

Tenet admits that "flawed analysis" was compiled in the Estimate. But he adds:

> It would have been helpful to have clarified [in the Estimate] that the use of the words "we judge" and "we assess" meant we were making analytical judgments, not stating facts.[47]

In defending the National Intelligence Estimate, Tenet writes at great length about the unusual steps that were taken in the classified document to include and even highlight the caveats, reservations and outright dissents that were part of the final product. In an extraordinary passage, Tenet writes:

> The dissenting views were clearly and extensively laid out in the [Estimate] . . . the dissenting opinions are not relegated to footnotes and, indeed, often appear in boxes with special colored backgrounds to make them stand out. These make up an unprecedented sixteen pages of the ninety page National Intelligence Estimate . . . the phrase "we do not know" appears some thirty times across ninety pages. The words "we know" appear in only three instances.[48]

George Tenet wants us to know that the intelligence analysts had many reservations about Iraqi weapons that they freely expressed in the classified document. But he states the compilers of the Estimate made some fundamental mistakes:

> Unfortunately, we were not as cautious in the "Key Judgments", a five page summary at the front of the document. The Key Judgments is written with language that, especially on chemical and biological weapons, is too assertive and conveys an air of certainty that does not exist in the rest of the [Estimate] . . . the chemical and biological judgments are stated as facts. They were *not* facts [emphasis in the original] and should not have been so characterized.[49]

After pointing out the errors and the distortions in the Estimate, Tenet turns his attention to the White Paper that he released publicly three days after the classified Estimate was produced. Calling the White

Paper a "major error," Tenet describes the mistakes in its preparation as a summary of the Estimate:

> Out went the "we's", and what remained were bolder assertions, such as "Saddam has." The classified NIE already had too few cautionary "we judge's" in the Key Judgment section. Now, with a few strokes of a keyboard, the unclassified paper—the only one most Americans would ever see—came out sounding far too assertive.[50]

This is the only admission I can find in the public record by any of the senior members of the Bush administration that their primary public document presenting their case for war in Iraq, the October 4, 2002 CIA White Paper, was a "major error" and was "far too assertive" in its claims about Hussein's weapons of mass destruction.

In the midst of this admirable candor in his memoir, I took notice of Tenet's comments about his need to miss a meeting of the Senate Select Committee on Intelligence on the morning of October 2, 2002 that was scheduled on short notice to discuss the contents of the Estimate delivered the day before:

> I was required to be at the White House at the same time, ironically, to meet with other congressional leaders.[51]

Unless the actual congressional leadership also showed up at the White House that morning without my knowledge, the meeting Tenet "was required" to attend was the briefing that he and Condoleezza Rice gave to my small group of congressmen that I discuss earlier in this book. While I cannot remember all of the attendees at that meeting, I am positive that there wasn't a "congressional leader" in sight. We were just a bunch of House backbenchers trying to learn what was going on in Iraq, without the benefit of access to the classified intelligence.

I was also amused to read Tenet's statement that the briefings he provided for almost every member of Congress "were fairly strident."[52] Given the problems that arose that morning at the meeting of the Senate Intelligence Committee, the public interest would have been better served if Tenet had answered the senators' questions instead of misleading us with his "strident" briefing.

Tenet writes how Deputy CIA Director John McLaughlin appeared before the October 2 closed Senate committee hearing in Tenet's stead, and testified that the likelihood of Saddam's initiating a terrorist attack in the foreseeable future was, in the CIA's judgment, "low", but if Hussein felt cornered, the chances of his using his weapons of mass destruction were "pretty high."[53] Democrats on the committee asked that this testimony be declassified and cleared for public release, and McLaughlin sent the requested letter to the committee on Tenet's behalf. When the testimony became public, the media wrote a flurry of stories suggesting the CIA's testimony contradicted President Bush's assertion that Iraq posed an imminent threat.

Tenet agreed to Condoleezza Rice's "frantic" request to speak to the *New York Times* to tamp down the controversy, and Tenet told the *Times* reporter, "There was no inconsistency in the views in the letter and those of the president."[54] This was the statement that caused me to discount the press reports about a discrepancy between the CIA and the White House the week of the House vote on the war resolution.

Tenet writes about this controversy:

In retrospect, I shouldn't have talked to the *New York Times* reporter at Condi's request. By making public comments in the middle of a contentious political debate, I gave the impression that I was becoming a partisan player.[55]

Of course, it was Tenet's deputy who created the "contentious political debate" in the first place by suggesting that the CIA had a different view from the President regarding the imminent threat posed by Saddam Hussein.

Tenet recounts how Condoleezza Rice asked the CIA in writing on July 17, 2003, after four months of American occupation of Iraq had uncovered no weapons of mass destruction, to declassify the Key Judgments and some other paragraphs from the National Intelligence Estimate on Iraqi weapons. The CIA complied, and the following day two senior White House officials held the famous background briefing for the press in which the declassified material was presented. Tenet believes the briefing was designed to absolve the White House of any blame for misleading the country about Hussein's weapons. Tenet writes about the White House briefers:

It was not clear to me then, nor is it clear now, whether they even understood the facts, but it was clear that the entire briefing was intended to convince the press corps that the White

House staff was an innocent victim of bad work by the intelligence community.[56]

If Tenet is correct, and I believe he is, that the White House declassified the Estimate and held the briefing on July 18 in the hopes of creating good publicity for itself, then it may be the biggest and loudest backfire in the history of White House manipulation of the news. The irony is that it was instantly apparent to the press corps, as soon as they read the Key Judgments and other sections of the Estimate, that the Bush team had been exaggerating the intelligence from the beginning. The reporters saw that the Estimate was full of caveats, reservations and dissents, none of which had been included or acknowledged in the public statements and public documents put out by the administration. The partial declassification and release of the Estimate by the White House on July 18, 2003 was the event that forever shredded George Bush's credibility with the American people.

The most fascinating entry in George Tenet's memoir is his proposal of what the National Intelligence Estimate *should* have said, given what the CIA actually knew on October 1, 2002, if the analysis had been properly done. He suggests the following:

> We judge that Saddam continues his efforts to rebuild weapons programs, that, once sanctions are lifted, he probably will confront the United States with chemical, biological and nuclear weapons within a matter of months and years. Today, while we have little direct evidence of weapons stockpiles, Saddam has the ability to quickly surge to produce chemical and biological weapons and he has the means to deliver them.[57]

We know today that even these "more accurate and nuanced findings," as Tenet describes them, are still fundamentally inaccurate. Saddam Hussein's weapons programs actually ended in the mid 1990's. He couldn't "quickly surge" or do anything "within a matter of months or years," particularly if international sanctions remained in place.

But if the Estimate had indeed been written as George Tenet suggests it should have been in light of what the CIA knew in October 2002, and if the public knew this Key Judgment, I do not believe Congress would have authorized war. We would have called for renewed inspections, and pushed for tougher sanctions, but we would not have voted to invade Iraq.

I wish the CIA had done its job better. George Tenet should have been more a defender of the Iraq intelligence and less an advocate of the President's Iraq war policy. Tenet's honesty in his memoir about the flawed intelligence and distorted use of that intelligence does not absolve him of responsibility for his original misleading statements and documents, but his candor is refreshing. In fact, his assumption of blame and responsibility is impressive, and very uncommon in Washington, D.C.

George Tenet's memoir is an important work that will help Americans and historians better understand what went wrong regarding the intelligence on Iraq. Similarly, Colin Powell's recollection about his U.N. presentation is a useful history and a powerful statement of personal regret.

The other memoirs by George Bush, Dick Cheney, Donald Rumsfeld and Condoleezza Rice are misleading in their comments about Iraq. They fail to come clean about their false statements before the war about Saddam's weapons of mass destruction. Additionally, they write deceptive and half-true descriptions about their prewar claims, and distort and misquote the official reports as if the expert findings validated the Bush officials instead of discrediting them.

In their memoirs, George Bush, Dick Cheney, Donald Rumsfeld and Condoleezza Rice are still trying to con us.

ELEVEN

Disclose the Intelligence

*Intelligence doesn't necessarily mean something is true. It's just—
it's intelligence. You know, it's your best estimate of the situation. It
doesn't mean it's a fact. I mean, that's not what intelligence is.*[1]

General Richard B. Myers
Chairman, Joint Chiefs of Staff
June 24, 2003

It is my contention that the United States Congress would not have
authorized military action in Iraq in October 2002 if every member
of Congress and their constituents had the opportunity to review the
classified intelligence findings on Iraqi weapons of mass destruction
before the congressional vote. The reservations, caveats and dissents
in that intelligence, particularly in the National Intelligence Estimate
of October 1 on Iraqi weapons, would have raised far too many doubts
about the adamant statements of fact coming from President Bush and
his top advisers. Congress and the public would have questioned how
the President could be so certain about Saddam Hussein's weapons
when the intelligence was so uncertain. I believe a majority of Congress
would have demanded a resumption of intrusive, unfettered inspections to determine the truth in Iraq, before considering any authorization of war.

It is my recommendation that the intelligence laws of the United
States be amended now to require the prior public disclosure of classified

intelligence findings whenever a president asks Congress to preemptively declare war or authorize the use of military force based on such intelligence, with appropriate protections to safeguard the sources of the intelligence and the methods of its collection.

Make no mistake. Presidents will be faced in this age of rogue states and faceless terrorists with intelligence reports of grave and imminent threats to the United States. Some of those threats may be large enough to require a military response greater than the generally accepted powers of the President to unilaterally order brief military strikes under the Constitution's commander-in-chief clause. The President may seek a congressional military authorization to bolster his authority and pull the country together in a time of peril. The President will surely seek prior congressional authority to declare war or to undertake major military operations such as invasion of another country.

If the President is required to disclose to the public the key judgments of the classified intelligence on which he is basing his call for congressional support for preemptive military action, then those findings will either make his case for him by their validity, or deny him support by failing to pass muster in the light of day. Either way, the country will be better off. Another foreign policy debacle like Iraq may be averted.

The lesson of Iraq is to disclose the intelligence before seeking congressional authority for preemptive use of American military power.

Preemptive use of military force is something new in American history. Generally, American armed forces are used in response to attack, in retaliation for provocations or under binding treaty obligations. Usually, the president cites some prior attack on Americans or American interests to trigger his call for a declaration of war by Congress, or to justify the retaliatory action he is taking under his constitutional powers as commander-in-chief.

According to a 2001 legal opinion from the Office of Legal Counsel in the U.S. Department of Justice regarding the President's war-making powers,[2] Congress has declared war just five times: the War of 1812, the Mexican-American War, the Spanish-American War, World War I and World War II. All of those declarations occurred after hostile acts or provocations by others or under treaty obligations.

According to the Legal Counsel, Congress authorized thirteen military engagements throughout our history without a formal declaration of war, including the Vietnam War, the Persian Gulf War in 1991, the war in Afghanistan in 2001, and the Iraq War in 2002.

Seven military engagements have been authorized in modern times by resolution of the United Nations Security Council, with American involvement subsequently funded by Congress, including the Korean War, the Bosnian war in 1992, and the 2011 intervention in Libya.

Finally, on at least 125 additional occasions, presidents have used military force overseas under their constitutional power as Commander in Chief without the prior express authorization of Congress. Hostile foreign provocations ranging from serious to slight generally preceded these military actions.

But never before in American history have we started a preemptive war against another nation.

An April 2003 Congressional Research Service report to Congress concluded that the United States had never engaged in a preemptive military attack against another nation. The report defined preemptive use of force as:

> The taking of military action by the United States against another nation so as to prevent or mitigate a presumed military attack or use of force by that nation against the United States.[3]

Similarly, no president had announced a formal doctrine of preemptive use of American military power until George W. Bush in 2002.

At a graduation speech at the United States Military Academy at West Point on June 1, 2002, President Bush declared:

> We cannot defend America and our friends by hoping for the best. We cannot put our faith in the word of tyrants . . . if we wait for threats to fully materialize, we will have waited too long . . . we must take the battle to the enemy, disrupt his plans, and confront the worst threats before they emerge . . .
>
> Our security will require transforming the military you will lead—a military that must be ready to strike at a moment's notice in any dark corner of the world. And our security will require all Americans to be forward-looking and resolute, to be ready for preemptive action when necessary to defend our liberty and to defend our lives.[4]

The Bush Doctrine of Preemption appeared in the National Security Strategy of the United States, published on September 17, 2002 by the Bush administration. The document provided:

The security environment confronting the United States today is radically different from what we have faced before . . . The greater the threat, the greater is the risk of inaction—and the more compelling the case for taking anticipatory action to defend ourselves . . .

To forestall or prevent such hostile acts by our adversaries, the United States will, if necessary, act preemptively in exercising our inherent right of self-defense.[5]

I agree with President Bush on the necessity for the doctrine of preemption as part of our national military strategy. The attacks of 9/11, the proliferation of weapons of mass destruction around the world, and the threats posed by terrorists and rogue nations should teach us that we might not want to wait to be attacked first before we act to defend ourselves.

But if we are going to contemplate congressional authorization of preemptive war in the future, surely we must have accurate and timely intelligence findings on which to rely. The popularly named WMD Commission, appointed post-invasion by President Bush, reported on March 31, 2005 that the intelligence community was wrong in almost all prewar judgments about Iraq's weapons.[6] Unfortunately, the commission was not mandated to investigate how policymakers had used, or misused, that intelligence.

As we bemoan the manipulation, exaggeration and outright lies by Bush administration figures regarding the intelligence about Iraq, we cannot lose sight of the fact that much of the underlying intelligence was indeed wrong. We must have intelligence that is accurate and not manipulated. We cannot afford to repeat the intelligence failures of Iraq in an age when preemptive use of force may be necessary. The best way to guarantee the necessary accuracy and transparency is to disclose the intelligence to public and congressional scrutiny when Congress is contemplating the authorization of preemptive war.

It is important to remember that Congress has no independent power under the law to gather national or foreign intelligence. Congress must rely entirely on the executive branch to gather, analyze and provide the intelligence information that legislators need to authorize and review national security policy and programs.

A review of the recent history of the use of intelligence, and the laws that authorize intelligence analysis and operations, gives needed perspective to the congressional oversight and executive accountability we should be seeking.

Dr. Mark Lowenthal, in his excellent 2012 book *Intelligence: From Secrets to Policy,*[7] argues that a strict dividing line must exist between intelligence and policy. Government is run by the policymakers, and intelligence has a separate support role that should never cross over into the advocacy of policy choices.[8]

Intelligence agencies exist to help the nation avoid strategic surprise in foreign and military affairs. The intelligence community provides long-term expertise and support to the policy process, and maintains the secrecy of information, national needs and collection methods.[9]

But intelligence weaknesses regularly appear. Some analysis ends up being not much better than the conventional wisdom on the subject at hand. Some analysis becomes so dependent on technology and data that it can miss the intangibles and the human element that may determine the importance or the success of the issue being evaluated. And the natural assumption that others will act like you, called mirror imaging, can cause analysts to discount or even ignore the possibilities of a random, irrational actor transforming the situation under study.[10]

Dr. Lowenthal believes the most important weakness of intelligence is the freedom that policymakers have to reject or ignore the findings.[11] I would respectfully add one more to his list of weaknesses: the freedom policymakers have to distort, exaggerate and lie about the intelligence, as we saw from the Bush administration regarding Iraq.

This weakness will last as long as we insist on classifying and thus keeping out of the public eye the critical findings and key judgments of the intelligence community that are used by policymakers to go to war.

The culture of secrecy in American intelligence comes from the nation's laws and executive directives, as well as decades of practice and procedure in the field. The National Security Act of 1947,[12] which gave legal status and structure to the modern intelligence community, authorizes secrecy and classification of information throughout its many sections.

The original 1947 Act specifically states the Director of Central Intelligence "shall be responsible for protecting intelligence sources and methods from unauthorized disclosure."[13]

The National Security Council created by the 1947 Act issued Intelligence Directive Number 11 on January 6, 1950, which stated each executive department "shall take steps" to prevent unauthorized disclosure of U.S. intelligence sources and methods, and the Director of Central Intelligence "will be guided" so that covert intelligence only goes to those agencies whose official duties require such knowledge.

Intelligence Directive Number 11 also contained the slightly paranoid demand: "No reference will be made to this agency [the CIA] whatsoever unless it is unavoidable, of course."[14]

Once Congress created the modern intelligence structure by law, it retained the right and the obligation to conduct oversight review of the performance of the intelligence community, no matter how much secrecy the intelligence professionals put into place.

The power of Congress to conduct oversight of the executive branch is established in the Necessary and Proper Clause of the U.S. Constitution, which provides that:

> Congress shall have the power . . . [T]o make all laws which are necessary and proper for carrying into execution the foregoing powers . . .

The courts have ruled the Necessary and Proper Clause grants the power to Congress to require reports from the executive on any subject that can be legislated.

Certainly, the most fundamental and far-reaching congressional oversight power is budgetary, the "power of the purse." The Constitution proclaims: "No money shall be drawn from the Treasury, but in consequence of Appropriations made by Law."

No Chief Executive can spend any money on intelligence activities unless Congress appropriates the funding first.

Other congressional oversight powers include conducting hearings to collect information and quiz officials, approving nominations of intelligence leaders, imposing reporting requirements, conducting investigations and issuing congressional reports.

The core congressional oversight issue is whether the intelligence community is properly carrying out its functions in four areas:

1. responding to policymakers' needs for accurate and timely intelligence,
2. asking the right questions to produce useful intelligence,
3. being rigorous in its analysis of the raw intelligence it collects,
4. maintaining the right operational capabilities to collect needed intelligence and conduct successful covert activities.[15]

During the Cold War, from the founding of the modern intelligence community after World War II until the Watergate revelations of CIA spying on American citizens, illegal wiretapping and other abuses, Congress provided little oversight of intelligence operations and demanded little accountability from the agencies. The Watergate Scandal, the loss of the Vietnam War and the CIA misconduct greatly undermined public faith in government in the early 1970s, and spurred calls for government reform and changes to the military and the intelligence community.[16]

Congressional oversight of the intelligence community increased dramatically after 1975 in response to the abuses and failures of that decade, and the congressional intelligence committees were established as a result. By 2002 Congress also became an independent intelligence consumer, directly ordering national intelligence estimates from time to time, such as the Estimate that October on Iraqi weapons requested by several Senators.

But even without much congressional attention, intelligence lapses during the Cold War were sometimes met with harsh reaction from the executive branch. Dr. Lowenthal describes how the failures of the military and the CIA regarding the botched 1961 invasion of the Bay of Pigs in Cuba was a huge embarrassment for the Kennedy administration, and led to the forced resignations of the CIA Director Allen Dulles and all of the members of the Joint Chiefs of Staff.[17] I believe this Kennedy-era accountability stands in stark contrast to President Bush's 2004 award to retired CIA Director George Tenet of the Presidential Medal of Freedom, even after the numerous failures of the Central Intelligence Agency regarding Iraqi weapons of mass destruction.

Congress and the executive branch have come to accept that the intelligence community needs to shed some of its secretive ways and communicate more openly and effectively within itself and with its customers, including the President, Congress and the public.

The Intelligence Reform and Terrorism Prevention Act of 2004,[18] the first major amendment to the National Security Act of 1947, reorganized the intelligence community, created the Director of National Intelligence, established the "Information Sharing Environment" and told the new Director "to ensure maximum availability of and access to intelligence information."

The Director of National Intelligence responded in October 2005 with a new strategy based on "need-to-share" information, rather than the traditional need-to-know approach. The policy stated:

The Deputy Director of National Intelligence for Customer Outcomes will oversee the development of plans to provide maximum access to intelligence information among intelligence community customers, consistent with applicable laws and the protection of civil liberties and privacy.[19]

This new awareness by the intelligence professionals of the need to share information with their "customers" is admirable, but is hampered by existing laws that limit significantly the ability of Congress to conduct oversight of and require accountability from the intelligence community. It is time for Congress to demand more transparency for the nation's intelligence and its use.

The National Security Act of 1947, 50 U.S.C. 401-442, as amended, provides the framework for congressional oversight of intelligence:

1. Section 413a(1) states the President "shall insure" that the congressional intelligence committees are kept "fully and currently informed" of U.S. intelligence activities, including any "significant anticipated intelligence activity."
2. Section 413b(b)(1) states the Director of National Intelligence and the heads of all the intelligence agencies, ". . . with due regard for the protection from unauthorized disclosure of classified information relating to sensitive intelligence sources and methods," shall keep the congressional intelligence committees "fully and currently informed" of all covert actions, including "significant failures."
3. Section 413b(c)(2) provides the President "may elect" to report only to the congressional leadership, popularly known as "the Gang of Eight," when he believes "it is essential to limit access" to information about a covert action.
4. Section 413d requires Congress to establish "procedures to protect from unauthorized disclosure all classified information, and all information relating to intelligence sources and methods" that is furnished by the executive branch.

This legal framework provides the authority and the requirement for the President, the Director of National Intelligence and the agency heads to keep the Congress "fully and currently" briefed regarding intelligence matters, but also severely limits those entitled to the information to the members of the House and Senate intelligence committees and the congressional leadership.

Additionally, the House and Senate adopted procedures under the law to restrict all intelligence information to only the designated, entitled members of Congress, and some few senior staff members. All are sworn to secrecy and not permitted to discuss with other colleagues or the public any intelligence information that comes into their possession.

Presidents have chosen to further restrict the access of Congress to intelligence information by electing as permitted by law to limit their briefings to the Gang of Eight, defined in the law as the Speaker and minority leader of the House, the majority and minority leaders of the Senate, and the chairs and ranking minority members of the House and Senate intelligence committees.

In recent practice, White House and intelligence officials often provide the most detailed classified information to the smallest congressional groups, such as the Gang of Eight or just the Gang of Four (the four party leaders from the House and Senate), and less information to the intelligence committees and occasionally other select committee chairs and committees.

At the time of the congressional vote authorizing the Iraq War, rank and file members of Congress did not have routine or regular access to classified information. However, as I described in Chapter Three, the Bush administration provided several "classified" closed-door briefings to the full House membership in September and early October, 2002 regarding Saddam Hussein's weapons of mass destruction.

But these briefings were not particularly helpful to rank and file members of the House because we heard merely the same positive assertions about the threat posed by Hussein that the Bush team was making on the evening news each night. I remember no persuasive classified intelligence offered to back up the assertions in the briefings. We did not see any classified documents. We were shown a number of grainy photographs purporting to show illegal weapons sites in Iraq, but the buildings in the pictures could have been any buildings anywhere. I recall that many of my colleagues shared my frustrations over these almost useless "classified" briefings.

Dr. Lowenthal's book provides a fascinating account of the dispute in 2009 and 2010 between the executive and legislative branches about intelligence briefings of Congress regarding intelligence operations. House Speaker Nancy Pelosi wanted more intelligence information for more members of Congress, reducing the use of briefings just for the

Gang of Four and the Gang of Eight, while Director of Central Intelligence Leon Panetta and President Obama resisted the call for more inclusive briefings. The compromise that was finally reached continues the primary use of the Gang of Eight briefings, while the full intelligence committees must wait 180 days after such a briefing to be notified of covert action findings. All intelligence committee members receive a general description of the briefing, but no details.[20]

Recently, primarily as a result of the inaccessible intelligence regarding the Iraq War, Congress and the Executive Branch have created two procedures to grant access to classified intelligence to all members of the House, in most circumstances.[21]

First, any member of the House may submit a written request to the chair of the House Intelligence Committee for access to a National Intelligence Estimate or other classified report in the committee's custody. The chair will bring the request to the full committee and a formal vote will be taken whether to grant the requested access to the non-member of the committee. Such access is generally provided.

Second, general agreement now exists between the Obama administration and the bi-partisan House leadership that all members can have access to many classified documents at the House Security Office, run by the Sergeant at Arms. Specific decisions regarding which documents are available are made on a case by case basis.

The Obama White House and the current House leadership seem genuinely committed to a far higher level of access for House members to classified documents than previously existed. This new policy was clearly demonstrated by the full briefings and document access granted to all members during the September 2013 review of chemical weapons abuses in Syria. President Obama announced that he wanted congressional authorization for any military action against Syria, and he clearly wanted all members of Congress to be fully briefed before taking any vote.

These recent reforms that improve congressional access to classified intelligence reports certainly are worthwhile. But we should not simply rely on the good faith and transparent instincts of a particular president to insure better public and congressional access in the future to critical intelligence assessments.

The current level of congressional and public access to intelligence information is simply not adequate when Congress is requested to authorize preemptive war. When the president wants congressional authority to use first-strike military force and commit the nation to war, all the policymakers, and the voters who put them in office, must have access to the same intelligence.

In my opinion, it is not enough to grant classified intelligence access only to Congress when the nation is deliberating whether to start a preemptive war. Public disclosure of the relevant intelligence findings is also essential, with full protection for the sources of the intelligence and the methods of collection.

The people who will pay for the war, fight the war, care for the wounded and bury and mourn the dead also have a right to know why the war should be started in the first place. In a democracy, the public should be informed and involved when the country is considering starting a preemptive war.

Public disclosure will keep everyone accountable. Members of Congress will pay the closest attention to the classified findings if they know that their constituents are seeing the same information the Congress is seeing. Media inquiries will be better informed and more incisive, keeping public officials on their toes.

The most important step Congress should take now is to mandate by law the public disclosure of the relevant classified National Intelligence Estimates, specifically the Key Judgments contained in those Estimates that summarize the findings, when Congress is asked to authorize preemptive war.

As we have seen, National Intelligence Estimates are the most authoritative written judgments of the Intelligence Community concerning national security issues and the likely course of future events. They are designed to help civilian and military leaders develop policies to protect U.S. national security interests. While Estimates provide information on current conditions, they are primarily judgments about likely developments, trying to identify the implications for national policy.[22]

Estimates contain summary sections at the front of the document called Key Judgments that present a concise synopsis of the entire document. Under current practice, entire estimates are almost never declassified, and Key Judgments only occasionally are publicly disclosed.

On October 24, 2007, Director of National Intelligence J.M. McConnell stated that his policy was that Key Judgments should not be declassified, but six weeks later the Key Judgments were declassified from the Estimate on Iran's nuclear capabilities.[23]

At least five National Intelligence Estimates have had their Key Judgments declassified, including documents on trends in global terrorism, the terrorist threat to the U.S. homeland, prospects for stability in Iraq, and the status of Iran's nuclear program.[24]

The intelligence professionals are understandably inclined to keep their work product classified. They deal every day in a tough and clandestine world, and they prefer to keep things a secret. But this secrecy can be taken to a level that is not in the national interest.

Some secrets must be kept. The identity of confidential sources of intelligence must not be disclosed, in order to protect those sources from retribution and to encourage the continuing flow of information. The methods of collection of intelligence must not be disclosed, in order to protect our own agents and to prevent foreign adversaries from figuring out how we gain access to their information.

But the findings and judgments in our intelligence reports are not as sensitive as the sources and methods of collection. They are just opinions, with various levels of certainty, about the current capability of an adversary, and what is most likely to happen. Exposing those opinions to public and congressional scrutiny could help determine the validity and necessity of the proposed public policy that is based upon those key judgments, particularly when Congress is asked to determine matters of war and peace.

It is time to change the National Security Act to guarantee congressional and public access to the intelligence reports and their key judgments when the executive branch seeks congressional authority to conduct preemptive war.

TWELVE

Cheney and Iraq:
Another Intervention?

Former Vice President Dick Cheney has been popping off lately about how President Obama is to blame for the current crisis in Iraq.

Cheney sees the alarming territorial gains by Sunni Muslim insurgents and al Qaeda jihadists, and the growing and regrettable influence of the clerics of Iran over the Shiite government of Iraq, and blames it all on the Obama administration.

Dick Cheney is wrong about Barack Obama and Iraq now—big time—just as he was in 2002 when he and President George W. Bush deliberately distorted classified intelligence about Saddam Hussein's weapons of mass destruction and misled the Congress and the country into the Iraq War under false pretenses.

Cheney and Bush are responsible for our invasion of Iraq, the greatest foreign policy blunder in our national history. They made mistake after mistake in Iraq in 2002 and 2003, and those failures, not President Obama, are directly responsible for the government dysfunction, sectarian unrest and growing civil war we see today in that divided country.

First, the President and Vice President intentionally lied to Congress and the American people when seeking congressional authority to invade Iraq. They stated publicly with complete certainty that Hussein had weapons of mass destruction, was getting more, and was willing to use them, and thus posed an imminent threat to the United States. But the classified intelligence being given to the White House at that time was full of reservations, doubts and caveats about the status of Sadd-am's weapons. Had Congress seen the classified intelligence before the vote to authorize war, instead of months afterward, I believe Congress would have voted against the war and for continued international sanctions and enhanced inspections. We would have avoided the American debacle in Iraq.

I was a member of Congress then, and I regret to this day that I believed the White House lies that convinced me to support the war in order to disarm Saddam Hussein. The fact is that when we invaded Iraq, Saddam Hussein was already disarmed.

But Cheney and Bush were just getting started with their mistakes. They believed the blowhard Iraqi exile Ahmed Chalabi who swore that Shiite Iraqis would embrace us as liberators, that Sunnis should be marginalized in society, that the Iraqi army should be disbanded[1] and former Ba'ath party members should be expelled from government (although they were the ones who could make the trains run on time).

For nine years we functioned not as liberators, as Cheney infamously promised, but as occupiers of a dangerously splintered country with a deadly insurgency. America's cost: 4,500 dead, 30,000 wounded and maimed, $758 billion in direct military spending, $2 trillion in total expenditures.[2] And our misadventure in Iraq has surely created more terrorists and extremists than we ever brought to justice.

Cheney and Bush believed that Iraq was ripe for a modern, pluralistic democracy, and the hostile clerics running Iran would be the next to fall. Those were two more sadly mistaken beliefs.

The fact is that Iraq has never recovered from the poor policy choices imposed by Dick Cheney and George Bush. The Iraqi army can barely function, as seen in their recent retreat in the face of the initial onslaught of ISIS, the Islamic State of Iraq and Syria. Civil Iraqi society is hamstrung by incompetent and corrupt managers. Our ouster of Hussein gave rise to an often vindictive Shiite majority rule in Iraq and directly expanded Iran's influence over their former adversary. Disaffected Sunni militants joined with al Qaeda offshoots and gave ISIS its golden opportunity.[3]

Now, in the face of all of this abject failure, Dick Cheney is saying that it is actually President Obama's fault. Really? Let's review Cheney's brazen hypocrisy.

In a recent opinion column in the Wall Street Journal,[4] Cheney wrote, "When Mr. Obama . . . came into office in 2009, al Qaeda in Iraq had been largely defeated." This totally ignores the fact that al Qaeda did not exist at all in Iraq before the Bush invasion. Saddam was a murderous tyrant, but he was contained by international sanctions and possessed only conventional weapons, and the vacuum caused by his overthrow and the subsequent government dysfunction gave al Qaeda a foothold in Iraq for the first time.

Cheney wasn't finished. He wrote, "Now, in a move that defies credulity, [Obama] toys with the idea of ushering Iran into Iraq." But it was Bush-Cheney policies that led to the vastly increased influence of the Shiite Iranian clerics over the dysfunctional Shiite Iraqi government. Dick Cheney, not Barack Obama, opened the door in Iraq for the hardline clerics of Iran to enter.

Then Cheney went on Fox News[5] and said, "When we left, Iraq was in pretty good shape . . . we had the situation pretty well squared away when we departed." Baloney. Iraq has been a mess from the time Dick Cheney started calling the shots there.

Commenting on the recent gains of ISIS, Cheney told Fox, "The Iraqi military just collapsed . . . so now we have a terrible, difficult relationship on our hands . . . primarily because of both Maliki and Obama." But it was Cheney and Bush that disbanded the Iraqi army in 2003, and it has never recovered. And it was the heavy-handed, punitive policies of Prime Minister Nouri al-Maliki toward the Sunni minority and the Kurds that caused increased sectarian violence and unrest in Iraq. Maliki was handpicked by the Bush administration in May 2006 to succeed the failed Prime Minister Ibrahim al-Jaafari, thirty-one months before Barrack Obama became president.

Cheney topped off his interview with the following, "President Obama is on track to securing his legacy as the man who betrayed our past and squandered our freedom." Maybe the right-wing Obama haters admire this overblown rhetoric, but it is unseemly for a former Vice President, regardless of party.

But clearly, Dick Cheney has secured his legacy as the vice president who misled our country into war in Iraq under false pretenses, then imposed a number of governing policies there that utterly failed.

It is true that President Obama has made some mistakes. He did not pay enough attention to the sectarian abuses and divisive policies of Prime Minister Maliki, who may lose his power because he wasn't willing to share any of it. Maliki's intransigence prevented an agreement with the White House for a continuing American military presence in Iraq after December 2011, so now President Obama has no strong hand to play to impose more inclusive leadership in Baghdad.

But President Obama must not send American troops back to Iraq at this point, or re-engage militarily in the current sectarian and civil strife. That would make no sense. We cannot resolve Iraq's problems for them. We cannot make the Shiites like the Sunnis, or the Sunnis like the Shiites, or either of them like the Kurds. America has no acceptable or sensible military solution today to the problems in Iraq, and we must face that reality.

There is always a critical role to be played on the world stage by robust American diplomacy, and that is still true in Iraq. But those needed efforts to bring a more inclusive government to Baghdad will have to be made behind the scenes, because our active presence there now, particularly in any military capacity, would do far more harm than good. Thanks in part to Dick Cheney and his failed policies, most Iraqis don't want America to meddle in their country anymore. The trick for our diplomacy will be to remove the grounds for supporting the insurgents and jihadists.

There is no question that the violent methods of ISIS in eastern Syria and western Iraq are a real threat to regional stability. The Muslim majorities in Syria and Iraq must be alarmed by the declaration of a conservative religious caliphate by ISIS in their midst. Such a caliphate claims the allegiance of all Muslims, yet the existing governments will surely not accept the extremism and brutality of this caliphate.

America should realize that the repressive leader Bashar al-Assad is going to retain his power in Syria for the time being, and that the conservative clerics of Iran are going to maintain their hold over Maliki in Iraq, and quite likely over any successor as well. Neither Assad, Maliki nor the mullahs of Iran are going to tolerate the caliphate created by ISIS in that part of the world.

The lesson of the 2003-2011 Iraq War for the United States is that never again should Congress authorize preemptive war without prior public disclosure of the key intelligence findings on which the President is relying to make the case for war. Had the intelligence been disclosed in 2002, I believe Congress would not have authorized the Iraq War.

The lesson for President Barack Obama in 2014 is that he must not order a major intervention in Iraq or against ISIS without prior public disclosure of the intelligence that would justify such a reengagement, and he must secure congressional authorization for such military action.

I do not suggest curtailing the President's constitutional powers as Commander-in-Chief to conduct limited military operations to respond to a threat against American personnel, retaliate after an attack, provide advice and training to an ally, or to collect intelligence.

I do suggest that President Obama must secure public approval before reinserting ground troops, conducting major bombing operations or taking sides militarily in the lethal disputes between the Sunnis, Shiites, Kurds and assorted jihadists.

After the mistakes of Bush and Cheney, such public approval will be hard to win. Most Americans now believe that Iraqis need to resolve their own problems without American military involvement. We cannot be the policeman of the Muslim world.

Afterword

It was late in the evening of Election Day, November 2, 1976. Maybe it was the early morning hours of November 3. All I remember now is I found myself suddenly out of bed, dancing barefooted across my darkened bedroom floor in my pajamas, bobbing and weaving, throwing a flurry of jabs and uppercuts, shadowboxing in the moonlight and laughing like crazy.

I was on top of the world. I was 26 years old and had just won my first election to public office. I was a Pennsylvania State Representative-elect and I was pumped. I wasn't about to go back to bed. I was too busy throwing devastating jabs and murderous haymakers as I floated like a butterfly back and forth in front of the window at the foot of the bed. I was beating hell out of the world.

That seems like a long time ago. Since then I have experienced many things in public life, most of them good, some of them even inspiring, a few of them bad. I still possess most of that youthful idealism, but I have come to realize that we have lost something in America.

It started for me before my first election, when I was working on Capitol Hill as a lowly congressional aide in 1973. It was the summer of the Watergate hearings and I spent many evenings in my apartment watching the replay of that day's Senate investigative hearing on the local public television station. I was amazed and dismayed by what we all learned about the inner workings of the White House and President Nixon's men. I came to the conclusion that my national government was lying to me.

That conclusion was reinforced by our failures in Vietnam where, despite the bravery of our soldiers, our national morale was sapped by the lies and dissembling of our political leaders.

But I was young and idealistic, and I stuck with it, working for open and honest government. I devoted my career to public service, believing that government at all levels is a necessary and valuable force for good in our society, helping individuals to reach their full potential and improving the quality of life for all.

Thirty years later, in 2003, after serving as a state legislator and county commissioner, I was proudly representing my community in Congress. As I have described in this book, I was directly involved in the decisions and the discussions about our military and foreign policies in Iraq. In particular, I focused on the threat of Saddam Hussein and his weapons of mass destruction.

I eventually came to the painful conclusion that, once again, my national government was lying to me. And this time, I was part of that government, and had voted for the disastrous invasion of Iraq, based on my belief that Saddam Hussein had to be disarmed.

I had come full circle. I was part of a national government that, once again, had misled the country. The fact the Bush administration had distorted the intelligence and taken us to war under false pretenses didn't make it easier for me. In fact, it made it worse. I should have figured it out and voted against the Iraq War. I was a fool to believe George W. Bush, and I was wrong to vote for the war.

We have lost something in America. The legacies of Watergate, Vietnam and Iraq remain front and center today. People basically don't believe their national government anymore. People no longer trust what the president says and doubt the sincerity of his policies.

President Obama experienced this national cynicism in 2013 regarding his policies toward the ruling regime in Syria and its use of chemical weapons against its own innocent civilians. He advocated the use of force in retaliation for Syria's chemical weapons use, but sought congressional approval first, thus demonstrating the restraint that many Americans say they value in their Commander-in-Chief. Americans have never been afraid of a fight, but they are wary of unnecessary foreign entanglements.

Yet President Obama was criticized roundly from the left and the right for his approach to this foreign policy challenge in Syria. Some critics saw weakness, and urged the President to go ahead and attack without waiting for congressional approval. Others criticized presidential uncertainty and fecklessness. Still others thought the President was just trying to trap congressional Republicans, and they complained about the policy in partisan terms. Few seemed willing to accept and evaluate the President's Syrian policy at face value.

Many citizens no longer seem willing to accept presidential leadership. They question the motivations of all national politicians, and seem to expect the president to be trying to pull a fast one, no matter what the subject.

I see this cynicism in my classes at Temple University in Philadelphia where I teach political science. These young people are very smart, and they are also very skeptical of government leaders. They wonder if government can ever do them any good. Yet these young Americans want to believe, and harbor the idealism I felt at their age. But their flame flickers, and I cannot blame them.

We have lost something in America, and it is time to get it back. The legacies of Watergate, Vietnam and Iraq, and a thousand sordid tales in between of greed and corruption, have taken a huge toll. Americans have been let down by their government time and time again, but they have not given up. Americans still understand that our self-government offers us great personal freedom and opportunity, if only we can have a government as worthy as the people.

Secrecy in government and a lack of transparency in the formulation of policy breeds mistrust and cynicism in the citizenry. People are smarter and more sophisticated than the politicians realize. If the people have all the correct information, they will recognize a four-flusher. Americans can handle the truth.

Government frequently fails and disappoints. Winston Churchill said that democracy is the worst form of government except all the others that have been tried.

We can do better. We must take an honest, clear-eyed look at the challenges we face in the public arena, including the past failures in our use and misuse of intelligence. We must determine what is working and what is not, and then fight for reform and improvement, with Churchillian resolve, in the classrooms, on the factory floors, in the boardrooms, in the union halls, in the neighborhoods, on Main Streets, in town halls and especially in the halls of Congress.

This is time for some youthful shadowboxing in the moonlight, to renew our zeal and idealism. We must all get to work revitalizing our democracy. We must make government work well for all of us, openly and honestly, restoring our confidence in our system of self-government and improving the quality of life for all Americans.

Appendix

I. THE NATIONAL INTELLIGENCE ESTIMATE

The first document is reprinted from the classified National Intelligence Estimate entitled "Iraq's Continuing Programs for Weapons of Mass Destruction," published October 1, 2002 by the National Intelligence Council. The Estimate remains a classified document to this day. However, the Key Judgments section of the Estimate was declassified by the Bush White House and distributed to the press at a briefing on July 18, 2003. This is the declassified document made available to the press, and it can be viewed on the website of the National Intelligence Council.

Iraq's Continuing Program for Weapons of Mass Destruction

Key Judgments

(from October 2002 NIE)

We judge that Iraq has continued its weapons of mass destruction (WMD) programs in defiance of UN resolutions and restrictions. Baghdad has chemical and biological weapons as well as missiles with ranges in excess of UN restrictions; if left unchecked, it probably will have a nuclear weapon during this decade. (See INR alternative view at the end of these Key Judgments.)

We judge that we are seeing only a portion of Iraq's WMD efforts, owing to Baghdad's vigorous denial and deception efforts. Revelations after the Gulf war starkly demonstrate the extensive efforts undertaken by Iraq to deny information. We lack specific information on many key aspects of Iraq's WMD programs.

Since inspections ended in 1998, Iraq has maintained its chemical weapons effort, energized its missile program, and invested more heavily in biological weapons; in the view of most agencies, Baghdad is reconstituting its nuclear weapons program.

- Iraq's growing ability to sell oil illicitly increases Baghdad's capabilities to finance WMD programs; annual earnings in cash and goods have more than quadrupled, from $580 million in 1998 to about $3 billion this year.
- Iraq has largely rebuilt missile and biological weapons facilities damaged during Operation Desert Fox and has expanded its chemical and biological infrastructure under the cover of civilian production.
- Baghdad has exceeded UN range limits of 150 km with its ballistic missiles and is working with unmanned aerial vehicles (UAVs), which allow for a more lethal means to deliver biological and, less likely, chemical warfare agents.
- Although we assess that Saddam does not yet have nuclear weapons or sufficient material to make any, he remains intent on acquiring them. Most agencies assess that Baghdad started reconstituting its nuclear program about the time that UNSCOM inspectors departed-December 1998.

How quickly Iraq will obtain its first nuclear weapon depends on when it acquires sufficient weapons-grade fissile material.

- If Baghdad acquires sufficient fissile material from abroad it could make a nuclear weapon within several months to a year.
- Without such material from abroad, Iraq probably would not be able to make a weapon until 2007 to 2009, owing to inexperience in building and operating centrifuge facilities to produce highly enriched uranium and challenges in procuring the necessary equipment and expertise.

  o Most agencies believe that Saddam's personal interest in and Iraq's aggressive attempts to obtain high-strength aluminum tubes for centrifuge rotors-as well as Iraq's attempts to acquire magnets, high-speed balancing machines, and machine tools—provide compelling evidence that Saddam is reconstituting a uranium enrichment effort for Baghdad's nuclear weapons program. (DOE agrees that reconstitution of the nuclear program is underway but assesses that the tubes probably are not part of the program.)

- o Iraq's efforts to re-establish and enhance its cadre of weapons personnel as well as activities at several suspect nuclear sites further indicate that reconstitution is underway.
- o All agencies agree that about 25,000 centrifuges based on tubes of the size Iraq is trying to acquire would be capable of producing approximately two weapons' worth of highly enriched uranium per year.

- In a much less likely scenario, Baghdad could make enough fissile material for a nuclear weapon by 2005 to 2007 if it obtains suitable centrifuge tubes this year and has all the other materials and technological expertise necessary to build production-scale uranium enrichment facilities.

We assess that Baghdad has begun renewed production of mustard, sarin, GF (cyclosarin), and VX; its capability probably is more limited now than it was at the time of the Gulf war, although VX production and agent storage life probably have been improved.

- An array of clandestine reporting reveals that Baghdad has procured covertly the types and quantities of chemicals and equipment sufficient to allow limited CW agent production hidden within Iraq's legitimate chemical industry.
- Although we have little specific information on Iraq's CW stockpile, Saddam probably has stocked at least 100 metric tons (MT) and possibly as much as 500 MT of CW agents-much of it added in the last year.
- The Iraqis have experience in manufacturing CW bombs, artillery rockets, and projectiles. We assess that that they possess CW bulk fills for SRBM warheads, including for a limited number of covertly stored Scuds, possibly a few with extended ranges.

We judge that all key aspects-R&D, production, and weaponization of Iraq's offensive BW program are active and that most elements are larger and more advanced than they were before the Gulf war.

- We judge Iraq has some lethal and incapacitating BW agents and is capable of quickly producing and weaponizing a variety of such agents, including anthrax, for delivery by bombs, missiles, aerial sprayers, and covert operatives.

  o Chances are even that smallpox is part of Iraq's offensive BW program—Baghdad probably has developed genetically engineered BW agents.

- Baghdad has established a large-scale, redundant, and concealed BW agent production capability.

  o Baghdad has mobile facilities for producing bacterial and toxin BW agents; these facilities can evade detection and are highly survivable. Within three to six months these units probably could produce an amount of agent equal to the total that Iraq produced in the years prior to the Gulf war.

Iraq maintains a small missile force and several development programs, including for a UAV probably intended to deliver biological warfare agent.

- Gaps in Iraqi accounting to UNSCOM suggest that Saddam retains a covert force of up to a few dozen Scud-variant SRBMs with ranges of 650 to 900 km.
- Iraq is deploying its new al-Samoud and Ababil-100 SRBMs, which are capable of flying beyond the UN-authorized 150-km range limit; Iraq has tested an al-Samoud variant beyond 150 km-perhaps as far as 300 km.
- Baghdad's UAVs could threaten Iraq's neighbors, US forces in the Persian Gulf, and if brought close to, or into, the United States, the US Homeland.

  o An Iraqi UAV procurement network attempted to procure commercially available route planning software and an associated topographic database that would be able

to support targeting of the United States, according to
analysis of special intelligence.

o   The Director, Intelligence, Surveillance, and Reconnaissance, US Air Force, does not agree that Iraq is developing UAVs primarily intended to be delivery platforms for
chemical and biological warfare (CBW) agents. The small
size of Iraq's new UAV strongly suggests a primary role
of reconnaissance, although CBW delivery is an inherent
capability.

- Iraq is developing medium-range ballistic missile capabilities, largely through foreign assistance in building specialized facilities, including a test stand for engines more
powerful than those in its current missile force.

We have low confidence in our ability to assess when Saddam would
use WMD.

- Saddam could decide to use chemical and biological warfare
(CBW) preemptively against US forces, friends, and allies
in the region in an attempt to disrupt US war preparations
and undermine the political will of the Coalition.
- Saddam might use CBW after an initial advance into Iraqi
territory, but early use of WMD could foreclose diplomatic
options for stalling the US advance.
- He probably would use CBW when he perceived he irretriev-
ably had lost control of the military and security situation,
but we are unlikely to know when Saddam reaches that point.
- We judge that Saddam would be more likely to use chemical
weapons than biological weapons on the battlefield.
- Saddam historically has maintained tight control over the
use of WMD; however, he probably has provided contin-
gency instructions to his commanders to use CBW in specific circumstances.

Baghdad for now appears to be drawing a line short of conducting
terrorist attacks with conventional or CBW against the United States,
fearing that exposure of Iraqi involvement would provide Washington a
stronger cause for making war.

Iraq probably would attempt clandestine attacks against the US
Homeland if Baghdad feared an attack that threatened the survival
of the regime were imminent or unavoidable, or possibly for revenge.

Such attacks-more likely with biological than chemical agents-probably would be carried out by special forces or intelligence operatives.

- The Iraqi Intelligence Service (IIS) probably has been directed to conduct clandestine attacks against US and Allied interests in the Middle East in the event the United States takes action against Iraq. The IIS probably would be the primary means by which Iraq would attempt to conduct any CBW attacks on the US Homeland, although we have no specific intelligence information that Saddam's regime has directed attacks against US territory.

Saddam, if sufficiently desperate, might decide that only an organization such as al-Qa'ida-with worldwide reach and extensive terrorist infrastructure, and already engaged in a life-or-death struggle against the United States-could perpetrate the type of terrorist attack that he would hope to conduct.

- In such circumstances, he might decide that the extreme step of assisting the Islamist terrorists in conducting a CBW attack against the United States would be his last chance to exact vengeance by taking a large number of victims with him.

State/INR Alternative View of Iraq's Nuclear Program

The Assistant Secretary of State for Intelligence and Research (INR) believes that Saddam continues to want nuclear weapons and that available evidence indicates that Baghdad is pursuing at least a limited effort to maintain and acquire nuclear weapon-related capabilities. The activities we have detected do not, however, add up to a compelling case that Iraq is currently pursuing what INR would consider to be an integrated and comprehensive approach to acquire nuclear weapons. Iraq may be doing so, but INR considers the available evidence inadequate to support such a judgment.

Lacking persuasive evidence that Baghdad has launched a coherent effort to reconstitute its nuclear weapons program, INR is unwilling to speculate that such an effort began soon after the departure of UN inspectors or to project a timeline for the completion of activities it does not now see happening. As a result, INR is unable to predict when Iraq could acquire a nuclear device or weapon.

In INR's view Iraq's efforts to acquire aluminum tubes is central to the argument that Baghdad is reconstituting its nuclear weapons program, but INR is not persuaded that the tubes in question are intended for use as centrifuge rotors. INR accepts the judgment of technical experts at the U.S. Department of Energy (DOE) who have concluded that the tubes Iraq seeks to acquire are poorly suited for use in gas centrifuges to be used for uranium enrichment and finds unpersuasive the arguments advanced by others to make the case that they are intended for that purpose.

INR considers it far more likely that the tubes are intended for another purpose, most likely the production of artillery rockets. The very large quantities being sought, the way the tubes were tested by the Iraqis, and the atypical lack of attention to operational security in the procurement efforts are among the factors, in addition to the DOE assessment, that lead INR to conclude that the tubes are not intended for use in Iraq's nuclear weapon program.

Confidence Levels for Selected Key Judgments in This Estimate

High Confidence:

- Iraq is continuing, and in some areas expanding, its chemical, biological, nuclear and missile programs contrary to UN resolutions.
- We are not detecting portions of these weapons programs.
- Iraq possesses proscribed chemical and biological weapons and missiles.
- Iraq could make a nuclear weapon in months to a year once it acquires sufficient weapons-grade fissile material.

Moderate Confidence:

- Iraq does not yet have a nuclear weapon or sufficient material to make one but is likely to have a weapon by 2007 to 2009. (See INR alternative view, page 84).

Low Confidence:

- When Saddam would use weapons of mass destruction.
- Whether Saddam would engage in clandestine attacks against the US Homeland.

- Whether in desperation Saddam would share chemical or biological weapons with al-Qa'ida.

Uranium Acquisition

Iraq retains approximately two-and-a-half tons of 2.5 percent enriched uranium oxide, which the IAEA permits. This low-enriched material could be used as feed material to produce enough HEU for about two nuclear weapons. The use of enriched feed material also would reduce the initial number of centrifuges that Baghdad would need by about half. Iraq could divert this material-the IAEA inspects it only once a year-and enrich it to weapons grade before a subsequent inspection discovered it was missing. The IAEA last inspected this material in late January 2002.

Iraq has about 550 metric tons of yellowcake and low-enriched uranium at Tuwaitha, which is inspected annually by the IAEA. Iraq also began vigorously trying to procure uranium ore and yellowcake; acquiring either would shorten the time Baghdad needs to produce nuclear weapons.

- A foreign government service reported that as of early 2001, Niger planned to send several tons of "pure uranium" (probably yellowcake) to Iraq. As of early 2001, Niger and Iraq reportedly were still working out arrangements for this deal, which could be for up to 500 tons of yellowcake1. We do not know the status of this arrangement.
- Reports indicate Iraq also has sought uranium ore from Somalia and possibly the Democratic Republic of the Congo.

We cannot confirm whether Iraq succeeded in acquiring uranium ore and/or yellowcake from these sources. Reports suggest Iraq is shifting from domestic mining and milling of uranium to foreign acquisition. Iraq possesses significant phosphate deposits, from which uranium had been chemically extracted before Operation Desert Storm. Intelligence information on whether nuclear-related phosphate mining and/or processing has been reestablished is inconclusive, however.

Annex A: Iraq's Attempts to Acquire Aluminum Tubes

[This excerpt from a longer view includes INR's position on the African uranium issue]

INR's Alternative View: Iraq's Attempts to Acquire Aluminum Tubes

Some of the specialized but dual-use items being sought are, by all indications, bound for Iraq's missile program. Other cases are ambiguous, such as that of a planned magnet-production line whose suitability for centrifuge operations remains unknown. Some efforts involve non-controlled industrial material and equipment—including a variety of machine tools—and are troubling because they would help establish the infrastructure for a renewed nuclear program. But such efforts (which began well before the inspectors departed) are not clearly linked to a nuclear end-use. Finally, the claims of Iraqi pursuit of natural uranium in Africa are, in INR's assessment, highly dubious.

II. THE WHITE PAPER

The second document is reprinted from the White Paper entitled "Iraq's Weapons of Mass Destruction Programs," publicly released October 4, 2002 by the Director of Central Intelligence George Tenet. Members of Congress and the media were asking for an unclassified version of the Iraq intelligence reports on which the Bush team was relying, and George Tenet presented the White Paper as the public summary of the classified intelligence. This excerpt contains the entire Key Judgments section of the White Paper. The White Paper can be viewed on the website of the Central Intelligence Agency.

Iraq's Weapons of Mass Destruction Programs

Key Judgments

Iraq has continued its weapons of mass destruction (WMD) programs in defiance of UN resolutions and restrictions. Baghdad has chemical and biological weapons as well as missiles with ranges in excess of UN restrictions; if left unchecked, it probably will have a nuclear weapon during this decade.

Baghdad hides large portions of Iraq's WMD efforts. Revelations after the Gulf war starkly demonstrate the extensive efforts undertaken by Iraq to deny information.

Since inspections ended in 1998, Iraq has maintained its chemical weapons effort, energized its missile program, and invested more heavily in biological weapons; most analysts assess Iraq is reconstituting its nuclear weapons program.

- Iraq's growing ability to sell oil illicitly increases Baghdad's capabilities to finance WMD programs; annual earnings in cash and goods have more than quadrupled.
- Iraq largely has rebuilt missile and biological weapons facilities damaged during Operation Desert Fox and has expanded its chemical and biological infrastructure under the cover of civilian production.
- Baghdad has exceeded UN range limits of 150 km with its ballistic missiles and is working with unmanned aerial vehicles (UAVs), which allow for a more lethal means to deliver biological and, less likely, chemical warfare agents.
- Although Saddam probably does not yet have nuclear weapons or sufficient material to make any, he remains intent on acquiring them.

How quickly Iraq will obtain its first nuclear weapon depends on when it acquires sufficient weapons-grade fissile material.

If Baghdad acquires sufficient weapons-grade fissile material from abroad, it could make a nuclear weapon within a year.

Without such material from abroad, Iraq probably would not be able to make a weapon until the last half of the decade.

- Iraq's aggressive attempts to obtain proscribed high-strength aluminum tubes are of significant concern. All intelligence experts agree that Iraq is seeking nuclear weapons and that these tubes could be used in a centrifuge enrichment program. Most intelligence specialists assess this to be the intended use, but some believe that these tubes are probably intended for conventional weapons programs.
- Based on tubes of the size Iraq is trying to acquire, a few tens of thousands of centrifuges would be capable of producing enough highly enriched uranium for a couple of weapons per year.

Baghdad has begun renewed production of chemical warfare agents, probably including mustard, sarin, cyclosarin, and VX. Its capability was reduced during the UNSCOM inspections and is probably more limited now than it was at the time of the Gulf war, although VX production and agent storage life probably have been improved.

- Saddam probably has stocked a few hundred metric tons of CW agents.
- The Iraqis have experience in manufacturing CW bombs, artillery rockets, and projectiles, and probably possess CW bulk fills for SRBM warheads, including for a limited number of covertly stored, extended-range Scuds.

All key aspects—R&D, production, and weaponization—of Iraq's offensive BW program are active and most elements are larger and more advanced than they were before the Gulf war.

- Iraq has some lethal and incapacitating BW agents and is capable of quickly producing and weaponizing a variety of such agents, including anthrax, for delivery by bombs, missiles, aerial sprayers, and covert operatives, including potentially against the US Homeland.
- Baghdad has established a large-scale, redundant, and concealed BW agent production capability, which includes mobile facilities; these facilities can evade detection, are highly survivable, and can exceed the production rates Iraq had prior to the Gulf war.

Iraq maintains a small missile force and several development programs, including for a UAV that most analysts believe probably is intended to deliver biological warfare agents.

- Gaps in Iraqi accounting to UNSCOM suggest that Saddam retains a covert force of up to a few dozen Scud-variant SRBMs with ranges of 650 to 900 km.
- Iraq is deploying its new al-Samoud and Ababil-100 SRBMs, which are capable of flying beyond the UN-authorized 150-km range limit.
- Baghdad's UAVs—especially if used for delivery of chemical and biological warfare (CBW) agents—could threaten Iraq's neighbors, US forces in the Persian Gulf, and the United States if brought close to, or into, the US Homeland.
- Iraq is developing medium-range ballistic missile capabilities, largely through foreign assistance in building specialized facilities.

Endnotes

INTRODUCTION

1. http://www.defense.gov/news/casualties.pdf

2. Nina Crawford and Catherine Lutz, "Economic and Budgetary Costs of the Wars in Afghanistan, Iraq and Pakistan to the United States: A Summary," *Costs of War Project,* Watson Institute for International Studies, Brown University, (2011)

3. Daniel Trotta, "Iraq War costs U.S. more than $2 trillion: study," *Reuters,* (March 14, 2013)

4. 103,000—113,000 civilian deaths by violence, between March 2003 and December 2011, http://www.iraqbodycount.org

5. "President Bush Discusses Iraq with Congressional Leaders," Remarks by the President on Iraq, The Rose Garden, White House, (September 26, 2002)

6. "President Bush Outlines Iraqi Threat," Remarks by the President on Iraq, Cincinnati Museum Center, Cincinnati, Ohio, (October 7, 2002)

7. "President Bush Delivers Graduation Speech at West Point," United States Military Academy, West Point, New York, (June 1, 2002). See further discussion in Chapter Eleven.

8. *National Intelligence Estimate on Iraq's Continuing Programs for Weapons of Mass Destruction,* National Intelligence Council, (October 1, 2002), partially declassified by the White House on July 18, 2003. See further discussion in Chapter Two.

9. *Iraq's Weapons of Mass Destruction Programs*, CIA White Paper, October 4, 2002. See further discussion in Chapter Two.

10. George Tenet, *At the Center of the Storm: The CIA During America's Time of Crisis*, with Bill Harlow, (New York: Harper Perennial, 2008), 334–5

11. *Report on Whether Public Statements Regarding Iraq by U.S. Government Officials Were Substantiated by Intelligence Information*, Select Committee on Intelligence, United States Senate, Senate Report 110–345, (June 5, 2008). See further discussion in Chapter Nine.

CHAPTER ONE: THE HARD SELL

1. Dick Cheney, speech to Veterans of Foreign Wars 103rd National Convention, Nashville, Tennessee, (August 26, 2002)

2. Donald Rumsfeld, statement to the House Armed Services Committee, hearing on "Threats Posed by Saddam Hussein, and U.S. Policy Toward Iraq," (September 10, 2002)

3. Bush, Rose Garden remarks regarding Iraq, (September 26, 2002)

4. Condoleezza Rice, interview with Wolf Blitzer, *CNN Late Edition with Wolf Blitzer*, (September 8, 2002)

5. Adam Schiff, telephone interview with author, (June 20, 2013)

6. Dick Cheney, interview with Jim Lehrer, *PBS Newshour*, (September 9, 2002)

CHAPTER TWO: INTELLIGENCE TRUTH AND LIES

1. Greg Bruno and Sharon Otterman, "National Intelligence Estimates," *Council on Foreign Relations* backgrounder, (May 14, 2008), and Richard A. Best, "Intelligence Estimates: How Useful to Congress?" *Congressional Research Service*, (January 6, 2011)

2. George Tenet, *At the Center of the Storm: The CIA During America's Time of Crisis* (New York: Harper Perennial, 2008), 322–323

3. *National Intelligence Estimate on Iraq's weapons,* see appendix

4. *White Paper on Iraq's weapons,* see appendix

5. *National Intelligence Estimate on Prospects for Iraq's Stability: A Challenging Road Ahead,* National Intelligence Council, (January 2007)

6. *Iraq—Key WMD Facilities—An Operational Support Study,* Defense Intelligence Agency, Department of Defense, (September 2002)

7. *Report on the U.S. Intelligence Community's Prewar Assessments on Iraq,* Select Committee on Intelligence, United States Senate, Senate Report 108–301, (July 7, 2004)

8. *Report on Whether Public Statements Regarding Iraq by U.S. Government Officials Were Substantiated by Intelligence Information*, Select Committee on Intelligence, *United States Senate*, (June 5, 2008), see further discussion in Chapter Nine

9. John D. Rockefeller IV, *Senate Intelligence Committee Unveils Final Phase II Reports on Prewar Iraq Intelligence*, Press Release of U.S. Senate Select Committee on Intelligence, (June 5, 2008)

CHAPTER THREE: THE RUN-UP TO WAR

1. Bay Fang, "When Saddam Ruled the Day," *U.S. News & World Report*, (July 11, 2004)

2. "The Anfal Campaign Against the Kurds," *A Middle Watch Report: Human Rights Watch 1993*

3. "War in Iraq: Not an Humanitarian Intervention," *Human Rights Watch*, (January 26, 2004)

4. Marc Santora, "On the Gallows, Curses for U.S. and 'Traitors,'" *New York Times*, (December 31, 2006)

5. http://www.un.org/en/sc/documents/resolutions/index.shtml

6. "Transcript of Blix's U.N. Presentation," *CNN.com*, (March 7, 2003)

7. Colin Powell press briefing, *historycommons.org*, (February 23, 2001)

8. *Associated Press*, (September 25, 2003), "Powell '01: WMDs Not 'Significant,'" *CBS/AP*, (February11, 2009)

9. Interview with Vice President Dick Cheney, *Meet The Press*, NBC News, (September 16, 2001)

10. Spencer Ackerman and John B. Yudis, "The Selling of the Iraq War: The First Casualty," *The New Republic*, (June 30, 2003), 15

11. James Risen, "Terror Acts by Baghdad Have Waned, U.S. Aides Say," *The New York Times*, (February 6, 2002)

12. "President Bush's Address to the United Nations," *CNN.com/U.S.*, (September 12, 2002)

13. Bush, Rose Garden remarks regarding Iraq, (September 26,2002)

14. Eric Schmitt, "Rumsfeld Says U.S. Has 'Bulletproof' Evidence of Iraq's Links to Al Qaeda," *The New York Times*, (September 28, 2002)

15. Ibid.

16. Ibid.

17. Bush, Cincinnati speech regarding Iraqi threat, (October 7, 2002)

CHAPTER FOUR: VOTING FOR WAR

1. Dennis Hastert, *Congressional Record,* (October 8, 2002), H7192

2. Michael Grunwald and Jim VandeHei, "Hastert's Team Mentality to Be Tested as Foley Scandal Unfolds," *Washington Post,* (October 16, 2006)

3. Ibid.

4. Hastert, *CR,* H7192

5. Ibid.

6. Ibid.

7. House Joint Resolution 114, "Authorization for Use of Military Force Against Iraq Resolution of 2002," 107th Congress, introduced October 2, 2002, signed into law by President George W. Bush, October 16, 2002, Public Law 107–243.

8. "Bills and Resolutions: Examples of How Each Is Used," *Congressional Research Service,* Report 98–706

9. see also Jeremy M. Sharp, "A Compilation of Legislation, Congressional Action on Iraq 1990–2002," *Congressional Research Service,* (October 1, 2002), reprinted in *Congressional Record,* (October 10, 2002), H7745

10. Senate Joint Resolution 45, "To Authorize the Use of United States Armed Forces Against Iraq," 107th Congress, introduced September 26, 2002.

11. For more on the House chamber, see www.house.gov

12. House Resolution 574, the rule for the consideration of House Joint Resolution 114, 107th Congress, adopted October 8, 2002

13. Tom Lantos, *Congressional Record,* (October 8, 2002), H7198

14. Joseph Hoeffel, *Congressional Record,* (October 8, 2002), H7198

15. "Amendment in the nature of a substitute No. 1 offered by Ms. Lee," *Congressional Record,* (October 10, 2002), H7739. Subsequent debate and voting on the Lee Amendment appears in the *Congressional Record (CR)* for October 10, 2002 on pages H7740–7751.

16. Barbara Lee, *CR,* H7740

17. George J. Tenet, "CIA Letter to Senate on Baghdad's Intentions," *The New York Times,* (October 9, 2002)

18. Lee, *CR,* H7740

19. *Congressional Record,* (October 9, 2002), S10154

20. David Firestone, "2 Critics of Bush Iraq Policy Say They'll Back Resolution," *The New York Times*, (October 10, 2002), see also Tenet, *Storm*, 336

21. See also Tenet, *Storm*, 335–336

22. Lee, *CR*, H7741

23. Henry Hyde, *CR*, H7741

24. Peter DeFazio, *CR*, H7741

25. John Linder, *CR*, H7741

26. Tom Lantos, *CR*, H7744

27. Sherrod Brown, *CR*, H7748

28. Jerry Lewis, *CR*, H7748

29. Steven Buyer, *CR*, H7749

30. Roll Call 452, *CR*, H7751

31. "Amendment in the nature of a substitute No. 2 offered by Mr. Spratt," *CR*, H7751. Subsequent debate and voting on the Spratt Amendment appears in *CR* for October 10, 2002 on pages H7752–7769.

32. John Spratt, *CR*, H7753

33. Henry Hyde, *CR*, H7754

34. Ibid, H7754

35. Tom Lantos, *CR*, H7755

36. Dana Rohrabacher, *CR*, H7756

37. Henry Hyde, *CR*, H7758

38. Hyde, *CR*, H7765

39. Spratt, *CR*, H7766

40. Ibid, H7766

41. Roll Call 453, *CR*, H7769

42. The leadership debate on H.J. Res. 114 appears in *CR* for October 10, 2002 on pages H7777–7780.

43. Nancy Pelosi, *CR*, H7777

44. Robert Dreyfus, "DeLay, Incorporated," *The Texas Observer*, (February 2, 2000)

45. Tom DeLay, *CR*, H7777

46. Dick Gephardt, *CR*, H7778

47. Ibid.

48. Paul Burka, "Why They Won," *Texas Monthly*, (December 1984)

49. Dick Armey, *CR*, H7779–7780

50. "Kucinich motion to recommit H.J. Res. 114 to the Committee on International Relations," *CR*, H7796. Subsequent debate and voting

on the Kucinich motion to recommit appears in *CR* for October 10, 2002 on pages H7797–7798.

51. Dennis Kucinich, *CR*, H7797

52. Hyde, *CR*, H7798

53. Roll Call 454, *CR*, H7798

54. Roll Call 455, *CR*, H7799

55. Armey, *CR*, H7780

56. http://www.un.org/en/sc/documents/resolutions/2002/shtml

CHAPTER FIVE: PREPARING FOR WAR

1. Donald Rumsfeld, Department of Defense news briefing, The Pentagon, (January 7, 2003)

2. Ari Fleischer, White House press briefing, (January 9, 2003)

3. Christopher Witkowsky, "Anti-war Protesters Meet Hoeffel Staffers," *The Reporter*, (January 21, 2003)

4. Greg Coffey, "Lawmakers Divided," *The Record*, (January 27, 2003)

5. Ibid.

6. George W. Bush, State of the Union Address, Washington, D.C., (January 28, 2003)

7. Keith Phucas, "Congressmen's Opinions Stick to Their Party's Lines," *Times Herald*, (January 29, 2003)

8. http://www.un.org/en/sc/members/elected.shtml

9. Colin Powell, presentation to the United Nations Security Council, eMediaMillWorks, *Washington Post*, (February 5, 2003)

10. Hans Blix, Statement to the United Nations Security Council, New York, (February 14, 2003)

11. "U.N. report reinforces Security Council divisions," *CNN.com./U.S.*, (February 14, 2003)

12. Mohamed El-Baradei, Statement to the United Nations Security Council, New York, (February 14, 2003)

13. Robert Windrem, "No 'direct evidence' of Iraq weapons," *NBC News*, (February 24, 2003)

14. For more on the Capitol building, see www.aoc.gov

15. Joseph Hoeffel, *CR*, (March 4, 2003), H1492

16. Lara Jakes Jordan, "Hoeffel won't support unilateral U.S. action," *Associated Press*, (March 5, 2003)

17. "Pa. Democrat Backs Away From Iraq Vote," *New York Times,* (March 5, 2003)

18. Margaret Gibbons, "Hoeffel criticizes Bush's 'cowboy diplomacy,'" *Times Herald,* (March 6, 2003)

19. Ibid.

20. "Congressman vs. cowboy: Hoeffel critical of Bush's Middle East policy," *The Intelligencer* editorial, (March 7, 2003)

21. Eric Seymour, "Representative's behavior is shameful," *The Reporter* letter, (March 9, 2003)

22. Christian P. Marone, "Iraq: the war, the motives, the protest," *Philadelphia Daily News* letter, (March 12, 2003)

23. "Sorry, Joe, we'll ride with the cowboy," *News Gleaner* editorial, (March 12, 2003)

24. Tom Waring, "Santorum weighs in on Iraq, France, Hoeffel," *Northeast Times,* (March 12, 2003)

25. Walt Scott, "The cowboy is in Iraq," *Intelligencer* letter, (March 14, 2003)

26. Tom Waring, "Hoeffel: Time for war debate is over," *Northeast Times,* (April 2, 2003)

27. Dom Giordano email to author, August 16, 2013

28. Hans Blix, Statement to United Nations Security Council, New York, (March 7, 2003)

29. Mohamed El-Baradei, Statement to United Nations Security Council, New York, (March 7, 2003)

30. Dick Cheney, interview with Tim Russert on *Meet the Press,* NBC, (March 16, 2003)

31. Ibid.

32. Dick Cheney, interview with Bob Schieffer on *Face the Nation,* CBS, (March 16, 2003)

33. George Bush, televised address to the nation, White House, Washington, D.C., (March 17, 2003)

CHAPTER SIX: WAR

1. Michelle Sale and Javaid Khan, "Missions Accomplished?" *New York Times,* (April 11, 2003)

2. David Zucchino, "Army Stage-Managed Fall of Hussein Statue," *Los Angeles Times,* (July 3, 2004)

3. Robert Collier, "Baghdad closer to collapse," *San Francisco Chronicle*, (April 9, 2003), "DoD News Briefing—Secretary Rumsfeld and Gen. Myers," U.S. Department of Defense, Pentagon, (April 11, 2003)

4. Reuters, "A Look at U.S. Deaths in the Iraq War," *Washington Post*, (October 25, 2005)

5. Ari Fleischer, White House press briefing, (March 21, 2003)

6. Donald Rumsfeld, *Face the Nation*, CBS, (March 24, 2003)

7. Donald Rumsfeld, *This Week*, ABC, (March 30, 2003)

8. Jodi Spiegel Arthur, "Opinions on the war shared with congressman," *Intelligencer*, (March 23, 2003)

9. Ibid.

10. Ibid.

11. Ibid.

12. Cary Beavers, "Hoeffel speaks his mind in Lansdale as 'Saturdays With Joe' kicks off," *The Reporter*, (1999)

13. Hoeffel, *CR*, (April 8, 2003), H2914

14. Wayne Lutz, "Constituent embarrassed," *Intelligencer* letter, (April 4, 2003)

15. George W. Bush, "Remarks by President Bush announcing the end of major combat operations in Iraq," USS Abraham Lincoln, (May 1, 2003)

CHAPTER SEVEN: THE AFTERMATH OF WAR, 2003

1. Hoeffel, *CR*, (May 13, 2003), H4001

2. Ibid, H4003

3. "Iraqi Mobile Biological Warfare Agent Production Plants," Central Intelligence Agency/Defense Intelligence Agency, (May 28, 2003), 1

4. Ibid.

5. Ibid, 5

6. Peter Beaumont and Antony Barnett, "Blow to Blair over 'mobile labs,'" *The Observer*, (June 7, 2003), Douglas Jehl, "State Department Disputes CIA View of Trailers as Labs," *New York Times*, (June 26, 2003)

7. Mike Allen, "Bush: 'We Found' Banned Weapons," *Washington Post*, (May 31, 2003)

8. Anne Applebaum, "Defending Bolton," *Washington Post*, (March 9, 2005), A21

9. John Bolton, *The Diane Rehm Show*, NPR, (November 12, 2007)

10. Hoeffel, *"U.S. Nonproliferation Policy After Iraq,"* Hearing before the Committee on International Relations, House of Representatives, 108th Congress, Serial No. 108–38, (June 4, 2003), 88

11. Hoeffel-Bolton dialogue, ibid, 88–90

12. Jim Wolf, "U.S. Insiders Say Iraq Intel Deliberately Skewed," *Reuters,* (May 31, 2003)

13. *Iraq—Key WMD Facilities—An Operational Support Study,* Defense Intelligence Agency, Department of Defense, (September 2002), leaked on June 6, 2003, partially declassified by the Department of Defense on June 6, 2003.

14. Warren P. Strobel, "Report cast doubt on Iraqi weapons," *Philadelphia Inquirer,* (June 7, 2003)

15. Greg Thielmann, "Questions Swirl Around WMD Charges," CBS/Associated Press, (June 7, 2003)

16. Jim Wolf, "Intelligence Historian Says CIA 'Buckled' on Iraq," *Reuters,* (June 7, 2003)

17. Ibid.

18. Ibid.

19. Walter Pincus, "Officials Defend Iraq Intelligence," *Washington Post,* (June 9, 2003)

20. Ibid.

21. Margaret Gibbons, "Hoeffel questions 'accountability' in weapons search," *Times Herald,* (June 10, 2003)

22. Bill Delahunt, telephone interview with author, (July 13, 2013)

23. Ted Strickland, telephone interview with author, (June 25, 2013)

24. Hoeffel, *CR,* (June 9, 2003), H5081

25. Delahunt, ibid, H5082

26. Hoeffel, ibid, H5083

27. Jonathan S. Landay, "Pro-war officials may have ignored CIA caution," *Philadelphia Inquirer,* (June 13, 2003)

28. Hoeffel, *CR,* (June 25, 2003), H5832

29. Sean Laughlin, "Bush warns militants who attack U.S. troops in Iraq," *CNN,* (July 3, 2003)

30. "Bring Reality On," *Philadelphia Inquirer* editorial, (July 6, 2003)

31. Dana Milbank, "Intelligence Dispute Festers as Iraq Victory Recedes," *Washington Post,* (July 17, 2003)

32. Walter Pincus, "White House Backs Off Claim on Iraqi Buy," *Washington Post,* (July 8, 2003) A01

33. Walter Pincus and Mike Allen, "Tenet stopped uranium remark in earlier speech," *Washington Post*, (July 13, 2003) A18

34. Delahunt, *CR*, (June 8, 2003), H6340

35. Rahm Emanuel, ibid, H6340

36. Greg Thielmann, press conference remarks, Arms Control Association, National Press Club, Washington, D.C., (July 9, 2003), four page statement provided by Thielmann to author in July 2003.

37. Matt Kelley, "Officials: Bush overstated Iraq links to al-Qaida," Associated Press, (July 13, 2003)

38. Dana Priest and Walter Pincus, "Rationale for Iraq war now suspect," *Washington Post*, (July 14, 2003)

39. John J. Lumpkin and Dafna Linzer, "Iraq nuclear evidence thin, experts say," Associated Press, (July 20, 2003)

40. Ron Hutcheson, "Report is cited as Iraqi evidence," *Philadelphia Inquirer*, (July 19, 2003)

41. Ibid.

42. Warren P. Strobel and Jonathan S. Landay, "After a year, Iraq case failing," *Philadelphia Inquirer*, (July 20, 2003)

43. Hoeffel, *CR*, (July 21, 2003), H7216

44. George Tenet, "Statement on the 2002 NIE on Iraq's Continuing Programs for WMD," Central Intelligence Agency, Washington, D.C., (August 11, 2003)

45. Strickland, *CR*, (September 9, 2003), H8073

46. Announcement by the Speaker pro tempore, ibid, H8074

47. Hoeffel, ibid, H8075

48. Margaret Gibbons, "Hoeffel criticizes Congress' Iraq Decision," *The Reporter*, (October 23, 2003)

CHAPTER EIGHT: THE AFTERMATH OF WAR, 2004

1. George W. Bush, State of the Union address, Washington D.C., (January 20, 2004)

2. Hoeffel, *CR*, (January 21, 2004), H66

3. Peter Slevin, "Powell Voices Doubts About Iraqi Weapons," *Washington Post*, (January 25, 2004), A14

4. Reuters, telephone interview with David Kay, (January 23, 2004)

5. David Kay, interview with Liane Hansen, *Weekend Edition—Sunday*, NPR, (January 25, 2004)

6. Fred Kaplan, "The Art of Camouflage," *Slate,* (January 26, 2004). See also David Kay, *New York Times* interview, (January 26, 2004)

7. *Philadelphia Inquirer* editorial, (January 27, 2004)

8. *New York Times* editorial, (January 27, 2004)

9. Bob Drogin and Greg Miller, "CIA Chief Saw No Imminent Threat in Iraq," *Los Angeles Times,* (February 6, 2004)

10. George Bush, *Meet the Press* interview with Tim Russert, NBC, (February 8, 2004)

11. Hoeffel, *CR,* (February 24, 2004), H555

12. Ibid.

13. "3 Iraq Strategists Honored by Bush," *Los Angeles Times/AP,* (December 12, 2004)

CHAPTER NINE: CONSEQUENCES

1. *Report on the U.S. Intelligence Community's Prewar Assessments on Iraq,* Select Committee on Intelligence, United States Senate, Senate Report 108–301, (July 7, 2004)

2. Pat Roberts, "Judging Intelligence: The Senators' Views and Excerpts from the Report on Iraq Assessments," *New York Times,* (July 10, 2004)

3. official title, *Comprehensive Report of the Special Advisor to the Director of Central Intelligence on Iraq's Weapons of Mass Destruction,* Central Intelligence Agency, (September 30, 2004)

4. Douglas Jehl, "U.S. Report Finds Iraqis Eliminated Illicit Arms in 90's," *New York Times,* (October 7, 2004)

5. Dana Priest and Walter Pincus, "U.S. 'Almost All Wrong' on Weapons," *Washington Post,* (October 7, 2004) A01

6. *Report on Postwar Findings About Iraq's WMD Programs and Links to Terrorism and How They Compare with Prewar Assessments,* Select Committee on Intelligence, United States Senate, Senate Report 109–331, (September 8, 2006)

7. *Report on Whether Public Statements Regarding Iraq by U.S. Government Officials Were Substantiated by Intelligence Information,* Select Committee on Intelligence, United States Senate, Senate Report 110–345, (June 5, 2008)

8. Rockefeller, Press Release of U.S. Senate Select Committee on Intelligence, (June 5, 2008)

CHAPTER TEN: THE BUSH TEAM MEMOIRS

1. George W. Bush, *Decision Points* (New York: Broadway Paperbacks, Crown Publishing, 2010)

2. Ibid, 242

3. Ibid, 240–241

4. Ibid, 262

5. Ibid, 244

6. Hans Blix, *An Update on Inspection,* United Nations Security Council, New York, (January 27, 2003)

7. Hans Blix, Statement to the United Nations Security Council, New York, (February 14, 2003)

8. Hans Blix, Statement to the United Nations Security Council, New York, (March 7, 2003)

9. Bush, *Decision Points,* 244

10. Mohamed El-Baradei, Statement to United Nations Security Council, New York, (January 27, 2003)

11. Bush, *Decision Points,* 270

12. Dick Cheney, *In My Time: A Personal and Political Memoir*, with Liz Cheney, (New York: Threshold Editions, Simon & Schuster, 2011)

13. Ibid, 389–390

14. Ibid, 391

15. Ibid, 394

16. Ibid, 413–414

17. Dick Cheney, speech to Veterans of Foreign Wars 103rd National Convention, Nashville, Tennessee, (August 26, 2002)

18. Cheney, *Time,* 404

19. Donald Rumsfeld, *Known and Unknown: A Memoir* (New York: Penguin Group, 2011)

20. Ibid, 481

21. Ibid.

22. Ibid, 449

23. Ibid, 432

24. Ibid, 433

25. Ibid, 442

26. Ibid, 712

27. Ibid.

28. Ibid, 435

29. Condoleezza Rice, *No Higher Honor: A Memoir of My Years in Washington* (New York: Broadway Paperbacks, Crown Publishing Group, 2011)

30. Ibid, 169

31. Ibid, 236

32. Ibid, 185

33. Ibid, 185–186

34. Ibid.

35. Colin Powell, *It Worked For Me: In Life and Leadership*, with Tony Koltz, (New York: HarperLuxe, HarperCollins, 2012)

36. Ibid, 287

37. Ibid, 289

38. Ibid, 294

39. Ibid, 295

40. Ibid, 296

41. George Tenet, *At the Center of the Storm: The CIA During America's Time of Crisis*, with Bill Harlow, (New York: Harper Perennial, 2008)

42. Ibid, 480

43. Ibid, 410

44. Ibid, 458

45. Ibid, 373–375

46. Ibid, 334

47. Ibid, 327

48. Ibid.

49. Ibid, 327–328

50. Ibid, 334–335

51. Ibid, 333

52. Ibid, 481

53. Ibid, 335

54. Ibid, 336

55. Ibid.

56. Ibid, 470

57. Ibid, 338

CHAPTER ELEVEN: DISCLOSE THE INTELLIGENCE

1. Richard Myers, "DoD News Briefing—Secretary Rumsfeld and Gen. Myers," Department of Defense, Pentagon, (June 24, 2003)

2. John Yoo, "The President's Constitutional Authority to Conduct Military Operations Against Terrorists and Nations Supporting Them," Legal Opinion, Office of Legal Counsel, Department of Justice, (September 25, 2001)

3. Richard Grimmett, "U.S. Use of Preemptive Military Force," Congressional Research Service, (April 11, 2003)

4. Bush, Graduation speech at the United States Military Academy, West Point, (June 1, 2002)

5. The National Security Strategy of the United States 2002, Department of Defense, Pentagon, (September 17, 2002)

6. *Final Report of the Commission on the Intelligence Capabilities of the U.S. Regarding Weapons of Mass Destruction*, (March 25, 2005)

7. Mark M. Lowenthal, *Intelligence: From Secrets to Policy*, 5th edition (London: SAGE, Los Angeles: CQ Press, 2012)

8. Ibid, 3

9. Ibid, 2–4

10. Ibid, 7–8

11. Ibid, 8

12. The National Security Act of 1947, as amended, 50 U.S.C. 401–442

13. Ibid, Section 101

14. Intelligence Directive No. 11, National Security Council, (January 6, 1950)

15. Lowenthal, *Intelligence,* 217

16. Ibid, 24

17. Ibid, 22

18. Intelligence Reform and Terrorism Prevention Act of 2004, Public Law 108–458

19. Enterprise Objective 5, National Intelligence Strategy, (October 2005)

20. Lowenthal, *Intelligence,* 232–233

21. Wyndee Parker, National Security Adviser to the House Democratic Leader, telephone interview with author, (January 31, 2014)

22. *National Intelligence Estimate on Prospects for Iraq's Stability: A Challenging Road Ahead,* National Intelligence Council, (January 2007), preface

23. Lowenthal, *Intelligence,* 149

24. Ibid, 149–150

CHAPTER TWELVE: CHENEY AND IRAQ

1. Trudy Rubin, "Again, Cheney is up to his old tricks," *Philadelphia Inquirer* (June 29, 2014)

2. see Introduction

3. Rubin, "Cheney"

4. Dick Cheney and Liz Cheney, "The Collapsing Obama Doctrine," *The Wall Street Journal* (June 17, 2014)

5. Interview with Vice President Cheney, *"Hannity,"* Fox News (June 24, 2014)

Index

10-14